GOVERNANCE
—— FROM THE ——
BOTTOM UP

GOVERNANCE
—FROM THE—
BOTTOM UP

ONE HUNDRED HORRIBLE EXAMPLES
FROM THE BOTTOM UP

CHARLES F. BINGMAN

GOVERNANCE FROM THE BOTTOM UP
One Hundred Horrible Examples From The Bottom Up

iUniverse books may be ordered through booksellers or by contacting:

iUniverse
1663 Liberty Drive
Bloomington, IN 47403
www.iuniverse.com
1-800-Authors (1-800-288-4677)

Because of the dynamic nature of the Internet, any web addresses or links contained in this book may have changed since publication and may no longer be valid. The views expressed in this work are solely those of the author and do not necessarily reflect the views of the publisher, and the publisher hereby disclaims any responsibility for them.

The views expressed in this work are solely those of the author and do not necessarily reflect the views of the publisher, and the publisher hereby disclaims any responsibility for them.

Any people depicted in stock imagery provided by Thinkstock are models, and such images are being used for illustrative purposes only. Certain stock imagery © Thinkstock.

ISBN: 978-1-5320-0799-6 (sc)
ISBN: 978-1-5320-0798-9 (e)

Library of Congress Control Number: 2016915969

Print information available on the last page.

iUniverse rev. date: 10/25/2016

CONTENTS

I

INTRODUCTION

Perhaps the most difficult thing that human beings are called upon collectively to do is to run a successful government. Many governments – perhaps most of them – throughout history have been very bad. Yet every government is an <u>opportunity</u> to succeed or to fail. Why do so many fail? Part of the answer is that governance is inherently so difficult that it cannot be mastered, and so confusing and chaotic that it simply overwhelms its practitioners, and much of this chaos stems from the inevitable complexity of millions of human beings and hundreds of thousands of organizations and groups and interests clashing and conflicting with each other. People deserve good governance, but it is increasingly clear that the odds are against it. Poor governments are not going to go away, nor can they be ignored or easily replaced. The message here is this: millions of people in countries all over the world must be less passive in their relationships with their governments. They must step up their own "bottom up" influence on their governments, to leverage them, or cajole them, or persuade them toward better and more human and more responsible governance. This is government from the bottom up.

There are 196 countries in the world. Perhaps 40-50 of them are very small or remote islands, important for those who live in them, but discounted on the world stage. Of the approximately 150 substantial governments, at least 105 of them, briefly summarized here, are in deep trouble. "Deep" trouble is defined by wars, insurrections, active internal conflict, serious mal-distribution of wealth, deep and widespread poverty, rampant corruption, serious lack of social services and public infrastructure, and an excess of plain old bumbling government incompetence, but the most discouraging reality is that many of these troubles are created and exacerbated by the governments themselves out of greed, viciousness and an insatiable lust for power.

Many of the prevailing concepts of governance are in fact based on a series of ancient human dysfunctions. There remain <u>eternal</u> conflicts between people in their families, clans, tribes, regions, races and religions. These are further complicated by equally eternal conflicts between men and women, old vs. young, rural vs. urban, rich and poor, and many, many others. There are modern conflicts deliberately created between political parties: Communists vs. democrats, State Socialists vs. everybody, and the totally inexplicable 1400 year history of Sunni vs. Shia. These human conflicts become the source of oppressive power. It is simply true that political leaders in all of those governments in deep trouble share the same corrosive sin of deliberately pitting their citizens against each other. Thus, people are taught to hate, and persuaded that conflict is necessary, and that opposing the leaders is somehow wrong and threatening.

In relatively well run countries, there is a reasonable recognition that the government does really important and necessary things, and does most of them reasonably well. There may be little difference between the levels of performance by public organizations and private ones. But still, for a majority of people in the world, it is "the People vs. the Government", and that every system is somewhere between acting oppressive and bullying, and being merely petty, mindlessly bumbling, messy and incompetent. Many feel that their government has gotten out of hand; is running amok and exceeding its reasonable roles. As the nature of governments becomes more authoritarian, the view from the bottom up becomes more fearful, involving feelings of increasing risk, and a growing constriction of freedom of action.

And of course, in the worst case situations, dozens of governments have pushed far beyond "unfair" to the point of being actively oppressive and dangerous. As reported in the summary later here, many top down governments have indeed become tyrannical, abusive, murderous and deadly, and even the average citizens are in constant fear for their own lives, their families, their property, their well-being, and their freedom. History is full of horrible, incredible examples of mammoth murders by governments of their own citizens: Major genocides include:

1915: Extermination of 1 million Armenians in Turkey (Ottoman Empire)

1930s: Famine in Ukraine – 6-7 million starved

1933-1945: The Holocaust in Europe – 6 million were murdered

1975-1979: Khmer Rouge in Cambodia – 500 thousand to 2 million killed

1983: Guatemala civil war – 200,000 deaths

1992-1995: Breakup of Yugoslavia – 200,000

1994: Rwanda – 800,000

2003- current: Sudan and S. Sudan – 2-400,000

But consider also such unbelievable "political" murders:

China under Mao, 1960-1976 - 30 million starved

USSR under Stalin, 1930s – 20 million starved in the Ukraine and beyond

Darfur, 2000's – The central Arab government attacked its own black citizens in Darfur, and 450,000 were killed, and 2.5 million were displaced.

Congo, Rwanda, Uganda, DAR, Burundi – An inexplicable hatred between the Hutu and Tutsi tribes displaced millions, and several hundreds of thousands were killed.

China: the displacement of Tibetans, Muslims.

Democratic Republic of Congo, 2008-2013: 5.4 million were killed, and 2.6 million were displaced.

Nigeria: Boko Haram has forced more than 1.5 million people out of their homes, and prevented agriculture and commercial functioning. 50,000 children are at risk of starvation.

Other states have had large displacements, such as in Mexico, Latin America, Jews from Europe and Middle East, China, India, Vietnam, Columbia, Philippines, N. Korea, and many others.

There are several general types of bottom up reactions to such top down tyranny. In places like China, North Korea, Iran or Russia, people somehow accept this top down power control as the natural order of things – the world is a tough place. The followers of Mao, or the Kims, or Vladimir Putin think that the concentration of power is ultimately a good thing, and they have been indoctrinated to believe that obedience to that power is the natural reaction. Other people see the power, going on forever, and believe themselves to be simply cogs in some great inevitable machine. Still others decide that the safe course is just to "go along to get along", hoping to dodge any stray bullets on the way. Some people decide that they might as well recognize the inevitable and join the oppressors. There is a kind of self delusion and absence of moral understanding that leads young men to join ISIS or al-Qaeda and blow up innocent civilians as an act of religious zeal, or as just a form of well paying employment.

But many people are willing and able to construct a counter power base which can offer some protection and provide a base for negotiations with the centrist regime. Local governments are able to argue their own interests versus the centrist elites. Special interest groups can bargain their support of the regime in exchange for protection and preferment. The military, the police, and lately the intelligence services always form their own power centers. Corruption can be used to strike deals between the crooked parties.

The bottom up world has two further levels of functioning. In the first, there will be people who oppose a regime, but do not try to overthrow it. Instead, they insert themselves into elements of the establishment, hoping to mitigate its excesses, and to push forward moderating positions and ideas. This is an extraordinarily long term approach, but it is often the one that works. Governments do moderate themselves. Old dictators die, younger leaders ascend, reality strikes, the people press forward.

The last level of bottom up activity is armed resistance to the regime: street protests, anti-government actions, attacks on government officials and facilities, insurrections, or civil war. These forms of action are excruciatingly difficult and dangerous. In some cases, regimes of crooks and scoundrels are overthrown, only to be replaced by a new group of crooks and scoundrels. But the glory is that many such drastic bottom up surges have triumphed.

Some of the patterns of governance are so horrible that they surpass rational understanding. The more one studies the roles of bad governments, the more one is forced to accept the fact of human evil. After all of the excuses are examined and rejected, and motivations explained and not believed, there remains a horrible number of human actions that are inhuman and insane, and utterly beyond rational explanation. Many of these actions are perpetrated by individuals or small groups, but these actions can inflict unbelievable death and destruction. Terror groups like Boko Haram in Nigeria, or al-Qaeda or ISIS may posture that they are saving people from corrupt and inept governments, but they cannot conceivably offer any explanation that justifies the nature of the hellish attacks against defenseless people and the deliberate slaughter of innocents, including even the smallest of children.

Some form of governance has existed among humans from the dawn of time, beginning with the coherence of families to the bonding of clans, on to a long and complex process by which power in human affairs evolved to become more concentrated and deliberately projected. Clans became tribes, and tribes became nations. The more or less democratic forms of clan chieftains and tribal councils became parliaments and almost inevitably, these systems concentrated power and control in the hands of often dictatorial leaders. Power became the legitimate instrument of the State – the power to decide, to create facilities and services, and to develop sub systems for performance and control. The power included the ability to extract resources from the country and to decide how to deploy them. It remains generally legitimate that government power can create and maintain a military to protect the nation; or to create and maintain a system of police and courts and systems of laws for the domestic safety and security of the nation's citizens. In developing nations where private enterprises were not sufficiently developed, the government has been a legitimate option for the creation or expansion of critical elements of the economy. The government is generally accepted as a force to limit crime or terror or other unacceptable citizen conduct. These roles of government are needed and constructive – until they become excessive and oppressive.

But it is inevitable and immutable that the tides of change are always flowing, and as the world changes, different demands are placed on people and their governments. Individual people adapt because they are forced to do so to live with the new realities. Human institutions both public and private have a certain degree of ability to choose their fate, and they have responded to change in a wide variety of ways. But every government ever created, for the last 10,000 years has possessed critical characteristics which oppose change. Government leadership has almost always been in the hands of relatively small, tight and highly centrist ruling elite. Such governments are strongly inclined to produce a powerful oppressive leader; they stoutly resist change because it might produce a loss of power and control. Thus, they cannot abide opposition or even criticism, however modest. Few people realize that any government can, if it wishes to do so, involve itself in virtually anything and everything in the country. Why and how governments do this is endlessly complex and muddled and conflicting; endlessly arrogant and often dangerous.

In a very real sense, the norm for governments has been authority from the top down, even in the face of a fair degree of social coherence, as for example the enduring strength of tribes, clans, regions and beliefs. But centrism is the father of preferment, which is the father of corruption. What is missing is the sense of the need for the government to be accountable or to be efficient and productive.

There are universities full of people who are studying the most worthy and noble modern theories of governance, but it is important to study governance on the dark side – the realities of hundreds of bad governments; how so many whole governments are broken or failing; and how government pathology is tied to human pathology. Governance is all too often the triumph of elitism, centrism and power hunger. So much of the decision making in governments is emotional and not essentially rational, and many of these motives are destructive – an urge for power, a greedy desire to get very rich, a cult of corrupt alliances, hatred of something or someone. Meanwhile, the general population is largely passive, feeling powerless and intimidated by oppression. The government itself will often create and exacerbate conflicts between elements of society; if people can be taught to hate each other, they may hate government less.

Governments are always "top down"; people are "bottom up". Governments are necessarily about the exercise of power. National leaders are almost by definition centrists in character, and most of the philosophies that have been developed about how to run a government are highly centrist as well, ranging from the pharaohs as gods, to the divine right of kings, to Communism, State Socialism or the Islamic Caliphate. Even representative democracy, in modern times, has a strong tendency to justify the supposed need for more and more direction from the top.

Consider for example the somewhat muddled debate about "drones". The U. S. and other countries have used drones effectively, but there have been losses of innocent lives as collateral consequences. Yet consider what the real "drone problem" is. It is the use of suicide bombers by terrorists. Every suicide bomber is a human drone, mindlessly controlled and sent to commit deliberate murder. The targets of their attacks are often not the government at all but deliberately against civilian targets. Suicide bombers are sent to blow themselves up in crowded market places where families will be shopping. And perhaps the most insane actions of all occur when Muslim suicide bombers are sent to slaughter Muslim worshippers outside of a Muslim mosque. Madness! Madness!

And the madness extends itself into official governments. Consider the example of the terror campaign of incomprehensible hatred mounted by the government of Sudan against its own citizens in Darfur, and against the Christian/Animist people of the south. Or consider the other pathologies discussed elsewhere in this book: the fantastic horror of the Khmer Rouge in Cambodia; the starvation of 30 million in China under Mao; or the slaughter of 20 million in the USSR under Stalin. These examples are sheer malicious evil executed by tyrants because they <u>wanted to</u> and they <u>could.</u>

Then, at another level, think of the nature of serious criminals who commit any form of horrible act in the name of profit or revenge – Mexican drug gangs, the Colombian drug cartels, oil stealers in Nigeria, the Yakusa in Japan, the Russian mafia, the pirates and thugs in Somalia. Such human evil has always existed, but the point here is to try and understand the evil here and now. Like it or not, one of the drivers of evil is religious zeal. (WP22Jan15) quotes the head of Boko Haram in Nigeria after a murderous attack on the town of Baga: "We are the ones who fought the people of Baga and we have killed them with such a killing as Allah commanded in his Book".

Perhaps there is more evil in the world because there are billions more people, and because life is more complex and confusing, and there are more sources of power to seize, and more money to grab. Every religion ever conceived (excluding some aberrations) has preached goodness and love, and the value of human kind. All recognize the reality of human evil and seek to oppose it. Each has defined evil, but none has ever fully prevented it, or explained why it is seemingly eternal.

While the intellectuals and the populists teach the virtues of representative democracy (as they should), the horrible truth is that the key to most governments is found in the practice of special interest politics. Special interest politics is far more than the expression of human interests. It is far more self-serving and is expensively pursued by very imposing professional organizations. The corridors of power are full of special interest lobbyists.

And it is simply true that, all over the world, the people still put their personal, family, or community interests above those of "the government", which is also probably hated and feared. Especially in developing countries, the older loyalties of families, tribes, clans, home lands and religions are far more important than loyalty to some remote central government, especially the horrible governments they are likely to possess. The world passes through its ideological waves – the divine right of kings, the Communist Revolution, State Socialism, or the Islamic Caliphate – and people cling hopefully to the value of "bottom up" loyalty and cooperation vs. "top down" oppression.

According to George Ayittey, "What Africans had was participatory democracy. A unique characteristic of Africa's indigenous systems of government was that they were open and inclusive. No one was locked out of the decision-making process. One did not have to belong to one political party or family to participate. No village was declared to be a one-party state, and the chief did not attempt to impose some foreign ideology on his people. There were village meetings at which the people expressed their views freely, and no one was arrested or detained for disagreeing with the chief. Larger political entities, like kingdoms and empires, employed extensive devolution of authority, and local communities enjoyed substantial authority to run their own affairs. This helps to explain why there remain over 2,000 distinct tribes in Africa today." [1]

Fairly rapidly, in the period after WW II, many African nations achieved their independence. This meant that each was creating **an opportunity** – to design and implement a good and responsive and humanistic government. And here begins an ominous and telling story of how country after country failed this opportunity and invented instead a series of governments that ranged from the seriously incompetent to the sadistically evil.

But the exercise of near-absolute centrist control almost always creates another absolutely incomprehensible phenomenon – the universal emergence of vicious, destructive and costly corruption,

---

[1]   Ayittey, George B. N., "Africa Betrayed", chapter 3; New York, St. Martins Press, A Cato Institute Book, 1992.

where the very centrist elite that touts its own value and wisdom, are the greatest and boldest corrupters, employing the very controls that were justified as the source of public good. Governments cannot and will not control corruption because they <u>are</u> the corrupt.

II

THE CORROSIVE NATURE
OF GOVERNMENTS

There is a basic human obligation: to provide for those who are at risk – children, the elderly, the disadvantaged and those forced to live in poverty. Therefore, it is a basic government responsibility to make such provisions, and see to it that every citizen at least has food and clothing and shelter, and protection and help when grown old. Every country has its poor, and almost every government acts in some way to help them. The concern is how often these government efforts are inadequate, ineffective or poorly run. Here again, corruption is present: money for the poor is often stolen or diverted. Public infrastructure is vital but very expensive. The unsavory truth is that many governments spend their money first on economic development, the military and on corruption, and social services and public infrastructure are inexplicably neglected.

It is also universally conceded that national governments are responsible for the nation's safety and security, and that this justifies the maintenance of national security forces, usually of a very complex and sophisticated nature. It will certainly provide for a classic military establishment: an army, a navy, an air force, and all of their supporting capabilities. The system may also include intelligence organizations both domestic and foreign, a national police force and a whole range of suppliers of weapons, equipment, supplies and materials, and everything else under the sun. Military leadership will also build up working relationships with local police departments and an array of support organizations.

The very size and complexity of these security capabilities mean that the people who populate them are very "bottom up" in nature: the sons and daughters of the people, bringing the mind set of the average citizen. It is of course true that the military – perhaps more than any other element of government – is heavily top down in character, and in a surprising number of cases, the army enjoys a pretty accepted relationship with the people, particularly in countries where the regular civilian government is really oppressive and hated. Then, the military may be urged to step in and play the national heroes by rising up and throwing out the hated regime.

Philosophically and intellectually related to the military obligation is the equally important obligation to provide an effective national legal justice system, involving the police, public prosecutors, and a system of independent courts and judges. This structure is the product of and parallel development of a body of laws defining the nature of governance, the authorities of public officials, the rights of individuals and organizations, and the limitations society wants to impose on them.

This legal system can and should be one of the greatest "bottom up" protections of people and institutions. At the same time, the justice system is one of the most important instruments that oppressive regimes use for top down control. Both the people and the officials of the justice system believe in its independence, and the equitable rule of law, and this put the system in constant conflict with the top down regime.

One of the most fundamental and cherished concepts advocated for any government is that "rightness" should be defined by "the rule of law": that is, the basic design and operation of governments as stated in constitutions, enacted laws, the enduring structure of the national justice system, a body of common laws and precedents, and a legal structure of governments in which powers and authorities are both authorized and limited. Citizen's rights are protected, and their obligations defined under these laws, and usually include the right to take legal action to protect themselves.

In most countries, there has been the warm and comfortable feeling that if only the rule of law is followed, all will be well. But perhaps the greatest source for the accretion of power has come through the philosophy that the good of the individual must be subordinated to the "good of the State", and that only the state is capable of defining its own good. Even where there is a substantial framework for the rule of law, those rules can be perverted because they rest on the often invalid assumption that the laws themselves are good and proper. This has been largely true in the United States and in most other developed countries, but it is increasingly apparent that keeping the laws good and proper is an enormously complex and sophisticated process. In many countries, rules of law and the institutions mechanisms to protect them do not exist or are not strong enough. Thus, laws themselves are perverted and made to work against the very people they are supposed to protect. Anything – any pathological, corrupt, perverse, outrageous and dysfunctional thing – can and has been made legal and the law of the land. Pathological politics has proved time and time again that it can frustrate the intent of the rule of law and turn it upside down.

Here are some of the perverse laws that regimes employ:

1. Prohibit free elections, forbid opposition political parties, or severely limit political activities – except by the government itself.
2. Create "designer" tax regulations that allow favoritism toward regime supporters, and punishment for opponents.
3. Prohibit any criticism of any policy or action of the government.
4. Deny without challenge the right of any group or person to start a business, construct a building or engage any almost any form of economic activity without the official approval of the government.
5. Make it illegal to have families of more than 2-3 children.
6. Give preference for access to public services to a specific ethnic, religious or tribal group – and deny services to others.
7. Appoint even top level public officials based on patronage, without regard for ability or merit.

8. Allow regime officials to give away or sell cheaply valuable national assets such as land, buildings, and mineral rights.
9. Award government contracts to anybody they choose, especially relatives and political supporters.
10. Direct banks in the country to lend to regime friends and deny opponents.
11. Use tax funds to replace financial losses of inefficient state owned enterprises.
12. Subsidize private businesses.
13. Make government loans to state owned enterprises or businesses – and later forgive the loans.
14. Create monopolies and give them exclusive control of part of the national economy.
15. Conceal all government activities, individual actions, and the expenditure of public funds.
16. Overstaff government agencies with no real relationship to work needs.
17. Appoint and remove judges at will.
18. "Selectively" enforce public regulations.
19. Use the police or military to suppress almost any form of civil activity.
20. Enter and search private homes and businesses, and remove anything.
21. Keep people in jail for long periods of time without charging them.
22. Direct public prosecutors to initiate or refrain from prosecuting certain organizations or individuals.
23. Sponsor and finance informal militias, paramilitary groups and other terrorist groups to attack insurgents.
24. Give government intelligence offices unlimited access to any information about private people and organizations.
25. Allow military officers to overrule elected officials.

This list could be almost endlessly extended.

Further, the ponderous apparatus of governments are, in most countries, so complex and poorly functioning that it is too costly and too time consuming for average persons or small organizations to use. When the government uses the legal system as its own tool, it becomes actually dangerous because opponents can be threatened and intimidated, and because of the likelihood that the "good guys" will lose. Public prosecutors and defenders suffer from the same problems and often refrain from performing their official roles simply because they would be wasting their time. The ultimate insult in some countries is that courts and judges also become corrupt, selling verdicts to the highest bidder. In sum, legal systems all over the world are proving to be poorly designed and wholly inadequate to deal even with legally precluded corruption, much less with the more sophisticated pathologies that politicians get into the laws themselves.

Thus, when corrupt or pathological laws are enacted, the whole justice system becomes an instrument for the enforcement of these rotten laws. Governments can create a dilemma in which people need to be protected not from other elements of society, but from the State itself. And from this power, there is little or no recourse. That is why it is vital, always, to look to the laws themselves and to prevent where possible those that embed tyranny.

Ultimately, the basis for any government is power since the state must control many legitimate sources of authority accepted as the mean to meet its obligations and serve and protect its people. Over the course of history, attempts have been made to define good governance and devise acceptable ways to deploy such governments and avoid that which needs to be opposed. Many form of government have emerged, and they are constantly evolving, and a distressingly large number are bad by any set or criteria.

One of the most important tides running in governments today is that of the universal presence and power of special interest politics. In the United States, Americans have grown up with the somewhat innocent belief that all groups that represent specific interests are "good" because they are presumed to be a form of democratic freedom of expression, and they help safeguard the public against an indifferent or wrong-headed government. But special interest politics have become far more sophisticated and, in most countries, far more ominous, and nobody particularly knows what to do about it since most political systems are ideally suited for it.

It is necessary to distinguish between special interests and "special interest politics". In essence, everybody is involved in special interests, some of them in conflict with others. Thus, a family could be concerned about the school system but oppose performance evaluation for teachers; be members of a union but vote Republican; worry about the environment but create trash and consume enormous amounts of energy, support a political party but not vote. Many special interests center on powerful ideas – environmentalism or women's rights or the well-being of minorities in society. It is therefore natural and normal for people to think and act around their special interests.

At the same time, since governments are so vastly extended and interventionist, a growing proportion of the population feels threatened by governments. Yet they want help in protecting their specific interests in the government arena, and advancing causes in which they believe.

Special interests tend to organize themselves so that they have collective influence and a more powerful voice. They will therefore tend to become more formal and bureaucratized, and much more assertive. Professional staffs are hired, recruiting stepped up, funds marshaled, a political agenda decided upon, and lobbying begun to search for allies or opponents. This leverage can initially be in the nature of information, education or persuasion, but as these groups press harder, they tend to phase over into "special interest politics" where they actively seek to change laws and regulations to favor their interests, or to capture funds and preferment to aid their cause.

From the political point of view, the practical consequence is that a trade takes place – a government asset for political support, or at least the absence of active opposition to the politician's agenda. Once these concessions are gained, they tend to be "forever" and vigorously defended. Subsequent retreat from such concessions is not only regarded as a defeat for the benefited interest group, but probably also as a "betrayal" by the political leadership. Governments therefore clash with, and collude with special interest political interests.

Special interest politics in most countries are very aggressive and heavily pointed toward the government and what concessions can be obtained – a new program, a subsidy, a tax break, a favorable policy or the overlooking of some wrongdoing. In many cases, there is a professional special interest bureaucracy that exists to lobby the government. These people have to gain something out of the political system from time to time in order to justify their work. And it must be perceived that the "something" that the government grants may be something that it was otherwise not inclined to provide. In other words, the ideal outcome for a special interest bureaucracy is to appear to have wrung concessions or resources from a reluctant government.

But the more ominous cases are those in which the influence of special interests is secret and carefully concealed, and deliberately intended as the absolute antithesis of "representative democracy". The history of countries is filled with this kind of "special interest" politics: the perverse collusion between corrupt officials and countless individuals and groups who are seeking to wrest wealth and power from a fumbling government.

What has emerged in every country therefore is a special interest political system based on the following elements:

1. A very broad range of national interests in the hands of the government, with the political system in charge of the decision-making apparatus, and capable of allocating huge resources with some degree of discretion, ranging up to 100% in dictatorships. The more public programs there are, the more special interest groups will be created, and the more intense special interest politics will become, seeking not just money, but power.

2. The system takes place at two levels: first, there will be forms of public debate such as legislative hearings, public utterances, press releases, and endless study commissions. Then, there is a second "back room" political process of negotiation and agreement, not visible to the public, which is usually where the real threats and promises are employed. The public operations of government are deliberately designed to be essentially bland assurances, to deflect the public concerns and avoid efforts to penetrate the back room process.

3. Government's own procedures and program delivery systems which are both massive and ubiquitous are both necessary and valuable, but they can become vehicles to deliver political preference to special interests. The most important are the public tax system, various forms of government regulations, selectively applied; items in the public budget; the award of government contracts; import and export controls, and of course, simple under-the-table corrupt payments. Both politicians and career civil servants are involved. One of the telltale signs of special interest government is when these delivery mechanisms become so extensive and so technically complex that they defy common understanding, thus giving the people in charge endless opportunities to punish or reward.

Special interest politics is enormously successful. The very broad public participation in so many forms of special interest gives them so much political credibility that political opposition seems almost unworthy. But while the "general public interest" is very broad and diffuse, special interest politics is usually very specific, and has a cutting edge that makes it easy to penetrate the political system and find backers to carry the freight. Organized special interest politics involves money, tactics and political clout specifically designed to bring pressure to bear at the key points in the political system.

It is usually the ambition of special interest politics to get concessions locked into statute or regulation, since they know that it is infinitely harder to change a law or regulation than to get it in the first place. Thus, these concessions tend to be "forever", with each special interest stoutly defending and protecting them. Special interest groups tend to be implacable, insatiable and immutable – and often insufferable.

In less developed countries, special interest groups are probably more influential in their dealings with the government because there are fewer constraints. The pattern is much more cynical and aggressive than in the United States, and is more oriented toward economic advantage. In developed countries, the range and variety of special interests in greater and more sophisticated in their dealings with the government.

Why do politicians cave so easily? Special interest politics is not just campaign contribution money or short term political support. It is more importantly about the forging of longer term alliances for mutual advantage. The special interest group will continue to provide support as long as the politician continues to deliver. And once a politician is committed publicly to a position, it would be embarrassing to abandon that position, even for just cause, for fear of being perceived as weak or inconsistent, but also for fear that it will outrage special interest backers.

In the last analysis, special interest politics, as with all politics, is first and foremost about power and money. While most special interests construct an edifice of public purpose for their position, few make any pretense of seeking for a balance of judgments about the broad public interest, nor are they concerned about the success of the government itself, or the ethics of governance. Special interests can be positive and constructive, but their performance, especially in developing countries, is seriously in doubt. Too many of these special interests stop representing the interests of their supporters, and their staffs become part of the elite of the establishment, working for their own advantage.

The key to an oppressive government can often be tracked in its use of law and regulations. In western countries, it is hopefully believed that the government regulates to protect its citizens, and to prevent threats and abuses within society. In most developing countries, people expect and receive far worse. Regulations, even at their best, are instruments of control, and people have learned that whenever government says it is "improving" a body of regulation, it usually means that it is being broadened and deepened, and made more compulsive. There is such a thing as "the regulatory mind", which thinks that the world is trying to do something bad, and it is up to them to prevent it, and that therefore, every regulation needs to be extrapolated as extensively as possible. The "red line" for the public is where these regulations become needlessly controlling, or petty and mean, or plainly beyond reason, or blatantly unfair, or excessively expensive – or all of the above. In every public opinion poll about the attitudes of people in developing countries, what disturbs people the most is the sense that their government has become the enemy, and that it is unfair, unfair, unfair.

The sources of dysfunctional preference are deep and strong. Every center of human life has created ancient and powerful traditions, customs and practices. What people wanted and hoped for from tribal chiefs and pharaohs is what people still want and hope for today. Every human community has evolved a form of religion or set of accepted moral principles that heavily influence what people accept as defining the nature of a decent government. Evolving further from such a base has been an enormous, unbelievably complex body of laws, regulations and procedures that vary from country to country, and there is a constant conflict to fill this great reservoir of confusion with those things that represent the best human values, and to oppose what sometime sees to be the irresistible forces of greed, oppression, error, and incompetence, and the yearning for power.

What are the best of these characteristics of well governed states? Surely the greatest is the dominance of democracy, meaning that the compelling power ultimately is determined from the bottom up, and the acceptance by the leadership of being instructed and compelled by the desires/demands of the citizenry. The needs of the people are political, economic and social; an economy that provides adequate work and income for all; a society that tries to make sure that the poor, the disadvantaged and the elderly can be cared for; the distribution and sharing of power to prevent tyranny; a very great acceptance of people's liberty and independence – for religion, for equality, for women and minorities, and for the civic and social organizations that people create to advance themselves and protect their interests. Religion is not a fit basis for defining governance: consider Europe up to the Reformation; Rome vs. the Saracens; the Spanish Inquisition; Muslims during the period of world conquest; Muslims in MENA; the Khmer Rouge in Cambodia. But religion and normal, sensible human beliefs and ground rules are very close together and reinforce each other. **Does religion produce good human beliefs, or do normal human beliefs produce religion?** It appears that the emergence of finer human qualities and motives has been the source of religion, and has been picked up, learned and extrapolated and formalized by religions. And no, religion does not guarantee good behavior in hundreds of millions of people. Does religion really set the base for government? Yes, in concept but not in practice. Religion is adamant when it insists that every decision or act is "Gods will" and cannot be challenged. Thus, it tends to produce governments that are rigid, doctrinaire, stagnant, and inefficient, and ultimately oppressive.

Fine. But the essence of this book is to record how difficult it is to find and achieve this grand level of governance, and how often our modern world has failed in that search.

The most important responsibility of governments is to create and support an adequate economy; one that provides enough wealth to fund the people's critical needs and enough jobs to give all an opportunity to provide for themselves. Many countries, especially among developing nations, still rest primarily on agriculture, animal husbandry, mining, fishing and other primary level economic activities which are not adequate producers of wealth. There have been exceptional strides made in the development of new modern technologies that can achieve remarkable improvements in agricultural productivity and profitability. Yet many nations simply fail to take advantage of this cheap, readily available technology which could improve farming and village life. There is a strange neglect of rural/village regions, and a prejudice in favor of burgeoning urban enlargement.

Also, there is a serious need to rethink the nature of the national workforce and the policies of labor protection. Technology, globalization and changing human desires have all changed the very nature of the work demanded. Unions which evolved to protect physical laborers, have had a hard time accommodating to the new workforce needs. Unions are often now just political lobbying groups of a very reactionary nature, but meanwhile, what workers really need is skills upgrading. The whole nature of the work itself is changing dramatically, away from mechanical and repetitive industrial production toward commercial and information activity which are far more intellectual, and demand a massive increase in the availability, the quality, and the sophistication of education. As people become more educated, they are tending to learn "portable" skills which can be practiced anywhere and are not tied to a production line or single location. Then, the higher education system itself must adapt to offer training in new and more intellectually and technologically challenging that more effectively prepare students for life in the increasingly more complex work environment.

It is possible for economic organizations to be either public or private, or both. In the period following WW II, many countries turned to State Socialism, and put the key elements of the economy, including the banks, in the hands of the government. But by the 1990s it had become apparent that the whole concept of state ownership and state management of economic elements through State Owned Enterprises (SOE) was seriously inadequate. State Socialism proved to be not liberating, but as the ideal intellectual justification for almost total top down control. SOEs including the banks could be manipulated by the government deliberately to aid and subsidize political allies and punish political opponents. Over the last 30-35 years, many of the world's greatest countries, including Russia, China, India, Vietnam, most of eastern Europe, Mexico and Brazil have been retreating from strict state socialism and moving, often reluctantly toward market based economies. Authoritarian regimes are especially reluctant to let go of the banks, but it is best if the banking function should be private and independent and regulated only for illegal or improper practices.

DEFINING ROLES: GOVERNMENT VS. THE PRIVATE SECTOR

A further and compellingly important element of the ability to limit the powers of a central government is to strengthen the power and independence of the private sector, and indeed there is a tide running, in the decline of state socialism, that is enabling exactly that. It is increasingly being recognized that governments, even in the form of State Owned Enterprises, is surprisingly ill equipped to manage the operational levels of the economy, and that the private sector is far superior in these skills. There does not seem to be any standard universal definition of what should be done by the government and what should be kept in the hands of private interests, but the following is reasonably accepted:

A. Roles that should be performed mainly by the national government:

* Welfare insurance
* National defense
* National security and justice system
* Certain kinds of regulation
* Government-to-government international relations
* National laws; maintenance of the Constitution
* Certain national transportation systems
* Certain environmental protections

B. Roles that are better performed mainly by local government:

* Elementary/secondary education
* Urban services and infrastructure (e. g. water
* Supply, sewage, trash disposal, streets, etc.)
* Parks, recreational and cultural facilities
* Welfare assistance
* Housing – public
* Power sources policy and regulation

C. Roles that can/should be shared with the private sector:

* Environmental protection
* Highways and public infrastructure
* Natural resources development and management
* Power generation and transmission
* Transportation: rail, road systems, airports, etc.
* Manufacturing: "national" industries vs. open industries
* Universities and training
* Entertainment
* Housing for most citizens
* Utilities ownership and/or operation

D. Roles that should be performed just the private sector:

- * All other manufacturing
- * Consumer consumption
- * Agriculture and food distribution

POLITICAL DILEMMAS

The people of the world are tired of malfunctioning governments. Malfunctioning is dominant in politics, government management, responses to society, and the determination of public priorities. It is one of the great dilemmas of history: why does power so often end up in the hands of dictators, tyrants, oppressors, thieves, liars and fools? Why is top down governance by power so universally successful? How can this "success" be mitigated? The American and French revolutions created a wave when, for about 200 years the trend, or at least the hope was toward representative democracy: "government from the bottom up." But in effect, the emergence of State Socialism shifted the tide in the other direction. Remember that Nazi Germany was a socialist state. Remember that Stalinist USSR was a socialist state. Remember the emergence of Mao Zedong as an extreme Socialist. The movement of State Socialism throughout Europe and in the newly independent countries of Africa and the Middle East provided the ideal philosophical and intellectual justification for top down centrist exercise of power and control. At its peak State Socialism and the emergence of "semi-socialist" states were dominant in at least 70 countries. In thousands of situations where leaders/ holders of power have opportunities to make good choices, they make bad choices instead. The main forms of decision-making are emotional and not essentially rational. Emotions include the urge for power, greed, preferment, hatred, fear, and personal gratification.

Public support is obtained by the uses of populist rewards and benefits used deliberately as a means of winning political support. Populism is deliberate and cynical and all about power. It is far more than the mere desire to be popular.

Consider also the concept of "creative ambiguity". Talk is easy and beguiling. "Spin" becomes the dominant form of analysis, with little relationship to something called "truth". Action is seen as difficult and often threatening, and thus becomes the source of political cowardice. The official acceptance of lying is now established public policy. For example, both China and N. Korea have large government agencies devoted to the generation of lies, misinformation, false information and statistics, false accusations, and endless "spin".

Special interest politics has become dominant throughout the world of governments, and it is inherently anti-democratic. But democracy is inherently decentralizing and devolving, and thus the inherent opponent of centralism and special interest self service. The success of nepotism, preferment, and favoritism especially in developing countries, and the older loyalties of families, tribes, clans, home lands, and religions are far more powerful than loyalty to the government, especially horrible governments. It is crushingly disturbing to recognize the popularity of conflict, hatred, malice, the desire for revenge

Big corruption also leads to little corruption. It is almost always true that, when the top people in an organization are corrupt, people at lower levels feel "entitled" to be corrupt as well. When the big guys steal big, the little guys steal little. And so often the standard defenses are too weak and ineffective: auditors, inspectors, police, the military, intelligence, political separatism, and failed elections. Finally, it must be recognized that the average citizen has been too passive in the face of these failures. The passivity stems from two main causes: first, the normal urge to keep out of sombody elses mess; and second, the success of official intimidation.

III

GOVERNMENTS SUFFERING
SERIOUS CONFLICTS

FAILURES FROM THE TOP DOWN

1. **AFGANISTAN:** The government was ousted by a major coup in 1973, but this threatened the USSR. The Soviets invaded in 1979 and lasted until 1989 when they were driven out by what became a serious and enduring upsurge of Islamic activism. There was a civil war won by the Taliban in 1994, and while they were dislodged, they continue to attack the government, and maintain alliance with the Taliban in Pakistan. Insurgencies of all kinds continue at high levels, involving the Afghan Taliban, the Haqqani Group, al-Qaeda, strange tie-ins with the Pakistani Taliban, and the Pakistani army Inter Services Intelligence organization (ISI). Faltering efforts at stabilization and rationality have lured more than 5.8 million Afghans to return to the country, mostly to the cities, where they are being largely sustained by foreign assistance. Thus, in a country with a population of about 30 million, almost 15% are supported by the United Nations High Comission for Refugees (UNHCR), other outside organizations, and remittances from expatriates. Foreign aid accounts for more than 90% of the $17. 1 billion national government budget, making it one of the most aid-reliant places in the world.

    Afghanistan has been a failed state for 200 years. It is rich in natural resources, especially in copper and natural gas, yet it has a congenitally underpowered and obsolete economy, far too few jobs, seriously disrupted social services, and a bumbling government seemingly unable to cope with anything. Unemployment still exceeds 30%. Yet it is considering an expansion of its army to more than 350,000 at a time when there is serious underfunding of education, health care and public infrastructure. The opium trade is the strongest element of the economy, making up more than a quarter of the declining GDP. The Afghan government complains and whines about "interference" while grabbing the money.

2.   **ALGERIA:** Independence from France was achieved in 1962. The military moved in and out of power, but a major event was the fact that an Islamic faction won a national election in 1991, which caused the military once again to take over power and cancel the results of the election. This led to an intense civil war, 1992-1998, when a civilian government finally got installed. Algeria suffers from constant attacks from al-Qaeda in the Magreb for the last 10 years. Despite these conflict, the country now is relatively stable.

3.   **ANGOLA:** Independence was obtained from Portugal in 1975, followed by 27 years of vicious civil war, ending in 2002. An estimated 1.5 million people were killed and 4 million were displaced. The country is overwhelmingly Christian and the government and most people are deeply suspicious of its Muslim minority, fearing it will fall under the spell of Muslim terrorist organizations. As a result, Islam activities have been banned or seriously limited, and all mosques have been shut down.

But meanwhile, the real national problem is economic. Oil is Angola's only serious export, and most necessities of life are imported. But the steep decline in oil prices has virtually destroyed the national economy. The failure of the government to diversify the economy means that neither the people nor the government have any money. More than 50% of the population is trying to live on less than $2 per day. The government is broke. Every government program is seriously underfunded. In some cases, workers, including police, fire fighters, doctors and teachers have not been paid for months. President Jose dos Santos, who has been in office for 47 years, is totally incompetent, presiding over a government famous for its corruption and mismanagement. Hospitals have run out of medications and supplies. Contagious diseases have had a resurgence. Angola has the highest rate of infant mortality in the world. Foreign donors, who favored Angola when it was rich, are now increasingly reluctant to lend to the hapless crooks that run the country.

4.   **ARGENTINA:** Once considered as one of the richest in the world, and a great nation of the future, Argentina fell into the hands of a series of governments run by tyrannical dictators, and bumbling incompetents. It is hard to find a better example of a country ruined by its own government. When Juan Peron came to power he instituted a series of socialist policies including aggressive protective import suppression. But the decline in imports harmed local companies for which certain imports were vital. It harmed average consumers who found themselves relying on poorer domestic products at higher prices. The three administrations prior to the current one were hounded out of office by rioters protesting the loss of subsidies – which in fact seems only to make everything worse.

5.   **ARMENIA:** Conflict with the old Ottoman Empire after WWI led to many deaths and the displacement of more than 1 million people. A war was fought with Azerbaijan from 1988 to 1994 over rights to Nagorno-Karabakh, and irrationally, fighting has persisted between the two countries for the last 20 years.

6.   **AZERBAIJAN:** See Armenia above. Recently, efforts are being made to negotiate a peace agreement between the two countries over their continuing low level fighting.

7.   **BAHRAIN:** Muslim Bahrain suffers from the usual problems of the region: an inadequate economy, high unemployment, lack of adequate social services, a corrupt and inefficient government. This in turn has generated a new wave of civil protest. The government is compounding the problem by unleashing its brutal, heavy handed security police who go after any form of protest even if peaceful. The punishment of peaceful activists is now producing a surge of additional resistance to the regime.

8.   **BANGLADESH:** Independence was wrested from Pakistan after a bloody war, supported by India, in which more than

300,000 people were killed. Pakistan has never forgiven India for its intervention. The country suffered from an oppressive military regime from 1981 t0 1991, but has been slowly improving both economically and politically since. But recently, the country has been threatened by a series of assassinations by Islamist terrorists, and there have been dark hints that the terrorists are linked by the opposition Bangladesh National Party (BNP), which is seen as linked with Jamaat-e-Islami as an ally. Thousands of people have been rounded up, but overall, the government has been accused of doing too little, and the police seem to have discovered a rich new source of bribe money to release many of those that have been arrested.

9. **BELARUS:** Independence from the USSR resulted in a 17 year dictatorship by a ruling elite that was heavily authoritarian and oppressive. There was little development of a structure of human rights or democratic organizations. Everything was made worse by the serious economic failures of the State Socialist government, where 80% of the workforce worked for the government and government sponsored enterprises. 80% of the people say that their personal financial situation has worsened under President Lukoshenko, and there are countless reports of police brutality, false arrests, beatings and property damage and theft by riot police who are driven by greed and not justice. Opponents of the regime are far too split up, and fearful of getting fired by their government employers. Everybody quite properly blames Lukoshenko.

10. **BENIN:** There were seven military coups in 12 years – 1960-1972. Then, from 1974 to 1989, there was essentially an oppressive Marxist-Leninist state.

    Economic mismanagement has left the country severely underdeveloped, and one of the poorest countries in the world. It lacks adequate social services and public infrastructure, but corruption is rampant, often involving senior government officials.

11. **BOLIVIA:** More than 200 coups and counter-coups over 150 years. The latest military dictator, Morales, is relatively benevolent.

12. **BOSNIA-HERZEGOVINIA:** These nations combined in 1991, and achieved independence from Yugoslavia in 1992. The country got caught up in the "Greater Serbia" movement sponsored by Serbia, leading to a serious civil war running from 1992 to 1995, involving Bosnian Serbs, Croats and Muslims with Serb elements of the population backed by Serbia. Serbia invaded the country in 1993 but failed to overthrow the Bosnian government. The country is still recovering and trying to rebuild cooperation between its contentious ethnic groups.

13. **BRAZIL:** The much lauded "B" in the BRIC group of designated notably developing countries (Brazil, Russia, India, China) has hit a bad speed bump. Brazil's bubble seems to have burst. The economy is mired in a deepening recession, thanks to a drop in oil and other commodity prices. The state owned oil company Petrobras has triggered the biggest scandal in the country's history, with dozens of business people, the President, and more than 50 members of Congress implicated in some $ 2 billion in kickbacks. Investments in the vaunted new oil fields have been cut back, even as Brazilians fume over the billions put into new sports stadiums. With Brazilian credit ratings in danger, President Rousseff is forced to impose the same austerity measures typically favored by the IMF, including cuts in energy subsidies. (Economist, 19 Sep. 15) The state of the economy continues to worsen: too many unprofitable state owned enterprises; too much anti private sector government meddling and regulation, loose questionable government budgets, lowering wages, rising prices, lack of investor confidence, loss of 500,000 jobs, government bonds classified as "junk" – all have caused a near collapse of the Gross National Product, and worse seeming about to follow. Largely as the result of her fiscal and monetary policies, and regulatory interventions, confidence in the economy has sagged, GDP shrank for the last three consecutive quarters, and is down a scary 4.5% from the same period last year, and inflation is pushing 10%. Meanwhile, Rousseff is accused of having a hand in the huge Petrobras scandal since she is the chair of its board of directors, and also of having made some shady budget maneuvers. Public pressure has grown so great that she was made to resign.

14. **BURKINA FASO:** Repeated military coups from the 60s to 90's seriously disrupted and confused the country. More recently, Touregs in the north, linked with tribal elements in Mali and Niger, have allied themselves with forces from Al-Qaeda in the Magreb (AQIM), which is linked with Al- Qaeda. These forces have been conducting raids and attacks around the country, incuding a horrible attack on a major international hotel in the capital in November of 2015. The strength and purpose of the terrorists is still very murky.

15. **BURUNDI**: The country suffered from a long horrible vicious conflict on ethnic lines: Hutus vs. Tutsis. Since 1993 when the government was ousted, the war raged, and millions have died and further hundreds of thousands fled or were displaced. External interventions helped achieve a peace agreement in 2003, but President Pierre Nkurunziza plunged the country into chaos again when he announced that he would violate the constitution by running for office for a third term. He has said to have ordered the assassination of more than 400 opponents of all types, and more than 250,000 people have again been forced to flee the country. He has essentially stone walled attempts to negotiate a settlement, sponsored by the United Nations and the African Union. Meanwhile, the economy has all but collapsed. The GDP shrank by more than 7% in 2015, foreign aid has been seriously retrenched, the violence has damaged many businesses, and the country is now rated by the International Monetary Fund as probably the poorest in the world. Nobody now expects any rational solution, and another civil war may be inevitable.

16. **CAMBODIA**: Independence from France was achieved in 1953. Then, seizure of the government by the Khmer Rouge in 1975 after a five year war produced one of the most murderous and vicious regimes in modern history. Cities were all but emptied as people were forced to live in villages and rural areas. More than 1.5 million people died during this period, including any educated person. Vietnam invaded in 1978 and the war lurched on for years. Vietnam finally left in 1988, but the war continued until 1999, when remnants of the Khmer Rouge, which had fled to the highlands, finally surrendered. In other words, the whole

nation was poisoned by irrational conflict for 24 years, suffering untold damage.

17. **CENTRAL AFRICAN REPUBLIC**: Independence from Belgium in 1960, led to bad and corrupt governments for the next 33 years. A civilian government did preside from 1993 to 2003, but then another military coup took power. There was a running war with the Lords Resistance Army has been running for the last 20 years, along with a collection of lesser terrorist groups. Terrorists hold big parts of the country. A deal for power sharing was tried in 2013 but failed, and terrorists siezed power in 2013. A so-called pro democracy movement was in the hands of trade unions, human rights activists, intellectuals and minor political parties; not really "the people".

18. **CHAD**: Independence in 1960 from France was followed by three decades of civil war, plus an invasion by Libya. A peace agreement in 1990 was shattered by rebel attacks from Sudan. In 2010, a peace agreement was concluded with Sudan, but it seems shaky. Meanwhile, the former president, Hissene Habre has finally, after 25 years of incomprehensible delay and fumbling, been brought to trial. His dictatorship in the 80,s was vicious and oppressive, and as many as 40,000 people died and countless others were tortured, starved, robbed and terrorized. Extraordinarily, his trial represents the first time that a former head of state is being tried with due process in an African court.

19. **CHILE**: An unpopular Marxist government was overthrown by military coup in 1973, and the dictator Pinochet ruled until 1990. Peace since.

20. **CHECHNYA:** Chechnya declared its independence in 1991, but is still retained by force as part of the Russian Federation. This is a rogue state in which Islamic extremists mix with Chechen independence freedom fighters, and a bunch of corrupt criminals running drugs and other criminal activities in Russia, Europe, Central Asia, and even the U. S. It is unquestioned that the Chechens have a long history of anti-Russian and anti-Soviet activity, marked especially by rebellions in the 19th century. Chechnya is also mainly Sufi – which is esthetic, moralistic, unorthodox, and mystical. In 1944, Stalin exiled more than 400,000 Chechens to Kazakhstan, and they were not permitted

to return until the 50's. After independence, a new constitution was drafted that was mostly about representative democracy and secular legal principles. Islamic law and principles were recognized, but the constitution had no reference to Islam, and instead religious liberty was emphasized.

But the Chechen conflict with Russia became one of the great targets and rallying points for the international Islamic movement, and drew Islamist fighters from across the Middle East. New Islamist religious and political leaders wrested a lot of power from the older more moderate Muslim leaders, and began the "Islamization" of the country, culminating in the declaration of an Islamic State in 1997. But it became obvious that Islamic slogans and the new laws could not provide a stable government, and government failures discredited the regime. Russia has kept control of the country, but armed conflict between the Chechen separatists and the Russian forces continues to this day.

21. <u>CHINA</u>: The Communists took power in 1946, and the dominating dictator, Mao Zedong created one of the worst oppressive dictatorships in the last 200 years. Reforms began only in 1978 after Mao's death. Huge economic progress has been made, and the reduction of the numbers of people in abject poverty has been absolutely miraculous. But the Communist Party has given up none of its dictatorial political power. There more than 3.5 million official party organizations at all levels of government involving more than 40 million workers. Civil rights are almost non-existent; the government is officially against "individualistic thought". Real elections still do not exist. The legislature is a sham, and the only legislation ever passed it bills originating with the Party. Debt financing of governments at all levels has made China the most heavily and dangerously debt ridden major country in the world.

22. <u>COLOMBIA:</u> There has been a fifty year war between the government and the guerrilla group the Revolutionary Armed Forces of Colombia (FARC), and recently, the government seems to have largely decimated it, with the very great help of the U.S., largely through the CIA. But criminal groups still are powerful

and aggressive, and it is feared that they will simply take over the illegal drug operations of FARC if the current peace treaty being negotiated really takes effect. A sort of peace accord was reached in 2012, but in fact, the government still continues actively to recover control over lost areas. The state is stable, but controls only about 2/3 of national territory, and more than six million Colombians have been internally displaced, one of the highest totals of any country in the world. Three private armies project their own power. Colombia has experienced the world's second highest per capita murder rate, the greatest number of kidnappings in the world, and had become the number one exporter of cocaine in the world, but the efforts of the current government are clearly bringing these sins under a greater degree of control. Finally, in 2016, a peace accord was almost miraculously concluded.

23. **CONGO, DEMOCRATIC REPUBLIC OF:** Formerly known as the Belgian Congo, the country was the personal property of King Leopold II of Belgium from 1885 to independence in 1960. Leopold stole a vast fortune through unbridled rapacity, wide use of slave labor and deliberate neglect of social services. Under his control, an estimated 10 million people died from starvation, lack of medical care, forced labor, and murders. The government of Belgium finally took over until 1960, when independence was finally granted. But the government fell into the hands of new domestic tyrants, with Patrice Lumumba as Prime Minister and Joseph Kasavubu as head of state. Then Kasavubu ousted Lumumba, and he in turn was ousted by a Communist insurgency led by Tsombe in 1965. Tsombe of course proved to be another tyrant who suppressed the population and all but ruined the economy. He nationalized much of the economy including the very important mining industry. He barred religious instruction and changed the name of the country to Zaire. Then – the tyrant Tsombe was ousted in turn by the tyrant Mobutu in 1965, who was ousted by the tyrant Laurent Kabila in 1997, who was assassinated in turn in 2001. After the election in 1993, protests by the losers precipitated a bloody, ethnically based civil war heavily subsidized by rebel forces from Rwanda. The opposition involved a number of

insurgent groups led by warlords after loot. The government won the war with help from Angola, but the country has a very weak economy with more than half of the population in poverty. The World Bank had to bail out the government again in 2002 with a huge $1.9 billion debt relief package. The country is rich with oil wells and diamond mines, but much of the revenue from these sources just evaporates. Laurent Kabila's son Joseph succeeded him as president and has managed, after a highly destructive four year civil war which killed an estimated 2.5 million people, to negotiate an uneasy peace with the help of the UN, which conducted its biggest peace keeping program ever.

Thus, as of 2014, an estimated 2.6 million Congolese have been internally displaced, and nearly 500,000 have fled, seeking refuge in neighboring countries, in what has been characterized as the bloodiest war in the world since WW II. An estimated 5.4 million people have died, including those who succumbed to war induced disease and famine, half of whom have been children. The country has suffered terribly from a sixty year period of horrible destruction and turmoil by a series of vicious, greedy and corrupt leaders which has destroyed the economy and left Congo one of the poorest countries in the world.

24.   **COTE D'IVOIRE**: The country achieved independence from France in 1960. There was a military coup in 1999, and an obviously rigged election in 2000 created widespread national outrage which culminated in the removal of the bad government. Another popular revolt tried to sieze control of the government in 2002, but failed, and the country then lurched into civil war that split the country in two. A shaky cease fire in 2003 led to a bumbling interim government until 2010. An election then was won by a former rebel head, but the armed forces – this time backed by France and the UN – have secured the government. Major political conflict contines.

25.   **CROATIA:** Independence from Yugoslavia was acheived in 1991. The new government was forced by Serbian intervention into a war with their own Serbian population which petered out in 1998.

26. **CUBA**: Independence was achieved by revolution in 1959, with Fidel Castro coming to power, along with a harsh centrist Communist power fixation. Cuba was a Soviet client state until 1991, and lately has been largely dependent of money, oil and weapons from Venezuela. US embargos helped to keep the country poor, but the major fault lies with the failed Socialist agenda. Cuba has been left in the 50's. The US has now taken steps to open up relations with Cuba.

27. **CYPRUS**: Independence was granted in 1960 by Great Britain. A co-government was designed because of the implacable positions of the Greek and Turkish populations which has frozen the country into two parts. There has been constant meddling by both Greece and Turkey which help to keep the island in turmoil. A peace agreement brokered by the UN seems endless, fruitless and forever "ongoing".

28. **CZECH REPUBLIC**: Invasion by Warsaw Pact troops in 1968 was used to back an unpopular Communist regime, and it simply led to worse repressions. The Czech Republic then separated from Slovakia in 1993, and it has abandoned much of the Socialist agenda, adopted a market based economy and become a more stable and prosperous country.

29. **EAST TIMOR:** In an extraordinary run of colonial assertion, Portugal entered the island of Timor in 1530, and remained in possession until 1975. during the period from 1613 to 1860, Portugal and the Netherlands fought over control of the island and eventually split in two – east and west. Portugal pulled out in 1975, E. Timor declared its independence, and nine days later, it was invaded and occupied by Indonesia. Not only were the people denied their independence, but they were then subjected to the rule of a tyrannical, oppressive, vindictive regime until 1999 – 24 very bad years. Indonesian rule was characterized by oppression, violence, neglect, violence against women, religious bigotry, lack of food and subsequent starvation; lack of medicine and consequent disease and death. The locals rebelled against the occupation, but the Indonesian Army suppressed the rebellion, including the training of local militia to fight against their own people.

E. Timor was finally able to declare its own independence in 2002 and hold a reasonable election. But Human Rights Watch claimed that 200,000 people (out of a total population of 650,000) were killed, and half a million forced out their homes at some point in time or another. Thus, the Indonesian occupation of E. Timor goes down as one of the worst atrocities perpetrated by any government in the last 100 years.

30. **EGYPT:** Egypt declared its independence from Great Britain in 1952, and it has been ruled ever since its independence by three dictators: Gamel Abdel Nasser, 1954 to his death in 1970; Anwar Sadat from 1971 to his assassination in 1981; and Hosni Mubarak from 1981 to 2011 when he was ousted from office be a huge upsurge of popular outrage. During this 51 year period there were virtually no stable elections. When an election was held in 2012, it was won by the MB candidate Mohamed Morsi. Morsi initiated executive orders changing the constitution and calling for the mandate of an Islamist government and national cultural practices. Again, at least two million people took to the streets of Egyptian cities demanding his removal, and in 2013, the army obliged. The government has returned to tight top down control, and harsh measures against the MB.

31. **EL SALVADOR:** There was a 12 year civil war, 1980-1992 against leftist rebels. Economist 1/31/15: El Salvador is one of the world's most gang ridden countries, which has horribly evolved into open war between two huge rival gangs, the MS-13 and Barrio 18. A truce, brokered by the government, lasted less than two years. The murder rate has climbed back up to 15 per day! In addition, the gangs have broadened their skills against average people: street violence, murder of police, extortion of shop keepers, kidnapping, and senseless terrorism. Bad politics seems to be a part of the problem. Both candidates for President fear being accused of being "soft on crime" and they thus oppose the truce. The sane course would, of course to try and build on the truce and make it work, instead of shouting out against it.

32. **EQUATORIAL GUINEA:** Independence in 1968 from Spain. Mbasogo ruled from 1978 to date, remaining in office through

a series of obviously flawed elections and very heavy centrist controls of everything.

33. **ERITREA:** Independence in 1952 from Ethiopea, when the UN helped it break away and form an autonomous region. Ethiopea re-annexed it in 1962, which triggered a violent civil war which lasted 30 years to 1991. Eritrea finally was able to declare its independence in 1993, but what the citizens got was a heavily repressive government, another two year war with Ethiopea (1998-2000), and constant bickering and fighting over border disputes.

34. **ETHIOPEA:** A very ancient country with large Christian traditions. Halle Salassi ruled as an emperor from 1930 to 1974, when the government was lost to a Marxist-Socialist group. Widely failed and hated, it was toppled by rebel forces in 1991. The government continues its bitter war with Eritrea, and has sent troops to Somalia to fight the terrorist insurgents there who have often attacked Ethiopea. In the UNDP Human Poverty Index, Ethiopea was ranked 99th out of 103 countries ranked, and and estimated 45% of its population (77 million) are living below the poverty line. And if the wars were not enough, the country has suffered from a major drought, epidemics, more than 130,000 refugees from other countries and massive internal displacements.

35. **GHANA:** Once again, Ghana is sliding into economic trouble because of the lack of intelligent leadership. The currency, the ceti, is sliding, having lost half of its value since 2008. Oil income was high for many years and the general economy prospered: up 14% in 2011, 8% in 2012, and another 7% in 2013. But where does the money go? 2/3 of the population live on less than $2/day (i. e. the World Bank definition of "near poverty"). Populist subsidies and crony capitalism suck up a lot. Public sector wages consume up to 70% of the national budget. General wages can't keep up with inflation. Much of the urban population lives in make-shift hovels with no real address. Huge numbers of youths graduate school and can't find any kind of job. Corruption is infamous, especially among the police, judges, sitting politicians, and petty bureaucracy. Ghanian labor unions are pursuing a pattern found elsewhere around

the world where they sell their votes, and oppose technology or any cuts in wages or benefits. Patronage is the core of election campaigning. All of this despite peaceful elections in 2000 and 2008, which seems to have changed little.

36. **GAZA STRIP:** Since 1948, it had been controlled by Egypt. Then it was conquered by Israel in 1967. It was transferred to the Palestinian National Authority in several agreements from 1994 to 1999. The Palestinian Authority lost a key election to HAMAS (The Islamic Resistance Movement) in 2006. The HAMAS is no real government; it is an organized guerilla army, and its sole purpose is make attacks on Israel. It is heavily financed by foreign mostly Shia donors and it is privately backed heavily by Iran. The economy and social environment are so bad that, in 2013 HAMAS and Fatah attempted to effect a merger in which some form of government would be administered by Fatah, but this whole scheme collapsed when HAMAS chose to step up its rocket assaults against Israel. The Gaza Strip is one of the most pitiful places on earth.

37. **GEORGIA:** The "Rose Revolution" ousted the corrupt, incompetent, and highly unpopular regime os Shevardnadze in 2003. It suffers from constant pressures and conflicts from Russia, from which it took its independence in 1991.

38. **GREECE:** 50 years of bad economic policies and populist politics had decimated the Greek economy, discredited the government and caused serious malfunctioning of the civil wellbeing of its citizens. These failures have been mitigated by long term reliance on huge amounts of aid and loans from international sources. In 2014, a crisis was precipitated when these outside lenders and donors, led by the European Union countries, declared their intention to cut off most of the money. This move was driven by increasing protests from the citizens of these countries as to why their tax money was being sent to Greece where it was inevitably and persistently squandered. While a compromise was reached about lending, the Greeks do not seem able or willing to make significant changes for the better.

39. **GUATAMALA:** The country suffered a draining guerilla war for 30 years, 1960-1996, with more than 200,000 people

killed and one million people displaced or forced to flee, with the native Maya Ixil population targeted for racist attacks by President Montt. (He was later convicted of genocide and crimes against humanity). An externally negotiated peace accord was finally achieved in 1996, but unfortunately, what emerged was a long period of governments infamously corrupt even by Latin American standards, and the country suffered from surges in gang, drug smuggling, extortion, murder and theft. This corruption reached the highest levels of the government, and Alfonso Portillo, a former president is in jail in the U. S. for bribery and money laundering. In recent months, the vice president resigned, and the directors of the state central bank and the social security agency have been fired.

As a result, the people have been so abused that protests of many kinds have become an almost daily occurance, and the President, Perez Molina, has launched a belated but substantial reform effort. New charges have been brought against senior tax officials and 22 other officials. A further 17 people have been arrested for an alleged contract bribe scandal. The interior and the environmental protection ministers have been kicked out. Yet the general public opinion still seems to be that not enough has been done, and that nobody in government can be trusted. The presidential term ends in January of 2016, and nobody knows what will happen then.

40. **GUINEA:** Independence was obtained from France in 1958, and the government that came into office was essentially Marxist. It severed relationships with France in 1965 and turned to the Soviet Union for support. There have been constant serious tensions between the military and the government for more than 30 years, including a military coup in 1984 and military rule until 2008, during which the Constitution was suspended. Thus, a state of turmoil has prevailed for 50 years.

41. **GUINEA-BISSAU:** Independence from Portugal in 1974 led to an oppressive regime with Pres. Vieira serving until 1999 when he was ousted by a military coup, which in turn was overthrown by another military coup, the assassination of the

president in 2009, and yet another military coup in 2012. Is this really a nation or a home for crooked generals?

42. **HAITI:** The poorest country in the Western Hemisphere suffered from the seriously corrupt, oppressive and incompetent rule by "Popa Doc" Duvalier from 1957 to his death in 1971, when his son, "Baby Doc" succeeded him. Duvaliers ruled by terror, much of it through a terrorist organization called the Tontons Macoute which continues to plague the country 60 years later. Aristide was elected president in 2010, was overthrown, was returned to office by the UN, and vacated the office. A horrible earthquake shook the island in 2010 and more than 300,000 people were killed and 1.5 million made homeless, with the government incompetent to do anything effective. Thus, Haiti has suffered for 200 years with the worst government in the hemisphere.

43. **HONDURAS:** A military coup in 2000 seems to have unleashed a continuing series of horrible governmernts: Francisco Maduro from 2002 to 2006, followed by Manuel Zelaya who was in turn overthrown in 2009, followed by Juan Hernandez. These successions seem to have been precipitated by militaristic power seeking, "right wing" vs. "left wing" politics, and hordes of criminal drug traffikers. The United States, the UN, the EU and other Latin American interests are all backing the return of Zelaya. Honduras is now seen essentially as a police state in which the economy is a wreck. High youth unemployment is dealt with by the government – by repression, attacks against youthful activists, violence against transgender people, 3,000 murders, a generally soaring unemployment rate, and widespread violations against civil rights and the rule of law. Thousands of Hondurans have fled the country, many to the US, and the American government is trying to get the Honduran government to develop a "return plan", but the people are developing their own "get out of Dodge" plans.

44. **INDIA:** After independence from Britain in 1947 great conflict between Hindus and Muslims led to riots and ethnic violence, and ultimately to partition in which the Hindus broke away and created Pakistan. Animosity continued, and the two countries fought three messy but inconclusive wars. Then, in 1971,

41

eastern parts of Pakistan revolted, broke off into the nation of Bangladesh, and were enthusiastically supported by India in fighting Pakistan. India and Pakistan have never been at peace. Much of the blame can be placed on the "secret government of the ISI" – the Inter Service Intelligence organization which is the implacable and incomprehensible enemy of India, and constantly poisons national politics. India also has serious armed conflict with a Naxalite sect in northeast India. One of the most stupid and vicious disagreements has persisted for more than 65 years is the dispute between India and Pakistan over control or influence in the Indian States of Jammu and Kashmir. (J/K). The lowlands of the state are predominantly Hindu. The Kashmir hills and valleys are mostly Muslim. For decades, Pakistan largely through the ISI, has meddled in J/K as part of their irrational conflict with India. There is also an independence movement in J/K damning both India and Pakistan and hoping for independence. So, a three way conflict has muddled along for 6 decades. Many of the J/K protesters have been young people, and many hundreds have been killed or jailed. Unfortunately, the state government has a bad and deserved reputation for bumbling and corruption. Last September, an unexpected flash flood in Srinagar in the Muslim area revealed badly maintained canal banks; thousands of people were displaced and many homes, public facilities and businesses were destroyed. Through it all, the local government totally failed to perform well. And as a consequence, the Hindu BJP has sensed an opportunity to unseat the current Muslim regime. And to make matters worse, there is a growing Sunni/Shia rivalry. Meanwhile, the Pakistani ISI continues to meddle; for them, bad news is good news. The J/K does not need this hostile and self-serving intervention. Meanwhile, the population of the country has reached more than 1.3 billion people, cities are being overwhelmed, and the government is unable to cope. India is a huge mess containing several billion sub messes.

45. **INDONESIA:** A history of two dictators: Soekarno from 1957-1965 when he was removed by a military coup, to be followed by Suharto who ruled for 31 years from 1968 to 1988. During both of these oppressive regimes, Indonesia was totally governed

by special interest politics of the worst kind, producing undemocratic, incompetent and corrupt governments. More recent governments have been surprisingly acceptable.

46. **IRAN:** After overthrowing the government of the Shah in 1979, the country became officially a religious theocracy, but in fact, control seems to be three cornered: one is the religious leadership which is officially in charge, and utterly conservative. The second is the official government of the president, the legislature and the ministries of government, which has swung from oppression to weak efforts to promote freedom. The third force is the Iranian Revolutionary Guard Force which, while officially part of the Ministry of Defense, is really an ominous separate entity, and it is the secret sponsor and supporter of terrorist organizations all over the MENA and even as far away as the Philippines. It is never clear who really runs the country and makes the decisions. Iran fought a bloody war with Iraq from 1980 to 1988, and it must be remembered that this war was the largest and worst in modern Middle East history, and it was classic Shia vs. Sunni. Iran has built a series of alliances with other governments in the region: Syria, HAMAS in the Gaza Strip, Iraqi's Shia government, Hezbollah in Lebanon, and most recently the Houthis in Yemen. But this is an alliance of losers: badly damaged and failed states. WP, 11 Aug. 15 : 29 Dec. 2011

47. **IRAQ:** Independence was achieved in 1958, but the government was later taken over by the military led by the tyrant Saddam Hussein. Iraq and Iran fought a bitter, costly war from 1980 to 1988, and then Hussein invaded and tried to conquer Kuwait in 1990. He was frustrated by U. S. and UN opposition which in turn led to a U. S. led invasion and ousting of Hussein in 2003, with American troops present until 2009. The subsequent bumbling Shia government isolated the Kurdish population, and punished the Sunni people of the north of the country, and the subsequent outrage ultimately led to the creation of the Sunni Islamic State of Iraq and Syria (ISIS). The post Hussein government proved to be one of the dumbest governments in the region, which is saying a lot

48. **ISRAEL:** Evers since its creation in 1945, Israel has faced implacable resistance by Arab governments and countless

wars and skirmishes, including an extremely important victory in what was called the Six Day War in 1967. 2006 saw a war against Hezbollah in Lebanon, and the victory of HAMAS in an election for control of the Gaza Strip. Wars have been fought against HAMAS in 2008-9 and a major conflict in 2014. Isreal continues to see Iran as an existential threat.

49. **JORDAN:** After achieving independence from Britain in 1946, Jordan fought a war with Israel in 1967 in which it lost the West Bank. Jordan has wrestled with conflict with a large population of Palestinians, and refugees from Syria and Lebanon. Uprooted Syrians are now one fifth of the population of Jordan, which already has had a large population of Palestinians. The government has done a remarkable job of coping with its 660,000 foreign refugee population, but it cannot find a way to resolve tensions effectively, so the country is in permanent uncertainty over its future, fearing that something will explode.

50. **KENYA: 3/21/15**: Kenya: Ever since independence in 1963, Kenya has been notorious for its government corruption. Finally – finally – this year, after ten years of muddled investigation, seven highly placed officials have been charged with many acts of corruption. "This is the first serious prosecution of senior politicians accused of corruption in modern Kenyan history", and "a revolution in the fight against graft." (Economist, 3/21/15). The seven officials have been charged with signing to fake contracts or over priced contracts, or "ghost" contracts involving huge sums; as much as 16% of the state budget; and thus, sucking money out of funding for valuable public programs. It is notable that the president finally acted in part because the public has finally risen up in support of – something!

Meanwhile, Kenya has become the destination of choice of more than 600,000 refugees fleeing the convulsions of civil unrest, terrorism, and ethnic violence in Sudan, South Sudan and Somalia, and the Dadaab camp, with 350,000 residents has become the largest such camp in the world. In addition, Kenya suffers from a new wave of terrorist incursions from al Shabab terrorists based in Somalia.

51. **KOREA, NORTH:** The country was occupied by Japan from 1905 to 1945. Then it was taken over by the Kims who have produced one of the weirdest and most oppressive regimes in the world. N. Korea launched war against S. Korea which precipitated U. S. involvement. The war lasted from 1950 to 1953, and ended in an armistice which still holds. Three generations of Kims have maintained a government of unbelievable oppression and viciousness for more than 60 years, in constant conflict with S. Korea, the U. S. and most of the rest of the world except China, which sees it as a client state. And it is often overlooked that N. Korea and Iran have had a 20 year partnership in the development of nuclear weapons systems, and N. Korea is perfectly capable of providing Iran with enriched nuclear materials or full missile based bomb delivery systems. Meanwhile, the arrogant and misguided policies of Kim Il Sung produced economic stagnation and a terrible famine in the late '90s that starved hundreds of thousands of people. The once adequate economy is now obsolete and in a shambles suffering from surging inflation which the government denies. More people are forced into the informal economy, smuggling, theft, all forms of public and private corruption. WP 29 June 15 Pope Francis (June 21): Knowledge of a tyranny or horror brings a responsibility to do something about it. After the holocaust, the world said "never again", but N. Korea is "again". N. Korea holds an estimated 80 to 120K prisoners in inhumane prisons. N. Korea is accused of "extermination, murder, enslavement, torture, imprisonment, rape, forced abortions and other sexual violence, persecution on political, religious and gender grounds, the forcible transfer of populations, the enforced disappearance of persons, the inhumane act of knowingly causing prolonged starvation." At stake for the world is the same moral issue raised by the Pope's statement at Auschwitz: "doing nothing is not an option". Both China and the West fear possible collapse; what would they have to do to rescue 25 million poor and unskilled North Koreans?

52. **KOSOVO:** Kosovo has suffered from conflicts with Serbia which tried to sponsor a rebellion against the mainly Albanian majority and government. Most of Kosovo's people are Muslim,

but the Serbs argued that Kosovo is the seat of the Serbian Orthodox Church, the site of its defeat by the Turks in 1389, and the victory over the Turks in 1912. Insurgency against Serbia in 1998 was brutally repressed by the Serbian military which committed brutal atrocities, and ultimately, more than one million people were forced to flee, and an additional 500,000 were displaced within the country where the total poulation was just 1.8 million. It took military intervention by the UN to force Serbia out of the country. Yougoslavia as such ceased to exist in 2003, and its replacement of Serbia and Montegro dissolved in 2006. Thus, almost by default, Kosovo was then able to declare its final independence in 2008. Low levels of conflict stubbornly persist.

53. **KUWAIT**: The invasion by Iraq in 1990 was highly destructive, especially of oil production facilities, and it took the UN to oust Iraq in 1991. But the turmoil has stimulated new insurgent activity by Shia groups and tribalists against the predominantly Sunni government.

54. **KYRGYSTAN**: After independence from the USSR in 1991, the government fell into the hands of a hard core dictator Akaev from 1991 to 2005, when he was ousted by Bakiev – who proved to be another tyrant, and who got ousted in his turn in 2010. Thus, the country has suffered from lousy, oppressive dictators for almost 25 years.

55. **LAOS:** A country of about 7.5 million that fell victim to the surge of Communist revolution that swept S. E. Asia in the 1950s into the 1980s. Laos was a French colony until 1953 when it became independent and established a monarchy. But a major conflict emerged with the formation of the Pathet Lao, a native Communist revolutionary group which was quickly backed and supported by the Communist regimes of North Vietnam and the USSR. By 1968, the Royal Army was much decimated, but the fighting persisted between the Communist forces and irregular troops of Hmong and other hill clans. The Americans, preocupied with the war with North Vietnam, undertook a massive bombing in Laos, supposedly to interdict North Vietnamese troops moving on the Ho Chi Minh Trail which passed through much of Laos. The resulting bombing,

largely futile, produced stupendous damage, and even to this day, Laotions are still having to deal with dangerous unexploded bombs.

The monarchy was finally overthrown in 1975 after 25 years of bitter civil war, and a Communist/Socialist regime took power. In the war, more than 100,000 Hmong out of a total population of 400,000 died, and 250,000 Laos refugees fled the country, largely to Thailand. The government has lately retreated from its Socialist policies and has begun to redevelop the country, but Laos remains the victim of its shattering conflicts. The economy remains very weak. After 40 years of Communist rule, 85% of the population is stilll tied to the land and agriculture, and more than one third of the population lives in poverty, as Laos remains one of the poorest countries in Asia. Adding insult to injury, Transparency International has labled Laos "one of the most corrupt countries in the world."

56. **LEBANON**: Independence from France in 1943. There has been secular conflict since, with a major civil war from 1975 to 1990 with more than 120,000 killed. Syria invaded the country in 1976, in support of Muslim interests, and did not withdraw until 2005. Hezbollah has created a Muslim enclave in parts of the country, and is an ally of Iran, and is often at odds with the Lebanese government. Hezbollah has attacked Israel often, and in 2006, Israel attacked Hezbollah in retaliation. Hezbollah has also been induced to send fighting men to support the Syrian government against both its moderate rebels and ISIS and other terrorist groups. In other words, Lebanon has been in a constant state of turmoil which has seriously harmed the country for more than 35 years. July 31, 15: After fighting a war last year the Israelis and Hezbollah have seemed to have learned nothing. Hezbollah ambushed an Israeli patrol on Jan. 28, killing two soldiers. Israel threatens reprisal; Hassan Nasrallah, the leader of Hezbollah threatened to "unleash thousands of rockets, and occupy Israel's northern towns." Both sides want to look tough. Hezbollah is mired in an unpopular war in Syria, aiding an unpopular dictator, having been suckered into the fighting by Iran. Israel in turn is fearful that Hezbollah will be able to

arm itself with anti-aircraft missiles stolen from Syrian army supplies, and thus will be motivated to build another front, possibly in the Golan Heights. This is an enduring hate between two bloody regimes that seems impossible to mitigate.

(**Economist 29/18/15**) In Lebanon, there is a growing question shouted out by the people: Wayn al dawlah – Where is the State?" The Lebanese government is a long term masterpiece of low level bumbling. Everything sort of works, but nothing ever seems to work adequately, much less effectively. But it is somewhat ironic that two tides are running strongly now: the willingness of Hezbollah to carry out the will of Iran by sending militias to prop up the al Hassad regime in Syria, and --- the growing mountains of trash and garbage that sits and rots and smells in the streets of Beirut and elsewhere. Summer time this year has been marked by tear gas and rubber bullets and fires and flying stones. The new street accolade for the government? "YOU STINK!"

But the garbage battle is only the latest of civilian outrages against an incompetent government. The root of the mess starts from a tortured form of governance, with power awkwardly shared among Sunni Muslims, Shia Muslims, Christians and Christian Druze. Everything political is sectarian and bitterly contested. Compromise is a forgotten idea. The various sects do not hesitate to turn to bribery and subsidy and illegal preferment to buy support. As a result, the electrical network produces daily shortages and failures produced by "the generator mafia". Water is scarce, especially in the hot summers, thanks to notoriously bad management. Internet services are among the worst in the world. And still, Lebanon sort of works.

57. **LESOTHO**: Independence was achieved from Great Britain in 1966, and the country has swung many times from weak civilian governments to military regimes, and this culminated in violent protests against the government and mutiny in the military, forcing SADEC, S. Africa and Botswana to intervene to restore order. It remains a badly run and desparately poor country.

58. **LIBERIA**: A military coup in 1980 ushered in the era of the vicious regime of Samuel Doe for 20 years, followed by the equally unsavory regime of Charles Taylor who got the country tangled up in a war with Sierra Leone. Taylor pursued the war mostly for money, but his actions were so vicious that he has been arrested for war crimes and is in prison. The UN was called in to stabilize the country and is still there.

59. **LIBYA:** Independence was achieved from France in 1951. Qaddafi came to power by a military coup in 1969, and he created a government that was a strange mix of Socialism, radical Islam, and a personal religious cult in which he declared a new Muslim religion. The fear that he was developing weapons of mass distruction led the UN to intervene, and there were also vigorous "Arab Spring" protests in 2010. Qaddafi was ousted in 2011 after 42 years of almost incomprehensible rule, but the succession to his regime is horribly contested by two terrorist oriented groups running their own governments and which are now fighting a real civil war. The UN has attempted to negotiate a compromise agreement, but with little success, and most public services and facilities are increasingly being reduced to collapse. Libya has become a case study of the utter moral and intellectual bankruptcy of terrorist organizations, which offers nothing but war and hate against "non-believers".

60. **MALAWI:** The recent shooting of a public official brought into the open a whole long series of accusations about the depredations of corrupt officials. This exposed scandal has led to dozens of arrests, including government ministers, and a freeze on foreign aid, which accounts for 40% of the national government's budget. The scam – dubbed "cash gate" - has raised deep questions about Malawi's dependence on aid, its stubborn poverty, and its inability to match neighbor's economic growth. Foreign investors and donors worry about pouring money into a leaking pot, especially since the government seems increasingly hostile to foreign investment. Malawi now ranks 171st out of 189 countries in terms of the cost of doing business, says the World Bank. The new president, Joyce Banda has made serious efforts to curb corruption, but she has a long way to go and not many allies. Meanwhile, in the mid 80s, neighboring Mozambique's

income per head was less than half of Malawi's, but now it is 40% higher, and Malawi's economic record remains the worst in the region.

61. **MALAYSIA:** 4/4/15 There has been a constant struggle between deeply conservative Muslim religious leaders and the rest of the country over the adoption (or re-adoption) of the strictest forms of Islamic Sharia punishment. Malaysia, like almost all of the rest of Islam, has drawn back from such cruel practices as cutting off the hands of thieves, heavy whipping, and death by stoning. These practices, called the *hudud,* had been anciently defined in Islamic law, but even in those countries that widely accept Islamic Sharia Law, these practices have long been abandoned. The debate is important in Malaysia because it has long enjoyed its reputation of Islamic moderation, in a legal system which has allowed two parallel legal systems, one secular, and the other a system of Islamic courts. One very confusing element of the national legal system is the existence of a large number of ethnic Chinese and Indians, plus a large number of ethnic Malays who tend to be more moderate. All of these ethnic groups fear some broad expansion of the worst of Islamic law. The political party in power, the United Malays National Organization (UMNO) has long opposed this expansion of such punishment, but is now waffling. Once again, what is being shown is the weak and vacillating policy of an inferior government, unwilling simply to say NO.

And now, Malaysia's leaders have added disgraceful corruption to the long list of their failures. Many political leaders have been implicated in the vast looting of a state owned and operated development fund called 1MDB. It is alleged that more than $3.5 billion dollars simply cannot be accounted for, and it is further alleged that more than $1 billion has been stolen by government officials who have used it to buy personal luxuries, hidden bank accounts and ownership of upscale properties, some of them in the U. S. The American Justice Department is now involved because much of this stolen money has passed through elements of the U. S. financial system.

62. **MALI:** Independence from France in 1960 produced military rule from 1960 to 1991. Over the following years, there have been continuing clashes with Islamic militants, especially in the north. Hundreds of thousands of people were force to flee these vicious conflicts, but the military claims that it has beaten the insurgents and won back the north since 2012. Mali is one of the west African countries most seriously affected by the Ebola outbreak.

63. **MAURITANIA:** Independence was achieved from France in 1960. The country tried to occupy about one third of Western Sahara in 1976 in conflict with Morocco, but the attempt failed. There was an oppressive dictatorship from 1984 to 2004, and then a military coup led to civilian government in 2005, but the president was once again deposed by a military junta in 2008. Mauritania is one of the poorest in Africa, and it continues to have serious, unresolved conflicts between whites and blacks, and the country is infamous for its continuing toleration of slavery – probably the worst in the world. In addition, these national conflicts have encouraged outside terrorist groups, including al-Qeada in the Magreb.

64. **MEXICO:** Mexico has been suffering for a long time from an inadequate economy, a constant war with the drug cartels, an incompetent governance. The drug wars disrupt large segments of the country and have produced tens of thousands of deaths. The Socialist use of SOEs has produced organizations that are not only losers but the sources of endless corruption. In recent years, the government seems to have become more honest, more market oriented and is finally getting on top of the cartels.

65. **MOZAMBIQUE:** Independence led to a long civil war from 1975-1992 against a Marxist guerilla regime. There is a horrible record of questionable elections and universal corruption. Mozambique's Socialist government with a centrally controlled economy and a single-party state produced one of the poorest countries in the world. Marxist-Leninist leadership socialized society, mobilizing key sectors thru mass-based organizations such as unions, youth organizations, women's groups, and professional organizations which were all designed as instruments of the regime. A movement away from this

mess has been occurring since the early '90s with a good deal of effectiveness, but 25 years later the country seems to have reverted to its bad economic habits and is once again in such serious trouble that many analysts are now predicting total collapse.

66. **MYANMAR:** The military was fully in control of the country for more than 50 years, and they turned a decent, resource rich country into a closed off and impoverished state. Military rule extended from 1962 to 2011, and it was characterized by oppression, lack of human rights, punishing ethnic conflicts, especially with the Rohingya tribe, control of communications, and the constipation of the economy. As a result, Myanmar (Burma) has ended up as one of the least developed economies in the world, heavily reliant on ties to China and condemned by the rest of the world. An election in 1990 was won by the opposition, but the military refused to relinquish power. Finally, another election in 2016 achieved a hand-off of power to a civilian government after 54 years of on-an-off military rule. But one of the big problems of this new government is how to deal with a still very powerful military which have anchored their position into the Constitution, and which, by law, still holds 25% of the seats in the country's Parliament and by law, are entitled to appoint the ministers of defense, border affairs, home affairs and one of the government's two vice presidents. One of the vital needs in efforts to reform the country lies in the need for serious changes in the Constitution, in the face of what will certainly be stubborn resistance by the military. As a valuable interim move, the new position of State Counselor was established by law, and the hugely popular and respected Nobel Prize winner Aung San Suu Kyi appointed to the position. This gives her, and her political party new, but as yet undefined authority, and strengthens their position against the puzzled military.

67. **NAMIBIA:** Namibia suffered from a long war with South Africa, seeking independence and an end of white minority rule. The war was fought by the South West Africa Peoples Organization (SWAPO), which wa sponsored by the UN and

it finally took over the government in 1990 after more than 25 years of turmoil.

68. **NEPAL:** Nepal finally shifted away from an ancient monarchy in 1951. In 1996, it fell into a serious fight with Maoist insurgence who were not subdued until 2006. Regimes since have been obsolete Communists.

69. **NICARAGUA:** Opposition in the country finally turned violent, and a civil war was won by a Marxist Sandinista group in 1979. The Nicaraguan government then got involved in aiding the Marxist rebels in El Salvador, causing the U. S. to sponsor an anti-Sandinista force. The Sandinistas were forced out of office from 1990 to 2006, but a revised versions of the organization was voted back in in 2012. There is widespread belief that the election that returned them to office was badly tainted. The country is a big source of refugees seeking to enter the United States.

70. **NIGER:** Independence from France in 1960 produced control by a single military party until 1993, but the elected government was subsequently ousted by a military coup in 1999. That government was ousted by a second coup a couple of years later, and the country seemed to have reasonable governance until 2010 when yet another coup produced a government that suspended the Constitution, dissolved the Cabinet, and constrained civil liberties. The long standing dissatisfaction of the Taureg native population broke out in open conflict in 2007. The Taureg national movement has been tied to the vicious Boko Haram, but the government itself has joined those of Nigeria, Chad and Mali in jointly attacking Boko Haram throughout the region. More than 50,000 people are internally displaced, and in an extraordinary twist of fate, more than 100,000 refugees from the horror in northern Nigeria flee for safety to ---Niger!

71. **NIGERIA:** The most populous country in Africa, Nigeria could be one of the richest and most important, but it has wallowed in a long period of military dictatorship until 1999, huge and universal graft and corruption, especially in the oil industry, bad ethnic and religious conflicts between the Muslim north and the Christian south, and now the hideous incursions of the Boko Haram in the north. It now also seems that the army

is weak, badly led, poorly paid, rebellious and totally unable to cope with the Boko Haram threat. The country is the happy home of thousands of smugglers, drug traffikers, criminal gangs, and illegal business operations. Smuggling is so serious that it has destroyed or damaged legitimate businesses, and it makes a joke of government policies for the promotion of local production, which has seldom worked in any country anyway. Meanwhile, the economy is sagging, despite reform efforts. Oil revenues are down, total government income is down about 30% from last year, and more than $ 8 billion has disappeared.

In northern Nigeria, pervasive poverty, worsened by unchecked government neglect and corruption, is as much of the problem as religious conflict. A stark economic contrast between the mainly Muslim north and the Christians and animist south is also fanning the flames. Literacy rates in the northeast are 2/3 lower than in Lagos, the southern business hub. Less than 5% of women are able to read and write in some northern states. Income per head is 50% lower in the north than in the Christian south. The lack of economic opportunities is driving some into the arms off radicals. An organization called the Boko Haram is pursuing a terrorist program in the north, but their ideology has very little support in the country. In a widely experienced pattern, they appeal mostly to dissillusioned youths, unemployed, and those living in poverty. But the organization seems to provide only murder and destruction. It appears to have no clear purpose or objectives, no defined structure or leadership, nor any meaning other than the creation of evil.

72. **PAKISTAN**: After India obtained its independence from Great Britain in 1947, serious religious conflicts between Hindu and Muslim caused the Muslim population to seek its own country, and they broke off from India to form Pakistan in 1947. Thus, this separation created an extraordinary opportunity – to create a high value government for a newly coherent Muslim population. But they failed. Instead, the leadership created a feckless, bumbling, vacillating oppressive and conflict burdened government. Pakistan and India fought wars in 1948 and 1965, and the dispute over who controls the provinces in Kashmir

goes on, willfully and stupidly to this day. Another war in the eastern part of Pakistan produced the independence of Bangladesh, a nation of 160 million people, and its war with the main government was heavily supported by India – a sin for which it has never been forgiven. The Pakistan military has repeatedly intervened to drive out the civilian governments and to rewrite the Constitution to augment centrist power. There is a long and sordid history of the military's central intelligence organization, the Inter Service Intelligence service (ISI), pushing its own agenda of meddling in the relationships with India, Kashmir, and Afghanistan, often in direct conflict with the policies of the central government.

73. **PERU:** The country had a long military dictatorship from 1968 to 1980, jusstified in part by the constant threats posed by the violent Maoist terrorist group Shining Path. Alberto Fujimori became president in 1990, and the country seemed to stabilize and make economic progress, but his regime was so oppressive that it led to his ouster in 2000. Much of this oppression was led by the chief of intelligence, Vladimiro Montecinos who used false arrest, blackmail, extortion, illegal imprisonment, and other horrors. When Fujimori was ousted, Montesinos fled the country, but he was later caught, arrested and imprisoned. The recent history of the country is far more positive. In the most recent 2016 election, Fugimori's daughter, Keiko had been front runner, despite the offenses of her father, and she has benefitted from the government's almost unbroken record of corruption and incompetence, and one major scandal after another, many involving members of her own party. In election final results, she lost by less than 1%.

74. **PHILIPPINES:** Independence from the U. S. was achieved after a brutal occupation by Japan from 1942 to 1946. Unfortunately, the Marcos adminstration, which ran from 1966 to 1986 was horribly corrupt and inept, and subsequent administrations from then to now are infamous for their corruption. The country also has suffered from Moro Muslim insurgencies in the southern islands, in part financed by Iran, and more recently 18 soldiers were killed and 52 wounded in an attack by a new group of Islamist extremists in the disturbed south.

75. **PUERTO RICO:** The Republic of Puerto Rico is really a territory of the United States, but manages its own affairs, with various kinds of support and assistance from the U. S. But this confusing arrangement is producing very dangerous results. The economy is in a shambles, and in the middle of 2015, Puerto Rico announced that it cannot repay debts adding up to more than $73 billion. In part, this near bankruptcy has been caused by rampant corruption; hundreds of millions of dollars have mysteriously been "disappeared". The island has lost a large number of its valuable people talents because thousands of people with portable skills have moved the the continental U. S. because of high and persistent unemployment and low wages at home.

76. **ROMANIA**: The dictator Ceausecu ruled from 1965 to 1989, almost 25 years of oppression and corruption. He was finally voted out of office in 1996, overthrown by a Communist government which was almost as bad. Things have been more or less stable, but never efficient, since.

77. **THE RUSSIAN FEDERATION**: The history of the Stalinist regime (1928-1953) was that of one of the worst and most vicious tyrannies in history. Millions and millions of people were deliberately killed, starved, imprisoned and displaced. Deaths have been estimated as high as 30 million. What is worse, many of the oppressions of the government were totally inexplicable. When the Soviet Union collapsed in 1991, the whole structure collapsed, and 14 new independent countries were created. When Russia faced its opportunity to create a decent and effective new government, it failed, choosing instead create one of criminal, crooked and bullying nature, with the tyrant Putin as president. The economy that emerged has been far too heavily dependent on revenues from oil and gas resources, and after more than 25 years of fumbling efforts to diversify the economy, it still remains in precarious condition, and the GDP has actually declined.

78. **RWANDA**: After independence from Britain in 1962, Hutus who had usurped the long standing kingdom, attacked the rival tribe, the Tutsis, killing thousands and displacing many hundreds of thousands more. The Tutsis then formed a rebel

group, including forces from refugee camps in other countries, to attack the Hutu government, and another million people were murdered in a remarkably hate filled civil war that lasted from 1990 to 1994. Thus 2 million Hutus in their turn, were forced to flee the country to avoid what was regarded as an attempt at total genocide. The conflict continues as spastic lower levels ever since within the country and slopping over into Congo and other neighboring countries. Things seem to have stabilized in recent years.

79. **SAUDI ARABIA**: The Saudi government has been at the heart of a coalition of Sunni Muslim governments and religious leaders against a comparable coalition of Shia governments led by Iran. This is at the heart of the troubles in the MENA. Saudi Arabia has a seriously stern Sunni conservative government, which is slowly and painfully easing toward a more open society and government, but the worse relationships become with the Iranian coalition, the more tense the Saudi government becomes. Threats posed by insurgents in Yemen, backed by Iran, precipitated a Saudi military attack on the country. Meanwhile, the decline of oil and gas receipts has emphasized the unbalanced and dangerous nature of the national economy, with oil revenues producing 90% of the state budget funding. There is a growing concern that the leadership has spent far too many billions of dollars on wasteful spending, much of it to pursue their interntional conflicts, or on populist subsidies for people, an overblown bureaucracy, and large numbers of inefficient state owned enterprises. Plans have recently been announced to sell of perhaps 5% of the enormous state owned oil enterprise, Saudi Aramco. There may be the introduction of a value added tax, cuts in subsidies, and new efforts to stimulate more capital investment.

Saudi Arabia is troubled but not in any great emergency. Its fundamental problem however is extraordinarily bad and highly intractable; it continues to foster an unremitting feud with Iran in the tortured Muslim world.

80. **SERBIA**: Slobodan Milosevic, an unreconstructed Stalinist Communist and populist was elected to head a multi-ethnic

government in 1989, and he immediately set out to create a "Greater Serbia" movement bent on dominating other ethnic groups, and in turn it was hated and resisted by them. This led to fierce resistance and ultimately the independence of Croatia, Slovenia, Macedonia and Bosnia in the period 1991-92. A major war conducted by Serbia against an Albanian insurgency in Kosovo in 1998 was a program of ethnic cleansing which drove more than 800,000 Albanians out of the country. This brutal crime caused NATO to send in a military force to prevent further civilian disaster. Milosovic was ousted by election in 2000, was arrested and turned over to UN forces, and ultimately died in prison in 2006 while under indictment by the International Court. Meanwhile, both Kosovo and Montenegro went independent in 2006. Thus, Milsovic created a human tragedy out of the former Yugoslavia, and stands as one of the most vicious and poisonous leaders of the century.

81. **SIERRA LEONE**: President Stevens in Sierra Leone (1968-1985) sold chances to profit from disorder to those who could pay for it, by providing services. He created a private military force to terrorize his own people, and to lock in control, especially in the diamond fields. As the official rule of law receded, the law of the jungle, presided over by Stevens, took its place. Institutions of government were broken and corrupted. The state became illegitimate, and a civil war over the spoils, encouraged and assisted from outside, turned failure into a collapse. The civil war raged from 1991 to 2002, creating a horrible oppression which led to the death of many thousands of people and the displacement in fear of almost 2 million. Again, the UN was forced to intervene in 2002 and stayed in the country until 2005, followed by governments that were simply unutterable failures.

82. **SOMALIA**: The country suffered a coup by a very authoritarian Socialist government in 1969 which was infamous for its oppression and brutality until its collapse in 1991. But this left the country open to utter turmoil among ill formed but conflicting interests. One group broke away and formed a government of the Republic of Somaliland in 1991, and other parts of the country have attempted similar breakaways. The miserable and

corrupt government was overthrown in 1991, and the following horrible turmoil led to a series of miserable "transitional" governments for almost 15 years. "Twenty years and many misadventures later, Siad Barre had succeeded in wrecking any semblance of national governmental legitimacy. Backed first by the Soviet Union and then by the United States, Siad Barre destroyed institutions of government and democracy, abused his citizens' human rights, channeled s many of the resources of the state as possible into his own and his sub clan's hands, and at the end to the Cold War deprived everyone of what was left of the spoils of Somali supreme rule. All of the major clans and sub clans, other than Siad Barre's own became alienated. His shock troops perpetrated one outrage after another against fellow Somalis. By the onset of the civil war of 1991, the Somali state had long since failed. The civil war destroyed what little was left, and Somalia collapsed."

Another UN intervention in 2006 including troops sent by Kenya and Ethiopia, but the country remains in a total terrible mess, with a shaky ineffective government, few public services, more than 870,000 people living on foreign support, and one of the highest levels of poverty in the world. Al-Shabab was able to grow because of the widespread failure of the government: poor revenue collection in a very poor country means that everything is neglected, including pay for the army troops. Al-Shabab was beaten back but there are now ominous signs it is resurging against both the central government and the sturdy clan structures. The army largely keeps its troops in central barracks because of the fact that, when deployed in small units in towns and villages, these units are far too vulnerable to attack. But the obvious incompetence and corruption of military leadership is causing foreign donors to rethink their support for the military. Complete chaos for almost 50 years, has meant that 3 generations have lived in misery and fear.

83. **<u>SOUTH AFRICA</u>:** Independence from G. Britain in 1961 produced a "whites only" government reflecting an aparteid policy that had been in effect for several years. Long liberation efforts by the black population led to a multi-race government

in 1996, and ultimate black majority rule. There have been long difficult conversions of elements of the economy into black ownership, and major social changes in the conduct of society. The successor African National Congress (ANC) controls what is a one party system, and consequently there are serious conflicts within the party and the country.

84. **SOUTH SUDAN:** There has been a long and bitter history of ethnic conflict between the Arab population that provides the government of Sudan, and which is entirely Muslim, and a black population in the south of Sudan that was predominantly Christian and Animist. This conflict precipitated a twenty year civil war which culminated in 2011 in the creation of the new nation of South Sudan, the youngest nation in the world. But the people of this new nation of about 4.5 million are wasting the great opportunity they earned. Instead of producing a stable governent and country, there has been extensive and unremitting deadly clashes between ethnic groups that have prevented any constructive advance, and instead have displaced more than 700,000 residents, and driven another 150,000 to seek refuge in neighboring countries. The whole country is a wreak and most social services have collapsed. People face starvation, lack of clean water, lack of adequate living places, and any form of safety or security. Outside aid is coming into the country, but the demand is so huge that starvation remains an ominous possibility. Nobody seems to believe that this pitiful failure will be corrected any time soon.

85. **SRI LANKA:** Independence in 1948 from G. Britain unleashed more violent conflict between the Sinalese majority in the country and the minority Tamil. A major war against Tamil rebels lasted from about 1983 to 2002 when a peace agreement was signed. But the truce was violated, and war was resumed against the Tamils who were eventually trapped and all but eliminated in 2009, when tragically thousands of innocent people were also killed, injured or displaced. Peace seems not to have brought recovery and development, and bitterness still marks the country.

86. **SUDAN:** From the start, the arrogant Arab Islamist oriented government ran an oppressive regime against the predominantly

Christian/Animist people in the south of the country. The government also sponsored the infamous Janjaweed terrorist militias in Darfur, and between them and government troops, more than 450,000 people died, two and a half million were displaced, leaving thr whole area and the remaining 4 million inhabitants destitute. The horrible war against the Christians and Animists in the south led to a further 400,000 deaths and displacements of 2 million people. The rise of resistance in the south and the intervention of the African Union led to the declaration of independence of these people and the formation of the new country of South Sudan. Sudan has also fought wars against Chad and argued with other neighbors. Sudan is surely one of the worst countries in the world, and has been for more than 60 years.

87. **SURINAME:** Since independence from the Netherlands in 1975, the governments and people have been embroiled in an unbelievably bad record of bad governments overthrown by worse governments. Every bunch of thugs and rascals that are overthrown are succeeded by a new bunch of thugs and rascals.

88. **SYRIA**: The French took over the country from the failing Ottoman Empire in 1918-1920. The British then took over, based on the post-WWI Sykes-Pinot treaty which divvied up most of the Middle East. Sykes-Pinot also promised to provide a home for the Jews.

Historically, Syria had been part of a larger grouping that included Jordan, Lebanon and Palestine. Lebanon was made independent in 1925, but Syria remained under the control of France until 1946. After independence in 1946 from France, the Syrian government suffered from a series of military coups and counter coups until it fell into the hands of Hafiz al-Assad in 1966. Syria fought a war with Israel in 1967 in which it lost the area of the Golan Heights. Syria meddled a lot in the affairs of Lebanon, including invasion and occupation for several years.

The regime of the al-Assads produced a declining country. It is a State Socialist government which, even before the current civil war, had produce a clumsy, muddled version of socialist policies which produced an obsolete, declining national economy, and an oppressive social environment. The current president, Bashar al-Assad had begun a confused and ineffective program of reforms. Big cuts were made in public subsidies for food, fuel, electricity, water, and transport, the result was an increase in the prices for these necessities, and little real progress. The government withdrew from a lot of control of prices, except the critical items of cotton, wheat and beets. But domestic production of food products remained very low and inefficient, more imports were needed, and they were more expensive. Some efforts were made to control property speculation and inflation to help local businesses, but they had become so weak that they are not very competitive and tend to lose out to foreign competition in both imports and exports. In sum, Syria has had a weak, obsolete economy, and the Assad war will destroy even that.

In the arena of social services before the war, everything was second rate. Elementary/secondary education has always been very poor, as was most health care, especially outside of major cities. The public long ago lost confidence in Bashar al-Assad and the fifty years of his family's failures, leading to the current civil war, but its consequences now seem to be the effective distruction of the country.

89. **TAIWAN:** 4/11/15 Taiwan may, after 70 years, finally be developing a viable "third force" in the political sense. "A year ago, a "sunflower movement" of popular demonstrations was mounted to protest the vague, murky and endless negotiations between the Taiwanese government and the Peoples Republic of China. There is a growing feeling that the 60 year conflict is out of date and a total failure, and some new and more moderate of middle-of-the road policy is needed, and that neither the KMT or the DPP can ever win an extremist position. In addition, the government has accepted another major change – the abandonment of its policy to obtain nuclear power.

90. **TAJIKISTAN:** After independence from the dissolved USSR in 1991, the country fell into a civil war lasting until 1997. The war seems to be mostly with self serving native clans and criminal organizations in a very poor and weak government

which seems unable to protect itself and its citizens. The leadership is very fearful about the threats posed by extremist Muslim organizations, and many laws and regulations have been installed to give the government more control.

91. **THAILAND:** The country has suffered from 40 years of unbridled political turmoil and internal conflict. A major civil war against Muslim "ethno-Nationalists" broke out in 2004, and thousands were killed, injured or displaced.

92. **TIMOR-LISTE:** After declaring itself independent from Japan, Timor-Liste was immediately invaded and occupied by Indonesia. This was bitterly contested and armed conflict persisted for more than 20 years with as many as 250,000 people killed. Later, a UN sponsored referendum in 1999 seemed to portend independence, but it was not observed by Indonesia, and another civil war ensued where more than 300,000 fled to safety in Timor. The country suffered badly from wide spread disruption, collapse of social services and advancing poverty. Finally, Australia intervened and sent troops to quell the fighting in 1999. Independence was reasserted by the UN in 2002; lesser insurgencies continued until about 2011 when the UN was finally able to leave. Thus, the country suffered from 36 years of conflict and distruction.

93. **TUNISIA:** After independence from France in 1956, Tunisia suffered from strict repression for the next 31 years under the regimes of Presidents Bourgieba (1957-1987) and Ben Ali (1987-2011). These dictators left a legacy of high unemployment, serious inflation, extensive poverty, corruption, poor social services, a destructive pattern of ethnic, religious and cultural conflicts, and an unbroken record of mismanagement and incompetence. Tunisia has benefitted from the consequences of the Arab Spring, and it has moved a good deal along the path to greater democracy, but the economy continues to be severely constrained by a continuing record of government corruption. Official nepotism and preferment has scared off investors, stagnated the economy, and produced youth unemployment of more than 20% in the cities and almost 50% in poorer regions of the country. Government regulations have long been sources of corrupt power for corrupt cronies of the old regime – and now

for the new. Now, Tunisia faces the possibility of an overflow of terrorist conflict imported from neighboring Libya, muddle and confusion among elements of the national security forces, and increasing impatience with the pace of reform.

94. **TURKEY:** The recent history of the country is one of a succession of weak governments and three military coups since 1950. Then, a government that was seen by the military as too "Islamic" was ousted in 1997, and a similar attempt was tried in 2016 but failed, with disasterous consequences to national civil rights. The affairs of the country are marred by long seemingly irreconcilable conflict with the nation's large Kurdish population, and by a subborn support of Turkish citizens on the island of Cyprus against the Greek government. The country has been substantially secular since 1924, and it is very tense about Islamic surges. Unfortunately, the Turkish economy suffers from a number of critical weaknesses: excessive inflation, a large stubborn current account deficit, lack of employment opportunities, and much of the economy that is of low quality, or carried in the huge informal economy.

95. **TURKMENISTAN:** This country has emerged as a very strange closed country and society, ruled with an iron hand by Saparmurat Niyazov who has created his own "cult" that has departed from the world of reality. He has outlawed any political opposition, reduced human rights, marginalized all kinds of minorities, restricted religious practices,drastically cut back public health care, badly degraded elementary and secondary education, and reduced an already weak public service almost to slavery. He has employed old Soviet techniques: assassinations, abductions, torture, beatings, house arrests, firings, control of all media. Since his ascendency in 1991, Turkmenistan has been a nightmare – one of the most repressive regimes in the world.

96. **UGANDA:** After independence in 1962 from G. Britain, Uganda installed vicious governments, infamous for their oppression and human rights violations. During the regimes of Amin and Obote (1971-1986) more than half a million people were killed in state sponsored violence. Remarkably the nation seems to have stabilized and civilized itself since 1986.

97. **UKRAINE:** Conquered by the USSR, murderous regimes locally and from Moscow created two famines to punish the locals, in 1923 and 1933, in which official figures say that 8 million people died, but more realistic estimates went as high as 30 million – one of the worst and most inexplicable horrors perpetrated by any government in modern history. Ukraine got its independence in 1991 with the collapse of the Soviet Union, and created its own bad government. The Orange Revolution caused the removal of the bad guys, but they got back in. Finally, Yanukoviych, after looting the treasury, was forced to flee to Russia. Russia, under Putin, then invaded Crimea and supported Russian sympathizers in the east of the country. What remains is a weak, poverty stricken and highly divided country. Recently, the Economics Minister resigned, saying that unrelenting pressure had come against him from allies of the President to make patronage appointments in key posts in the state owned enterprises which have monopoly control over many of the country's most profitable organizations, and that implacable resistance by entrenched interests make real economic reforms almost impossible, and many reform officials have resigned in disgust. These outrages forced the resignation of the Prime Minister in 2016, probably to be replaced with another creature of the country's greedy, self servicing insiders.

98. **UZBEKISTAN:** The breakup of the USSR in 1991 created many opportunities for newly independent countries like Uzbekistan to sieze the **opportunity** to form a good and decent government. But instead one of the former Communist Party leaders, Islam Karimov siezed power and produced one of the most vicious and oppressive governments in the region. Karimov has run roughshod over this country of 30 million imposing a harsh dictatorship that eliminated almost all form of human rights, and attacked hundreds of thousands of citizens through arrests, imprisonments, beatings, stolen assets, and total suppression of free speech or the right of assembly. Political or citizen opponents were simply exterminated. Every so called election is simply rigged, the to usual methods of governement feature bribery, preferment, theft and rampant corription. Despite a wealth of assets including oil, cotton production, and gold

mining, this wealth is usurped by the ruling elite and there is widespread poverty, unemployment and the deliberate neglect of public services. Even religious observances among the mostly Muslim population are regidly controlled.

Adding insult to injury, both the European Union and the United States have lifted previous sanctions against this dictator, applied by the World Bank and the International Monetary Fund, because Uzbekistan is used as a base for actions against the Taliban in Afghanistan. It seems to be impossible to get the world to stop making this stupid kind of mistake. Karimov is now seriously ill, and it is certain that there are many prayers offered – for his departure.

99. **VENEZUELA:** The country was relatively moderately run in the 40 years from 1959 to 1999 when Hugo Chavez was elected. He achieved high public popularity by providing massive forms of subsidized goods and services to the lower income population, but at the same time, he installed an increasingly authoritarian regime totally dedicated to the concepts of State Socialism, at a time when state socialism was clearly seen as a failed experience, and in retreat around the world. Chavez created a layer of communes usurping much of the authority of local governments. He installed a centrist, elitist "Marxist Communist regime", took over the courts, suppressed freedom of expression, applied strict controls on prices, controlled licensing of private businesses, politicized the military and the police, and tolerated a new surge in government corruption. As a direct consequence of these Socialist oppressions, the economy has seriously deteriorated, to the point that economic development, capital investment, unemployment and the rate of inflation are judged among the worst in the world. Chavez died in 2014, but his successor, Nicholas Maduro, has continued his policies. But despite the subsidies, less than a third of the people support this "21st Century Socialism", and 80% say they want to go back to the retention of private property. The national conflicts and deterioration are now so utterly overwhelming that the possibility of total national collapse is highly likely.

100. **VIETNAM:** When the French were defeated by the north Vietnam Communist regime in 1954, and the Americans withdrew in 1973, the country was unified. What followed was a very confused period in which the government reluctantly admitted the failures of Communist State Socialism and began a slow, halting retreat to a market based economy. But tight political control remains over both the economy and society, and efforts to go modern have been slowed by stubborn resistance from the old guard to liberalization of any kind. But still, some progress has been made.

101. **WESTERN SAHARA:** This has been disputed territory since Spain withdrew in 1976. Morocco, Algeria and Mauritania all claim parts of the country, with Morocco controlling about two thirds. UN attempts to conduct a referendum following an insurrection against Morocco in 1991 have floundered for years. The result has been little or no governance and development for 38 years.

102. **YEMEN:** This country of about 25 million people is one of the world's poorist countries, and it has tortured itself by a long and serious split into North and South. The government in the South was Marxist, oppressive and vicious, and hundreds of thousands of people were forced to flee to the North. The country managed a form of unification in 1980, but bitter divisions were never alleviated. In 2004, the Houthi tribes, historically Muslim, initiated a local insurrection which proved remarkably successful against a weak and divided government, despite backing from the U.S. and others. The Houthis have been heavily supported by Iran, and local Shia insurgent groups have assisted the Houthis. Iran's motive is perverse: it is really about threatening Saudi Arabia, and the interests of Yemen are irrelevant. In 2015, a very threatened Saudi Arabia began air attacks against the Houthis, and it is probable that further military assault will follow. This conflict has also sucked in Bahrain and the UAE supporting Saudi Arabia, the U. S. and European nations, and reflects conflicts of the world around it as well as its internal conflicts. Once again, here is another very poor country which has been all but destroyed by incompetence and internal hatred and violence, and by the meddling of its

neighbors. Now, half of the population is in dire need, with the collapse of public services, national shortages of food, fuel, medicines and much else. More than 700,000 are having to be fed by the World Food Program. 334,000 people have been displaced by the Saudi attacks, adding to the estimated 300,000 already displaced by the government/Houthi civil war. Schools have been closed. Agricuture has failed and most wheat now has to be imported, but not much can penetrate a blockade, nor could it be paid for if it did. Patient visits have fallen almost 50% and many, including children and the elderly have died from lack of treatment, especially from diarrhiea from polluted water. It is horribly ironic that Yemen, over the last several years has received more than 2 million people from elsewhere – coming seeking "safety"! Looking more deeply, this poor, poor beleagered country and the whole region has been in a murderous self inflicted killing frenzy for almost 40 years. Yemen's fate, and that of the millions of refugees and displaced persons in the region are tied to the Syrian war, the endless Iranian interventions, the dangerous meddling of the Muslim Brotherhood, the terrorist attacks of al-Shabab out of Somalia, and the long, historic and implacable and wholly incomprehensible hatred and conflict between the Sunni and the Shia.

103. **YUGOSLAVIA:** Yugoslavia was never a very coherent country. It was always a collection of ethnic and religious minorities held together for a long period by force, and in more recent years by the hope that a confederation of semi-separate political entities could succeed. The country was torn apart by the aggressive use by the Serbian government of Serbian minorities in now independent parts of the old Yugoslavia. These Serbian minorities were used to agitate against the local governments in Slovenia, Bosnia/Herzegovina, Croatia and Macedonia. Wars and local insurrections were fought as each of these entities spun off their own independence, leaving Serbia to the tender mercies of the criminal government of Slobodan Milosevic whose only motives were for criminal corruption. Milosevic was finally overthrown when even the majority of Serbs had

enough of him, and he was arrested and brought trial by the International Criminal Court.

If one wonders why Slobodan Milosevic was put on trial in the International Criminal Court, the best answer lies in the fact that he "criminalized" a whole country. The normal structure of the ministries and agencies of the government were deliberately put into the hands of crooks and thugs, all appointed by the president. These ministers and their cronies almost totally ignored their primary responsibilities for delivering the social programs of the government which deteriorated to somewhere between incompetent and nonexistent, in large part because public funds were systematically looted into the pockets of the leadership. Where the state had funds to spend or assets to allocate, public need no longer determined who got what. Almost all business was done on the basis of bribery, illegal preference, diversion of funds to illegal uses, and as leverage for perpetuating the power of the ruling elite. Any pretensions of proper accounting and control of government finances was abandoned, and most ministries developed "black budgets" to conceal the funds used for pathological purposes. The legal tax system was perverted to reward the crooks and punish the honest. State assets ranging from land and buildings to business licenses and regulatory controls were awarded by the regime to its political cronies. Factories or office buildings were "sold" to loyalists at a small fraction of their real worth, thus robbing the public of most of their collective value. Since the former Yugoslavia was a centrist socialist regime, the state owned enormous resources to loot. Lower level employees of state organs, taking their lessons from their top leaders, invented corrupt activities of their own to get a small "piece of the action."

Banks were state owned and controlled and were a powerful instruments in exercising criminal control. Subsidized loans were made to political favorites, and denied to any borrower who was in disfavor with the central clique. Often, even these highly subsidized loans were simply never paid back, and were used by the borrowers to buy up other national assets. These false loans were, of course, perfectly legal but totally pathological. Bank officials were so corrupt that the credibility of the banking system as a whole was all but destroyed. Limited amounts of money available in the country were diverted from legitimate to corrupt activities and denied to those who might have used them to improve a desperately bad economy. The corruption was so bad that whole segments of the economy simply wasted away. Businesses and individual citizens kept out of the formal funding channels of the state owned enterprises because they were so corrupt, and falling into the clutches of government organizations could be actively dangerous. Foreign investment withered as well, since it was a dead certainty that investments would be either wasted, or stolen or diverted to further enrich the already bloated corrupt elite. Much of the Serbian economy remained in the hands of the state owned enterprises which were not only highly corrupt but totally inefficient and deteriorating. Usually, their reputation was that of delivering inferior goods at excessive prices. It was fruitless to think that any of these SOEs could ever be brought up to a level of effectiveness that would allow them to compete in the international economy.

SOEs and in fact many private businesses were blackmailed into making "voluntary" contributions to Milosevic's Socialist Party. At the same time, if they resisted such pressures or tried to support opposition parties and candidates spies in the organizations would report them to government officials who took punishing retaliatory measures against them. Thus, the whole government under Milosevic had been criminalized. The rule of law had been perverted and the legal, ministerial, regulatory, and administrative authority of the state was turned upside down, and the very protective mechanisms that had been designed to aid and protect the public were employed instead to serve the material advantage of the small centrist elite, and against the people.

104. **ZIMBABWE:** A "whites only" government ruled the country after independence from G. Britain was finally unseated in 1979. Mugabe, the hero of liberation and the first and only president has been a horror. President Mugabe personally led Zimbabwe

from strength to the edge of failure. His highhanded regime (PM: 1980-1987; President: 1988 to present) has been seriously corrupt; he has deliberately stolen state resources and put them in his own pockets. He has squandered foreign exchange, discourage domestic and international investment, damaged local commerce, harassed the press, subverted the courts, and driven his country to the very edge of starvation." There have been forced land seizures. More than 4,000 white farmers were forced off of their land, along with more than 300,000 farm workers, mostly black. Two thirds of the appropriated land has been reallocated to poor black families, but the rest has gone to Mugabe's relatives and supporters, many of whom never intended to farm. As a result, agricultural production has slumped, and one of Africa's biggest food producers has been reduced to being one of the main food aid recipients. Of 6,500 white commercial farmers in 1980, only about 500 remain, but the government is still trying to get rid of them. The government now finds itself presiding over a failing economy, rigged elections, destruction of property, political oppression of opponents of the regime, and rampant corruption. An important election in 2008 was heavily rigged and condemned by international analysts, but it is dangerous to criticize the government. Mugabe clings to power by any means.

IV

THE RISE AND DECLINE OF STATE SOCIALISM AND STATE OWNED ENTERPRISES

The great wave of government creation and reform following WW II was not toward representative democracy but toward State Socialism. Some 77 of the countries of the world of that time turned either to a full blown Socialist form of governance or toward the adoption of many of the key political, economic and social policies characteristic of Socialist systems, which made them sort of "semi-Socialist" in nature. This was especially true about the creation in all of these countries of State Owned Enterprises (SOE) where major portions of the economy were controlled by entities created and controlled by the state.

The following is a list of these Socialist or Semi-Socialist countries and governments:

Albania, as part of USSR
Armenia
Azerbaijan, as part of USSR
Belarus
Belize
Bolivia – Morales
Cuba
Bosnia-Herzegovina
Bulgaria
Cambodia – under Khmer Rouge
Cameroon – SOEs

Chile – briefly Marxist
China
Croatia – as part of USSR; also many SOEs
Cuba
Czech Republic
Dominican Republic – state ownership/SOEs
DRC
Egypt
El Salvador
Eritrea – SOEs
Estonia – only under USSR, not since
Ethiopia
France – "social socialism" and economic socialism
Georgia
Ghana
Greenland – SOEs
Guyana
Hungary – Socialist to market
India
Iran
Iraq
Italy
Jordan – SOEs
Kazakhstan
Korea, North
Kosovo – as part of Yugoslavia
Kyrgystan – SOEs
Laos
Latvia
Libya
Lithuania
Macedonia – as part of Yugoslavia
Madagascar
Molawi
Mexico
Moldova
Mongolia
Montenegro

Mozambique
Nicaragua (79-90)
Norway – economic, SOEs
Oman – state control, SOEs
Pakistan
Papua New Guinea – state ownership
Poland
Portugal – retreat
Romania
Russia
Serbia
Slovakia
Slovenia – state ownership
S. Africa – SOEs
Spain – Franco until 1975
Sweden – social socialism and much state ownership
Syria – Ba'ath Party is socialist, many failures
Tajikistan – former USSR influence, many SOEs
Tanzania – heavy SOEs, neglected private sector
Turkmenistan – SOEs
G. Britain – heavy public ownership and social control
Ukraine
Uzbekistan – still very controlling with little reform
Venezuela – Chavez = socialism
Vietnam – slow to change
Yemen – Marxist; conflict with S. Arabia since 1970. Hundreds of thousands have fled to S. Arabia.
Yugoslavia
Zambia – copper industry finally being privatized
Zimbabwe – more oppressive and control oriented than former socialism.

The emergence of state owned enterprises (SOEs) was seen as the most significant force for Socialist economic domination. These economic entities were seen as a middle ground between a standard government ministry or bureau and a true private sector organization. The key is that the SOE was designed so that it could function like an independent private entity for economic efficiency purposes, but would still be under the policy direction of the government so that each would implement some presumably valid public purpose. State ownership was justified in part by an opposition to the private sector which was in itself pathological policy. This anti private sector philosophy also rested on the premise that somehow, officials in governments would always act correctly, and that public decisions about the use of national resources would somehow always be "right". It was also argued that there was some serious risk that private sector firms might achieve a monopoly position and thus be able to dictate exorbitant prices for their goods and services. This reasoning is especially ironic, since there are very few private sector monopolies but there are hundreds of thousands of government monopolies created in the form of state owned enterprises. The irony is more compelling in that the supposed defense against private sector monopolies would necessarily be laws and governments. But what are the protections against tyrannical government monopolies?

What have been the most frequent uses of SOEs? Power generation, telephone and telegraph, railroads, ports, highways, urban transport, auto/truck production, railroad rolling stock, airlines, shipping radio and TV broadcasting, media and book publishing, agricultural services including irrigation, fertilizers, food and beverage processing, agricultural credit, and crop purchasing. Also, they extend to construction, heavy engineering, machine tool production, electronics, industrial credit, and small business credit. There are specific industry sectors considered critical to the national economy including iron and steel, aluminum, copper, petroleum and petroleum products, petrochemicals, and electronics. Many countries have gone so far as to control consumer durables and nondurables, retail and whole trades, textiles, hotels, tourism, food and beverages. In most cases, the government will control banking and insurance, and the flow of foreign trade, both in and out of the country, and even social services such as hospitals.

According to Waterbury, "the empirical record shows that managers of public enterprises doctor their books, hoard goods, evade taxes, hide profits, and collude with other enterprises to defraud the government. So many enterprises ran forever as loss makers that the cost of propping them up contributed greatly to the fiscal troubles of their governments, and their failure meant that often decades of potential real economic development were wasted in the fruitless task of attempting to make SOEs work."[i]

There were many perverse and corrupt ways in which governments can "game" their relationships with SOEs. Most governments exercise control of SOEs through a supervisory government ministry. For example, a Ministry of Energy will supervise all SOEs that produce oil, gas, electricity, water power, and energy distribution. This supervision usually involves review (and control of) borrowing, product lines, business location, capital investments, labor rates and prices. Governments can keep foreign competition out of the country in order to protect their domestic SOEs and private companies. Such protections include denying the right to import goods or services; imposition of heavy tariffs on imports; quotas limiting the quantity of goods that can be imported; or technical regulations that prevent certain goods from entering. Similarly, governments are usually very defensive of their SOEs. It becomes politically important that SOEs succeed -- or at least appear to succeed. This has led to the evolution of many practices which give SOEs advantages over private competitors, including the granting of a national monopoly; licensing regulations that prevent private company entry into certain markets; limits on foreign investment and/or ownership; forced allocation of market access.

The old Soviet Union, through its command and control economic planning "perfected" highly corrosive techniques for control of prices of goods and services. This might involve overall price control structures for all goods and services; selective controls on the sale of goods or services (e. g. what is paid to farmers for wheat; what prices wheat processors and distributors are allowed to charge; and what prices bakeries are allowed to charge customers). There may be mandated limits on SOE charges and profits, and forced exchange rates between SOEs. Also, the government may tamper with the costs charged for government controlled services such as power or raw materials such that some organizations are penalized while others are subsidized. The government may use regulations, or back room pressures, to control payments between SOEs and even private companies to subsidize favored SOEs. In Egypt, which used to be famous for the quality of its medical treatment, the quality of care in state owned operated hospitals is so bad that many people, including national government rulers, simply avoid the state run system. Health insurance covers only about 54% of the population and almost none of these recipients use state facilities. People with no health insurance spend their precious money in private sector facilities. As a result, nearly 75% of health costs are paid from personal funds. Meanwhile, public run hospitals continue to be of low quality, under staffed with poorly paid doctors and technicians, obsolete and overcrowded.

The government can control the rate at which the local currency can be exchanged for foreign currencies. This makes goods either cheaper or more expensive to import or to export, based on the exchange rate

The government often controls labor relations through special privileged relationships with labor unions. This gives them additional leverage over SOEs, and that can be both good and bad. The government can mandate worker pay and benefits, and can mandate levels of employment in general, or in specific industries. Typically, governments have mandated excessive hiring for political reasons. Many SOEs are forced to carry as much as 40% of the workforce in redundant employment which all but destroys their ability to be cost competitive with private sector and foreign competition. Governments can also vest unions with power to effect SOE management decisions, including denial of technology upgrading, and privatization. In many cases, unsupervised union control over large pension funds has led to wide-spread theft and corrupt practices.

It is clear that any of these policies could become corrupt and they usually did. Many of the practices are inherently complex and technical, and cannot be seen or understood by the general public. Corrupt practices including the taking of bribes and/or kickbacks for preferential treatment (access to loans, access to licenses to do business, award of government contracts, insider knowledge on transactions, avoidance of audits or investigations, ignoring excessive and illegal charges, excessive prices and profits, etc.) Typically, government audit, oversight and investigation agencies are weak and understaffed -- often deliberately.

Most of the 100 plus governments discussed earlier have added another failing to their political and economic portfolio – almost all of them operate their governments at a very low level of effectiveness. They are simply very badly managed. Facilities such as electricity production and distribution, water supply, waste management, housing availability, schools, hospitals and clinics, transportation or welfare services are far too often seriously inadequate or poorly delivered, or both. City bureaucracies are widely loathed for their excessive paper shuffling, their slowness and their attitudes of indifference. Consider for example two horrible cases. In India in 2014, the country suffered an enormous power failure and blackout – now rated as the biggest electricity failure in history, anywhere in the world. This failure affected a staggering 640 million people. India's electricity system, long neglected by the top down government, is now so run down and poorly maintained that more than 25% of its power is simply lost through leakages, or by deliberate theft by thousands of "customers" who tap illegally to power lines. And almost 300 million people – 25% of the national population – are not even served by the system.

This kind of neglect of a critical element of public infrastructure is very characteristic of developing countries, and the problems seem destined to get worse. If the populations of Asia are destined to increase by 7-8% each year, it is hard to see how the current infrastructure, already far behind demand, will ever be able to keep up. India already has 68 cities with populations over one million, and the population of cities across Asia is expected to increase from 350 million now to almost 600 million by 2030.

Or take the horrible case of Venezuela, which is very rich – the world's 9th largest oil producer – but very stupid. The country suffers from a totally unreal Marxist-Socialist government and economy where bewilderingly bad economic policies have all but ruined the country in about 15 years. Venezuela suffers from a sagging, stagnant economy, a debilitating inflation rate of almost 20%, a plunging currency, serious and continuing shortages of vital civilian needs including food, heating oil, medicines and much else. As the economy collapses, crime, corruption and despair are rocketing up. Heavy subsidies paid by the government to people to buy political support are being reduced because the government is running out of money. The electricity system is so bad that in the "best" locations, it runs 3-4 hours a day, and in the worst places it runs not at all.

The need for massive reform extends also to the arenas of social policy. Most modern governments are largely anti-social. They work very hard to create and maintain top down <u>control</u> – often to the point of active oppression. They have no intention of addressing the question of what "the people" really want and need. "Bottom up" representative democracy is almost always seen as a threat, pressing the unacceptable concept that the people can direct their leadership. The famous dictum of the Soviets that government provided all "from the cradle to the grave", really came to mean that the government <u>controls</u> everything from the cradle to the grave. Everywhere, the obvious failures of Socialist regimes are finally forcing them to retreat toward a looser and more market competition based economy, but they are retreating as little as possible, as slowly as possible and as reluctantly as possible. And these retreats are mostly economic and not political. Regimes cling to political power and some of the worst elements of public policy, such as the zeal for military conflict, or the tendency to reward friends and punish enemies, or the enthusiastic retention of sophisticated forms of corruption.

To a remarkable degree, the emergence of a market based economy has led to almost miraculous improvements in national economies, such that, even after the looting and corruption, more wealth has been acquired by the average citizen. Two remarkable social changes are occurring. First, a marvelous tide has been running, mostly in the Far East, that is raising hundreds of millions of people out of abject poverty. Second, a new and important Middle Class has been evolving, even in China and India, and it will be very important to see how they can and will function in what usually remains a top down, centrist regime. Will the new middle class change the social balance, or will they just make money? Will they be more inclined to adapt valuable western concepts such as civil rights, gender equality, self reliance, and a new pattern of more intense moral and ethical values? In many places, "bottom up" may really mean "middle up" if the new class chooses to push for political dominance. It is a hope at least that the new middle classes will be more inclined and able to press for the upgrades needed to help the poor and to create adequate social services delivery systems and public infrastructure. One of the most significant changes that must somehow emerge is the abandonment of many governments of policies that deliberately pit one element of society against others as perverse instruments of power.

INDIA: STATE SOCIALISM'S UNREAL WORLD

"India is one of the colossal failures of state socialism: the Industrial Policy Resolution in 1956 reserved 17 industries exclusively for the public sector. The reserved sectors included iron and steel, mining, machine tool manufacture, and heavy electrical plants. This led to massive expansion of what became known and the License Raj. An untrained army of underpaid, third-rate engineers at the Directorate General of Technical Development, operating on the basis of inadequate and ill-organized information and without clear cut criteria, vetted thousands of applications on an ad hoc basis. The low level functionaries took months in the futile micro review of an application, then send it for approval to the administrative ministry. That ministry again spent months reviewing the same data before it sent the application to an inter-ministerial licensing committee of senior bureaucrats who were equally ignorant of entrepreneurial realities. Once this group was cleared, the application was finally sent to the Minister for approval. But even after approval of the general application, there were dozens of sub actions that had to get similar approval. If financing was required, a similar process for the funding had to be followed." **(Das, Gurcharan, "India Unbound")**

It became clear fairly early that the Nehru version of state socialism was delivering neither growth or equity yet the government stubbornly continued on the wrong path through the whole 70s and 80s, even when it was clear that these Socialist policies were failing, and the "mixed economy" was leading to a dead end. Then – Indira Gandhi's government compounded the felony by becoming even more rigid, introducing more controls, and becoming even more bureaucratic and authoritarian. It nationalized banks, discouraged foreign investment in the name of import substitution, and at the same time, placed more controls over domestic enterprise. Much of this control was highly political, to reward backers and friends and punish opponents.

VENEZUELA: WILLFUL SOCIALIST SELF DESTRUCTION

President Hugo Chavez became very popular because he supplied huge amounts of subsidized goods and services to the average citizen. But he also was a dedicated State Socialist in a time when State Socialism has been in serious worldwide retreat for its failures. Chavez installed a "Marxist communist regime" in Venezuela. He took over the courts, and maneuvered stricter control over state and municipal governments. The legislature approved a law creating communes: "a socialist entity" with legislative, judicial and executive functions" and which would operate SOEs to replace the "capitalist economy". Each commune was designed to "regulate social and community life and guarantee public order, social harmony and the primacy of the collective over individual interests." State and municipal governments were forced to transfer part of their revenues to the commune, and since communes can span municipal borders, they could reallocate funds to supportive areas. And, bouyed by floods of petro dollars, Chavez bought public support with a system of subsidies to the poor and near poor, and succeeded in cutting poverty by almost 30% in the early years of the regime.

But now, only 31% of the population supports this "21st Century socialism", and 80% favor private over communal property. The current government is in serious trouble of its own making, since the miserable socialist economy, and the cost of free or subsidized goods and services has all but bankrupted the country, and built up public resistance, especially in the national legislature. Even among corrupt countries in Latin America, Venezuela stands out. Transparency International ranks it as the ninth most corrupt country in the world. Now, people line up at stores where the shelves are mostly empty; doctors and hospitals admit they lack even essential medicines; the electric power system can't meet demands. The heavy investment in state owned enterprises (SOE), including the vital oil company was almost universally disappointing, with many operating at losses, draining money out of the social services elements of the economy. The oil company was so poorly managed that it failed to maintain its facilities, and as a result, production fell about 25% in the period of 2000 to 2014, at a time when the world price of oil had plummeted by almost 50%. Now, unemployment is out of sight, and The International Monetary Fund says that the country has "the world's worst pace of economic growth, the worst inflation, and the 9th worst unemployment rate." The currency has lost more than 90% of its value over the last three years, and the horrible economic debacle has caused wide-spread social collapse, with climbing crime rates of all kinds, and a surge of infant mortality, murders, and other crimes and an even greater opportunities for corrupt officials to pick off the carcass. The failed economy then drives off potential investors, and many businesses are going under. Complete national collapse is increasingly probable, yet President Maduro remains a stout Socialist.

AFRICA: VAMPIRE GOVERNMENTS (AYITTEY, 1ST BOOK, P. 20)

"The vampire parasitic elite minority groups have produced "a meretricious fandango of imported and borrowed institutions, the end product of which is a ludicrous monstrosity – a mass of confusion and an internally contradictory system – no rule of law, no accountability, no democracy of any form, and even no sanity! Common sense has been murdered and arrogant lunacy rampages with impunity. The ruling elites refuse to implement any real reform and thus will continue to produce never-ending crises on the whole continent. African governments have failed to upgrade much of their all important agricultural sectors and the life of farmers and villagers. They have failed to indentify the tide of growing industrialization and commercialization, and they have failed to understand and utilize the information and automation tides." (Ayittey, "Africa Betrayed")

Today African countries import more than $80 billion worth of food annually, having dissipated its past record of being a major food exporter earning $65-70 billion annually. Instead, they now rely on (increasingly reluctant) foreign aid totally more than $18 billion (2000) to buy food. In fact, in general, African governments got stuck to the State Socialist policy of national "industrialization" and never quite understood the whole wide range of economic development strategies that have emerged that are more attuned to the world economy. Finally, most governments did not understand the increasing importance of the consumer services sectors of a national economy. The ultimate failure has been governments where the population and economy is still heavily rural/village, have almost totally neglected the opportunities for rural development and the upgrading of village life.

Part of the African problem is a persistent lack of what could be called "functional literacy." For example, the Agency for International Development (AID) has constantly supported efforts to introduce modern technology into the agricultural sector. General illiteracy on the continent is appalling: around 90%. So even when new tractors and other farm equipment become available, few know how to use them effectively, and even fewer know how to repair them. While the world has become more complex and difficult, demanding more sophisticated skills, African governments simply have not gotten it, and they have allowed their education systems to remain in the last century. The key to these obsolete leaders is still "production", when the demand is for relevance and quality. There has been a constant struggle between the political need for fuller employment, and the tendency of modern technology to be less and less labor intensive.

THE ULTIMATE: CAMBODIA AND GOVERNMENT BY INSANITY

Cambodia has long been a kingdom, with the king held in much esteem, but it has long been a country run by oppressive dictatorships, and a series of opposition organizations. Many of them were inspired by the Marxist/Leninist models of the USSR and China, and active support from the powerful Communist regime of North Vietnam. As with most of the communist parties in less developed nations, the Communist leadership was not the "proletariat" of workers and peasants, but an intellectual elite more typically from the universities and the civil service. From this Communist background rose up something called the Khmer Rouge, destined to create the absolute worst and most evil government in the history of the modern world.

The Khmer Rouge grew up out of the Cambodian Communist Party, which grew up out of the Vietnamese Communist Party. The VCP was an organization of grand ambitions, fed by China. Mao himself thought that his revolution could be widely exported and would be eagerly sought in S. E. Asia, and Chinese leaders thought that Vietnam was the key to what was to become an irresistible surge. Thus, China and N. Vietnam meddled endlessly in the affairs of Cambodia, Laos and Thailand, making the bad situation in these countries infinitely worse. In Cambodia, the Premier was in and out of power; governments came to office, proved incompetent and corrupt, were replaced by another group equally bad. The result, ultimately, was civil war at various levels of intensity, which limited economic development, and prevented to creation of an adequate base of critical national social services and public infrastructure. Cambodians lived for decades in a muddled mess of their own devising.

Thus, there was a good deal of justification for the oppositions to the regime that developed, and because of the strong advocacy for Communism and State Socialism in the region, it is not surprising that the government's most formidable opposition was among the Communists. These forces were essentially local, but they had a lot of support, and a lot of "guidance" from their comrades in N. Vietnam. In the early years, from 1960 up to 1975 the nature of the Khmer Rouge was as an insurgent group in the Communist galaxy, with a strange record of shifting loyalties – sometimes an ally of the regime, and sometimes it implacable foe.

Then, in the early 70's, the nature of the conflicts seemed to change, and the "Khmer Rouge" went through a horrible change; a change so enormous and so inexplicable and so stunningly evil that, after almost 50 years of trying to understand what happened, no satisfactory explanation has emerged. The Khmer Rouge that emerged is a classic example of how human beings can descend into pure evil. This new Khmer Rouge seized the government of Cambodia in 1975 and it installed a reign of terror unparalleled in human history. The Wikipedia article entitled "Khmer Rouge" compellingly summarized the horror. "In power, the Khmer Rouge carried out a radical program that included isolating the country from all foreign influences, closing schools, hospitals and factories, abolishing banking, finance and currency, outlawing all religions, confiscating all private property and relocating people from urban areas to collective farms where forced labor was widespread. In cities, people who refused to evacuate would have their homes burned to the ground and they were then immediately killed. The evacuees were sent on long marches to the countryside, which killed thousands of children, elderly people, and sick people. The Khmer Rouge sought to turn Cambodia into some form of classless society, where the only class was simple farmers living in agricultural communes. These communes were in fact labor camps where inmates were expected to work 12 hours a day without rest, adequate food, or physical care. These camps became death camps producing massive deaths through executions, work exhaustion, illness and starvation.

Commercial fishing was banned, resulting in a loss of a critical source of food for 80% of the population. Money was abolished, books were burned, teachers, merchants and almost the entire intellectual elite of the country were murdered. Banks were closed, and all currency and records were burned", thus creating instant bankruptcy and total poverty for most of the population.

"All religion was banned by the Khmer Rouge. Any people seen as taking part in any religious rituals or services would be executed. Several thousand Buddhists, Muslims, and Christian were simply killed. Family member could be put to death for "communicating." Freedom of travel was abolished. Postal and telephone services were abolished." (Creuvellier, Thierry)

"Modern research has located 20,000 mass graves from the Khmer Rouge era all over Cambodia. Various studies estimated the death toll at between 740,000 and 3,000,000, most commonly estimating between 1.4 million and 2.2 million, with perhaps half of these deaths due to executions, and the rest from starvation, disease and

85

exhaustion. These estimates reflect the death of from 25 to 40% of the entire national population. In addition, a further 300,000 have said to have died after the expulsion of the Khmer Rouge from the government, largely as a direct consequence of Khmer Rouge horrors."

The Khmer Rouge remained a force outside of the government, and the national stupidity persisted in the considerable number of Cambodians in Khmer Rouge areas continued to support Pol Pot. Slowly, turgidly and often reluctantly some of the senior Khmer Rouge leaders have, after 25 or 30 years, been arrested and brought to trial. It is still not clear how many will actually punished. Finally, in 2009, the bumbling, incompetent government of the time permitted the teaching of the Khmer Rouge history.

NIGERIA: EVERYTHING THAT COULD GO WRONG HAS GONE WRONG

"Pervasive poverty, worsened by unchecked government corruption, is as much of the problem as religious conflict. A stark economic contrast between the mainly Muslim north and the Christians and animist south is also fanning the flames. Literacy rates in the northeast are 2/3 lower than in Lagos, the southern business hub. Less than 5% of women are able to read and write in some northern states. Income per head is 50% lower in the north than in the Christian south. The lack of economic opportunities is driving some into the arms of radicals. An organization called the Boko Haram ("western education is forbidden") is pursuing a terrorist program in the north, but their ideology has very little support in the country. In a widely experienced pattern, they appeal mostly to dissillusioned youths, unemployed, and those living in poverty. But the organization seems to have no clear purpose or objectives, no defined structure or leadership, nor any meaning."

The pathology of oil in Nigeria is a pathetic example of bad economics mired in corruption. Nigeria is Africa's biggest oil producer, but the country is always short of gas and oil. The government subsidizes the price of fuel for the public, but at such a low price that local refiners cannot profit from the local market and choose instead to sell abroad. This creates an artificial shortage in the country, with long lines at retail outlets, where fuel is seldom available. Instead, fuel is diverted to the black market which is often supplied by government officials. This artificial shortage in turn creates corruption, where users have to bribe SOE or government officials to get fuel allocated to them. Even individual car owners have to bribe gas station attendants. At the same time, the people in the oil producing areas are desperately poor and benefit little from the oil wealth of the region. In July of 2000, over 1,000 people were killed and others injured in riots while stealing fuel from deliberately punctured state owned oil pipelines. Some were locals, but much of the damage was done by organized criminal gangs who steal to sell to black market channels, and these criminal activities are now a settled way of life

While peasants were siphoning off fuel, officials in the state owned enterprise and government ministries were busy siphoning off oil profits for themselves. A previous president of the country is under investigation for allegedly stealing income and assets totaling more than $4.3 billion. Reformers in the present government find that attempts to eliminate public fuel subsidies and put fuel prices on a more market established basis are strongly opposed both by the vested corrupt interests, and by the public, which has mounted violent street protests against any increase in the subsidized price of fuel. Thus, having locked itself into a damaging economic policy, the government is almost helpless to correct its own past mistakes.

ARGENTINA: CREEPING SLOWLY FORWARD

In Argentina, 50 years of the use of SOEs may have enriched government officials and SOE managers, but the country is far less sound economically than it used to be, and the gap between rich and poor has seriously widened. Starting in 2001, the government under President Menem began a serious program, as sweeping as any in Latin America, to sell off these SOEs to private interests, including water, electricity, gas, telecommunications and the state owned oil company. Since most of these enterprises were losing money and having their deficits covered by the taxpayer, their sell-off relieved the government of an enormous burden. At the same time, the effectiveness of these services improved. The new private owners finally put up the new development money that the government could never manage to produce, and service has begun to improve. For example, the waiting time for new telephone subscribers has been brought down to less than three weeks, where, in the past, many months and even years passed without response, and the total number of telephone lines in service doubled to more than 8 million in just the last three years. But these advantages were mixed blessings in a sense, because the private owners had to charge rates that made up for the loss of the subsidies regularly paid to the former SOE operators, and many service bills to consumers have risen substantially. But still -------.

CHINA: PERVERSE ECONOMIC REFORMS

Two main fears have haunted the thinking of Chinese Party leaders: first, that, when some greater degree of economic freedom was allowed, the pressure for more and more would be irresistible and would overwhelm the government and destroy the command and control economic system that has been at the heart of state socialist theory and justification; and second, that a stampede to economic freedom would also undermine the ability of the government to provide the "cradle to grave" social services that the government uses to control society. In short, the Party worried that society and the economy would learn to manage without them, and people would start asking "Who needs the Party?"

The Party finally and reluctantly recognized that the old system would have to give way to a new and more market based economy, but they felt that the economy could be opened up in controlled ways without the loss of ultimate centrist political control. Four main mechanisms were to be relied upon to retain that essential control: government's continued control of most of the land; the retention of a substantial number of critical State Owned Enterprises; control of the national banking system; and the redesign and retooling of the centrist state bureaucracy, including the creation of the capacity to regulate the new market economy – and everything else.

In order to put together more development capital for investment in its "new wave" market economy, the Chinese government has finally been forced to face up to the inefficiencies of its state owned enterprises. At first, in the 1980's, the Chinese government sought to upgrade the performance of SOEs by pressing for better management, usually through the form of performance management contracts between the government and each enterprise. This effort failed in large part because the motives for difficult upgrading did not exist, and in part because of the limits placed on SOEs by the government itself (e. g. no funds for new technology). In another effort, the central government fobbed off many enterprises onto provincial and municipal governments and told them to cope.

But now, fiscal and economic reality is closing in and forcing what the Chinese government has most dreaded --the closure of many SOEs that have not been able to respond to improvement efforts, and can no longer afford to carry millions of redundant workers on the payroll. The Chinese government is notoriously unwilling to publish any reliable figures about its economy, but sources seem to indicate that an extraordinary 24 million jobs have been lost in failed SOEs in the last 4-5 years. Most were in the economic areas such as agricultural collectives, mines and primary manufacturing, including many of the very large manufacturing SOEs.

But despite these draconian reductions, still more cutbacks and closures appear necessary. In banking for example, some 45,000 offices have been closed, and 250,000 people laid off. The shear magnitude of the reductions simply highlights the degree to which these enterprises were overstaffed in the first place. Many of the workers who have been unemployed will receive a stipend for three years while they seek other employment; these workers are not counted as unemployed until the stipend is completed, but unemployed they are. Millions will not succeed in finding new jobs in the private sector, and will have to be absorbed into the informal economy, thus increasing competition, and lowering incomes for all. Others in rural areas can retreat back onto family farms, but this is the same marginal economic environment from which they fled to the cities in the first place. In all, the official government figures suggest an unemployment rate of 3-4% or about 8.4 million workers but the truth may be that it is closer to 11-12% and 20-25 million. Chinese economic development policy faces two additional dilemmas: first, the kind of high tech economic organizations that they need to meet the standards of the international economy, are also the types of organizations that have least to offer in the way of creation of large numbers of jobs to help soak up all of that unemployment. Second, there is growing concern about the fact that the forced pace in expansion has produced a glut of overproduction in critical areas: steel, coal, aluminum, chemicals and even oil, where refineries are running at about 65% of capacity. In effect, the government failed to understand the demand side for many products and services. State owed enterprises are once again operating under utilized factories producing goods that they cannot sell.

Another major way in which the Chinese government has sought to retain control of the economy is to continue the policy of state ownership and control of almost all land. This gives the government control of who is allowed to use the land, and thus it has control over the location and pace of development of housing, factories, businesses of all kinds, shopping centers, and various forms of transportation. As this form of government control was decentralized to provinces and municipalities, it quickly got out of hand, and became an evergreen source of corruption. All potential land users found that "who do you know" and "how much will you pay" had become the criteria on which land use permits were determined. The continued use of land also rested on willingness to continue some form of "kick-back" forever. In addition, public officials became dictatorial and perverse in throwing people off land holdings to make way for economic development, and there is now a rising tide of public indignation against such abuse, especially since the government often failed to provide adequate compensation or movement of displaced persons to other locations.

Banks of course were part and parcel of these abuses. Government corruption often extended to forcing banks to lend to favored developers including local governments and SOEs, usually with totally inadequate security, and without regard to actual risk or asset quality. When it came time for the borrowers to repay their loans, they often declined to do so, and relied on their political allies to protect them. As a result of these practices, China's banks have outstanding loans in excess of 145% of GDP – the highest ratio in the world. The stock market meltdown of early 2015 badly frightened Party leadership, in part because it exposed flaws in the stock market system and part because it exposed flaws in government policy. In response the Party acted typically; it decided to expand its regulatory control. It is proposing to create a new "super regulator" which combines the functioning of three separate regulatory agencies in the financial system to monitor all financial organizations: banks, insurers, brokerages, trading enterprises, hedge fund managers and so on. Of necessity will be creating some greater degree of control over asset management enterprises, especially at local government levels, that borrow huge sums with virtually no limit or supervision. But being China, it will almost certainly prove the old reality that regulatory "reform" almost always produces more regulation, and meanwhile, **China remains the most debt ridden country in the world.**

According to the Economist, "The country's debt has now increased just as quickly over the past two years as in the two years after the 2008 crunch. Its debt-to-GDP ratio has soared from 150% to nearly 260% over a decade. Problem loans have doubled in two years and, officially, are already 5.5% of banks' total lending. The reality is grimmer. Roughly two fifths of new debt is swallowed by interest on existing loans; in 2014, 16% of the 1,000 biggest Chinese firms owed more in interest than they earned before taxes. China requires more and more debt to produce less and less growth." (Economist, May 7, 2016).

If (or when) this debt cycle turns, the consequences will be enormous. Both asset prices and the real economy will suffer serious shock, and the consequences will be world-wide. China is the world's second biggest economy; its banking sector is the biggest, with assets equivalent to 40% of global GDP, and its stock market, at $7.5 trillion is the third largest. The government still owns many of the nation's largest banks – and most of their huge debt packages. Already, $65 billion in bank loans have gone bad, frauds in the system have "disappeared" another $18-20 billion, and hundreds of millions more is fleeing the country. Lots of money has been quietly leaking into less formal and less regulated "shadow lending". Banks are covering up by insisting that risky loans are safe and that losses are less than reported. China urgently needs to face up to reality and stop lying to itself. The facts make it clear that the government needs to curb debt, stop bailing out everybody, accept some defaults, close failed companies including state owned enterprises, and protect business and individual depositors. But these actions are stoutly resisted because they reveal just how much bad politics by the CCP is threatening the financial system and the national economy.

A new law from the Chinese government revealed a problem that nobody outside of China knew they had. In 2008, Zheng Yumin, chair of the commerce department of the CCP said that China had 43 million companies, 93% of them private, employing 93% of the workforce. Non-government owned or controlled enterprises now produce 2/3 of industrial output. Most service organizations are private. The SOEs have been a declining factor for about 8 years. But the government still owns/controls the commanding heights and a huge percentage of national wealth. Loans to small and medium sized enterprises are still less than 4% of the lending portfolios of the four major banks. This forces borrowing outside of the banking system, at significantly higher rates, and it has forced money strapped governments to go heavily into debt.

The new law would terminate the practice of local governments guaranteeing the indebtedness of so-called "local investment companies" which are special financing entities specifically created to circumvent previous national laws which restricted direct borrowing by the governments themselves. Local governments created these entities, made an initial capital investment for startup, and often pledged land rights or other assets as collateral. Then, the local investment companies borrowed heavily from banks and state insurance companies, and lent it in turn to local enterprises for transportation, energy, water, urban infrastructure and public housing. Suddenly, the national government became aware of the fact that these entitites had piled up debts in excess of 11.4 trillion yuan ($1.7 trillion) and had further commitments totalling an additional

12.7 trillion yuan. Because of a long past history of debt abandonment, it is estimated that as much as 25% of local investment company loans will go bad – then state banks and insurance companies will be in trouble – and the bad debt will once again descend on the central government.

At the same time, the national government is doing much the same thing through its economic stimulus package, since 3 trillion of the committed 4 trillion yuan is supposed to come from local governments. Local governments must assert that most of their commitments to the national economic stimulus package are through these local investment companies, since they can't mount two expensive programs at the same time. Meanwhile, as usual in China, much of the economic development program is caught up in shady deals between developers and local officials, and not a lot of reform has actually happened. Bank loans have increased by 15.4% in the third quarter of 2015, compared to the same period last year. The expansion of the economy has begun to slow, while overall debt has risen from about 160% of national output to a level of about 240%. In the past, the national government has often had to step in and bail everybody out at huge cost. In some cases, debt is simply forgiven. In other cases, debt is bought out by the government at heavy discount. Lately, debt has simply been pushed into the bond market which has risen by 67% over last year.

Now, there is increasing concern that the government's own money management policies have pushed the crucial financial system into a very dangerous condition. How long can the government afford to do it's usual expensive salvaging? If and when investors lose confidence in the prospects of government bailout, how hard would a crash become?

ALSO: CHINA AND COAL MINING IN A DEEP HOLE (ECONOMIST, 07/08/15)

For hundreds of years, rural Chinese have used small local coal mines for fuel. But for decades, these mines and others owned by some government have been miserable examples of both government and private greed, corruption, danger and contempt for human life. Thousands have died from lung disease, mine accidents and total neglect of safety features. But recently, coal mining has become a major government interest and concern. China runs largely on coal. Coal output has been doubled to feed China's growing economy. Many of the small mines have been consolidated into large state owned enterprises, or closed. China now produces 3.9 million tons of coal each year, about half of the world's total. As these structural reforms were taking place, the Communist Party in 2003 promised major programs to improve mine safety and miner health. But over the next three years, there was absolutely no improvement, and some 18,000 miners died, by the government's own account. In 2014, another 900 plus miners died in mine accidents. Deaths from black lung disease exceeded 14,000 in 2013 by the government's figures, but there is evidence that the actual total has been far greater, but no evidence that the government is really doing anything about it.

The debate about deaths has revealed another facet of the problem. China has an estimated 5.8 million miners, compared, for example, to the United States which is the next largest producer, with just 80,000. What this shows is that the mining industry is <u>vastly</u> inefficient. And as a matter of great significance, the Chinese government is pushing hard to expand its centrist government control over the entire energy sector of the country. Coal mining therefore is increasingly under the control of state owned enterprises (SOE), and these are notoriously inefficient. At present, despite recent efforts to improve mine safety, these SOEs "had a death rate three times worse than comparable large mines in India over roughly the same period, and some of the improvements being initiated are what most countries managed decades earlier, leaving China trying to brag about safety equivalent to what Great Britain had in the 1960s. Chinese families entitled to compensation are bought off. Accident reports to higher authority are often manipulated.

MEXICO: PEMEX IS DRAINING

In Mexico, the state owned enterprise Pemex, a huge energy conglomerate, is in serious decline. Twenty-three of the thirty-two biggest oil fields are suffering from declining production. For example, the largest, Cantarell, used to produce in excess of 2 million barrels per day, but is now down to about 600,000 barrels per day. Pemex has long been the jewel in Mexico's Socialist government crown. The nation's oil revenues account for more than 40% of government income. In a famous case, deep suspicion of the private operation of oil production led to the seizure and nationalization of foreign oil companies in 1938, and the Constitution was actually changed to prevent private investment in "hydrocarbons" in any form. But Pemex suffers from all of the standard sins of SOEs; seriously inefficient, riddled by corruption, nepotism and preferment for political allies, exorbitant executive salaries and benefits, and softness toward its powerful unions. As a consequence, the enterprise, which employs more than 140,000 people is said to be overstaffed by as much as 30%. Much money simply evaporates, and there are serious burgeoning problems of lack of repair and maintenance, and excessively high wages. Deep water drilling technology is now technically feasible, but Pemex is very slow to adapt it. Pemex people seem never to have latched on to such concepts as production efficiency, cost consciousness or cost-effectiveness.

The government often controls labor relations through special privileged relationships with labor unions. This gives them additional leverage over SOEs, and that can be both good and bad. The government can mandate worker pay and benefits, and can mandate levels of employment in general, or in specific industries. Typically, governments have mandated excessive hiring for political reasons. Many SOEs are forced to carry as much as 40% of the workforce in redundant employment which all but destroys their ability to be cost competitive with private sector and foreign competition. Governments can also vest unions with power to effect SOE management decisions, including denial of technology upgrading, and privatization. In many cases, unsupervised union control over large pension funds has led to wide-spread theft and corrupt practices.

It is clear that any of these games could become corrupt and they usually did. Many of the practices are inherently complex and technical, and cannot be seen or understood by the general public. Corrupt practices including the taking of bribes and/or kickbacks for preferential treatment (access to loans, access to licenses to do business, award of government contracts, insider knowledge on transactions, avoidance of audits or investigations, ignoring excessive and illegal charges, excessive prices and profits, etc.) Typically, government audit, oversight and investigation agencies are weak and understaffed – often deliberately.

GREECE: THE GREEK ATTITUDE

Bad economic policies: congenital fiscal deficits; patronage and populist subsidies that have swollen the public debt; toxic special interest politics; poor balance of payments; failure to stimulate economic development, to the point that very high levels of unemployment are endemic (except in the vastly overblown civil service); dependence on import substitution; waste, obsolescence and high cost/low value programs. Failure to control inflation; perversion of bank lending policies; neglect of maintenance and repair; failure to adapt technological improvements; rampant tax avoidance; uncontrolled smuggling; etc. And finally – a weak and cowardly government that lacks the skill and the willpower to undertake vital reforms. This is the miserable portrait of the Greek government and much of Greek society.

The West provided huge amounts of aid and support for more than 50 years – from 1950 to early in the 2000's. There is a growing feeling that many of the developing nations either wasted these funds or stole them, or that the funds were used to prop up tyrants. Therefore, there is a growing feeling in the West --- "the hell with them!"

The "Greek" argument in its own defense is so false: "We are in bad financial shape because of those nasty lenders." And "structural adjustment is a plot against us by foreigners". And "why do they want to stop lending to us just because we are unable and unwilling to repay the loans?" and "why are the taxpayers of lending countries so unwilling to give us their money free?" Nobody seems to want to discuss how Greece could act to become able to handle its own finances, reverse all of the economic failures listed above, and find ways to force the wealth of the country to be more wisely shared – and not through the equality of poverty.

COMPETITION FOR MONEY

Beyond Greece, in many countries, there is a withering of investment both from internal sources and from potential foreign investors. There is a world-wide shortage of capital investment money, and attracting capital is a competitive situation where "command and control" socialist countries could not or would not address. The Soviet Union, for most of its life, maintained a "closed border" policy which actively prevented foreign involvements in domestic Soviet economic affairs because the real motive of the government was to favor the SOEs that they had created and to protect them from formidable foreign competition which they could not match. But this cut off huge amounts of money that might have been attracted, and contributed mightily to the stagnation of the economy. Investments in the USSR looked far less attractive than options available to investors almost any place else.

Wages and salaries too became stagnant. There was little understanding about the relationship between productivity and management efficiency and the ability to increase wages as a consequence. Wage increases were most often granted for political reasons. The motives of the regime were mainly to buy loyalty, or at least to mitigate labor unrest as workers suffered from the consequences of an incompetent economy. Such increases almost always proved inflationary, and produced high discontent among other workers because the real motives of both management and workers was to conceal the failures of these structural mistakes. In fact, despite government efforts, unemployment – real or hidden – went up. Worker redundancy was as high as 40% in some industries occurred because workers and political leaders combined to keep it that way.

The pressures of stagnation caused governments to fail to deal with modernization and new technology potentials that might have improved productivity. Funds for modernization simply were not available, and even maintenance of current production facilities was neglected, leading to further declines in efficiency. In many socialist countries where government social services were inadequate, state owned enterprises became the providers of basic social services such as housing, education and health care for their own workers and even in part for the general population in their communities. This added to the fixed costs of the enterprises and made it especially difficult to cut costs in the face of declining economic usefulness. These high costs and rigid government price controls made state owned enterprises very expensive in comparison with their international competitors. As Russia and other former command and control economies lost the ability to control their borders, the essential weaknesses of local enterprises became glaring.

In many cases, the state tried to cover up these problems in the short run by lying about them, or by running larger deficits, or shifting resources between parts of the economy. In many less developed countries, such economic pathologies have been covered by overseas borrowing from both public and private sources. The decline in economic value led inevitably to a decline in public revenues and a growing inability to deliver social services. And the decline in productive work created a growing demand for such social services, especially unemployment compensation and welfare. Domestic public opinion could, in the short run, be constrained by the pursuit of false subsidy measures like cheap food, low rents, and subsidized fuels, but this made the eventual economic reckoning only worse.

INDIA: STATE SOCIALISM IN RETREAT

This portrait of failure was equally telling in India, but less drastic. The economic structure was defined and strictly enforced by the extremely popular President Pandet Nehru who was intellectually enchanted by the early Soviet model, plus some elegant but mistaken Fabian socialist theory from Great Britain. Economic policies were enforced by the iron fist of regulatory controls over the private sector, the spreading stain of inefficient public enterprises, and an inward-looking trade and investment strategy. This produced not merely dismal economic performance, but also the added sense of a mindless adherence to policies that have long been seen by others to have produced little real success, plus the perception that national policies have been "wittingly foolish." Dr. Bhagwati thus frames one of the key elements of governmental pathology – the stubborn clinging to policies or doctrines that are generally recognized as failures. Governments are, or should be, the leaders in testing reality and instigating change where needed. Instead, they are all too often tend to obscure the reality of change, and refuse to adapt even in the face of overwhelming evidence of its need, and become obstacles to those forces in their societies that are urgently trying to emerge.

Many governments have subsidized both their state owned enterprises and some purely private companies, usually justified by a philosophy of import substitution. But the problem then becomes that even temporary aid tends to become permanent. Government motives to protect their native producers and political allies were thus essentially political, but India also fell into the trap of thinking that subsidizing big SOEs was a short cut to achieving rapid economic growth. In fact, the need for salvaging huge loss-making SOEs seems to have so preoccupied the attention and resources of governments that they neglected opportunities they might have seized to foster and assist small businesses. Many small businesses are the kind that can use the services of the less skilled and less educated in such arenas as light manufacturing, construction, consumer services, and transaction oriented activities such as handling payments, generating information material, or processing paperwork. This potential is especially important in developing countries that lack an advanced education system for large numbers of people, such as India where elementary and secondary education was, foolishly, not compulsory.

Economic development is never easy; financial resources are limited and competitive around the world. Economic development must compete with urgent priorities for the provision of social services and the mitigation of poverty. When economic development is interrupted for any reason, it may stop or even collapse. India's 25 years of lack luster socialist economics was a cul de sac from which India must now spend further years in withdrawing. The total collapse of the Soviet style of command and control economics has left Russia and perhaps 30 other nations with the enormous task of reinventing their economic institutions. Tyrannies such as that of Saddam Hussein in Iraq, or Robert Mugabe in Zimbabwe, forcefully pursuing false motives, produced economies in protracted decline over 15-20 years – ground that may never be made up. Wars, rebellions, warlords, tribal feuds, terrorism, all interrupt any serious prospect of vigorous economic development.

CHINA: A NEW ANTI-CORRUPTION CAMPAIGN

Many of those in China who are being caught up in the unusually serious anti-corruption campaign of the central government have proved to be top officials of State Owned Enterprises (SOE), owned and controlled by the government under top officials directly appointed by the Chinese Communist Party (CCP). Accusations have been lodged against the former chairman of the China Resources Group conglomerate; the former chairman of Sinopec, China's huge state run oil company; the former chairman of Petro China, and in October of 2015, the arrest of Sam Pa, a murky middleman in various contracts won (or bought) with governments in Africa. While people in China continue to lack health care or retirement protection, China now has more billionaires (596) that the United States.

Business leaders in China now have three main worries; first, that the economy continues to slow down; second that the popular and successful corruption relationships may be at risk; and third, that their political allies may not always be able to protect them. At its very worst, it may be feared that the government, to maintain its absolute political control, may return to the anti-business policies of its Maoist past. Yet, by far, most of the estimated 100,000 people indicted for graft have been public officials, or officials of SOEs. The hope is that China's leadership has really grasped the fact the most of the economy is now in the hands of private interests, and they are now more important to the government than bureaucratic crooks and incompetent managers of loss-making SOEs.

V

GALVANIZING CHANGE IN THE MUSLIM WORLD

THE WORLD THAT NEVER EMERGED

The Muslim world is in a state of rapid change. Nobody know exactly how this change will emerge, but perhaps the greatest examples of opportunity for better governments lies within the Muslim world. But for 1400 years, nobody has been able to explain why Muslims cherish and perpetuate the hideous and incomprehensible conflict between the Sunni and the Shia in the Muslim world. Nobody.

Some say that it is because of crucial and powerful differences in religious interpretation. Yet even when Islamic scholars attempt to explain the differences, they sound weak when compared to the ways that Sunni and Shia Muslim people are essentially the same. Some say that the conflict is because of the concern that today's Muslims have moved too far away from the moral life that Allah has mandated for them; but this mandate presumably applies to both, and scholars in both branches argue the same points. Some say that it is because Sunni and Shia have serious differences in their understanding of Allah's writ as expressed in the Quran, along with the Sunnah and the Hadith. Yet beyond certain areas of immutable truth, the Quran has been subject to interpretation during its whole existence. This kind of intellectual conflict may be troubling to some, but it seems usually to be satisfactorily accommodated within the Muslim world. In addition, there is an even murkier perception about the nature of Sunni and Shia relationships with governments. Shia seem to be more militant in believing that only Allah can rule, and that governments are all improper and immoral usurpers of Allah's authority. Sunni, to some degree are more inclined to see governments as acceptable – as long as they obey spirit of the Quran. Yet in fact, all Muslim groups, whether religious or not, or legitimate or not, must face the reality of the growing power of formal governments and their increasing unwillingness to be "guided" by religious leaders. But this in turn produces another powerful Muslim motive: the urge of Mullahs to retain, or even to win back the dominant position in the Muslim world that they once possessed.

There is now a greater willingness to reject the traditionalist assertion that the Quran cannot be interpreted, and the Muslim religion is frozen into the definitions demanded by the clergy. In fact, the tide running seems to be to examine such interpretations, beyond an immutable basic core of the Quran, and various forms of more moderate interpretation are gaining ground. For example, it is increasingly realized that the view of women's place in the world is not set by the Quran, the Sunnah and the Hadith, but by long standing male ground rules which often actually run counter to the sacred documents. The constant pressure for religious conformity has acted to stultify intellectual freedom and make education very narrow and defensive. This stultification was not only over the introduction of new technology, but over the concept of <u>change.</u> In truth, change happens whether the conservative leadership wants it or not, and the values of the new things of the world (computers, cell phones, TVs, autos, refrigerators, etc.) are eagerly absorbed by Muslims along with everybody else. The new possibility is one of hope and <u>opportunity:</u> think not what Islam used to be; think about what it can become. The historic Muslim religion and the culture of the Arab world seem very conservative by modern standards, and this has contributed to the slow pace of change in both the Middle East and the Far East – in India, Pakistan, Bangladesh, and Indonesia.

Finally and perhaps most powerfully, both Shia and Sunni have forcefully condemned the bad, bad governments that most Muslims suffer under. It may come across as propaganda, but the fact is that, all over the Muslim world as evidenced by hundreds of opinion polls, people hate and despise their governments, have suffered from their incompetence and oppression, and rage at the greedy and corrupt nature of their own leaders. For these oppressed people, the religious leadership, however oppressive themselves, still hold out the prospect of a return to the great moral and richly rewarding life that Allah has offered in the Quran.

The ultimate question is whether Muslims themselves will take the primary responsibility to control their radical elements. Many governments have had to do so to save their own skins. But it is not clear how much the average Muslim is willing to do under conditions of heavy risk. Opposition to Islamic terrorism is not really an attack against religion. Most terrorists are motivated by nationalistic issues (usually Arabism), but they cloak themselves in religion, and as "liberators". (See Fuller, Chap 5 summary). Terrorism can't be handled by regular police/military because terrorists hide themselves in the general population, creating the risk of a lot of collateral damage. It is helpful to note that fundamentalist Islam has succeeded to power in only three cases – Iran, Afghanistan and Sudan, all three of which came to power by undemocratic means. All have bred eternal conflict and pain, and none have offered any real solutions for people's needs.

It is very encouraging to observe the emergence of stronger civil society, however slow and halting, and this is tied to the shift of populations from the traditionally conservative rural/village world to urban areas which tend to be more open and progressive. If Islamic politics is to succeed, it must largely abandon its more conservative aspects, accept cultural diversity, accept the challenge to carry its popularity into power without turning dictatorial – in other words, learn how to be relevant to a far broader constituency. It must stop thinking of non-believers as barely tolerated inferior infidels. It must also learn to mitigate its internal conflicts, some of which have been painful for 1400 years. To date, too little of this seems to be happening among Islamic organizations, but it is happening among the people themselves. All of this is perfectly consistent with the holy documents, but not with the interpretations of reactionary leaders. Important examples of the ability of Muslim regimes to coexist are India, Turkey, Egypt, Malaysia.

At the same time however, rival claimants as sources of authority in Islam are expanding exponentially, with independent and self appointed religious interpreters issuing directives through multiple forms of media, including <u>fatwa</u> centers all over the world. Originally, the *fatwa* was seen as a local authority issued by an Imam for the guidance of his own flock. The new "electronic *umma*" can be both a vehicle for the encouragement of diversity and broader public participation, or a device to rally the faithful to the wrong causes. The imposition of Sharia law is not supposed to apply to non Muslims, but if it becomes the official law of a country, this concept is negated.

Islam seems to be emerging in a situation where the world is increasingly pluralist, not all citizens are Muslim, not all Muslims are the same, nor are all Muslims religious, and where Muslim theology and interpretation fails to take account of what exists in the real world. Conservative interpretations can be too rigid, failing to meet the acid test of politics which is negotiation and compromise, and they can be a drag on economic development. How can a Muslim citizen and family lead a devout Muslim life while still getting all of the advantages of a modern society and economy? State Socialism/Communism failed this test. Some version of relaxed Islamism is possible, and it is increasingly recognized that the force of secularism is growing globally, while reactionary Islamism is acquiring an evil reputation. In the last analysis, religion in Muslim terms has become subordinate to the State – even now in Iran. People grow tired of old theology and now increasingly want Islamist theologians to stop thinking of "democracy" and "materialism" as threats and start thinking of them as desirable goals.

What is the Western challenge? Islamist apologists like to make it sound like the challenge is military, political or economic. In fact, much of it is cultural, and not deliberate. Muslims who are deprived are now seeing and hearing too much about the successes of <u>people</u> in the West to continue to believe the propaganda handed out by their governments – or by Islamist liars. At some point, Muslims in many countries will start to realize that the source of their problems is not the U. S., but themselves.

Muslims are learning, for example, that "women's lib" does not really come only from the West, but is more importantly coming through Muslim women themselves and is taking place well within the framework of Islamic movements. Thus, the women's movement is anti-clerical. Women want clerics to stop supporting inhibiting customs invented by men, really outside of the meanings of the Quran and Sharia law. A good example is the prohibition in many countries against women driving cars, which is totally unrecognized and unsupported by Islamic law, and is ignored in 90% of the Muslim world. New players are shattering the old order. The sleeping majority is awakening. The wider Muslim world is increasingly rejecting extremism. The Arabic world is where the many forms of militancy – from the venomous Sunni creed of al Qaeda to the punitive Shiite theocracy in Iran – have proven costly, unproductive, and ultimately unappealing. Jihadists have failed to provide anything constructive. But meanwhile, "In any mall in the Arab Gulf states, where teenage boys in bright white dishdashas, baseball caps, and Converse All Stars wait in line for first run Hollywood action films, while their teen age sisters in black burkas and designer sunglasses balance armfuls of shopping bags from American retail outlets while chatting on their iPhones." Increasingly, this new world for Muslim youth is less seen as mimicking America, but as becoming "modern Muslims." (Robin Wright, "Rock the Kasbah").

Increasingly, U. S. policy seems to be shifting from dealing with suspect regimes toward efforts to talk directly to Arab and Muslim people and their "bottom up" organizations. But also recognize that, as Smith puts it "none of consensual governance had ever been practiced in the actual course of Muslim politics over the last fourteen hundred years." And: "The fundamental problem with Arab democracy isn't Islam or Islamism but the norms of Arab politics and governance of which Islamist politics is merely one aspect. The problem is systemic and organic."

A second and absolutely vital tide running in the Muslim world is the counter-jihad, which is unfolding in the wide bloc of 57 countries with Muslim population majorities, as well as among Muslim minority populations worldwide. The counter-jihad is the rejection of specific violent movements, as well as the general principle of violence to achieve political goals. Every reliable citizen poll since 2007 shows steadily declining support for the destructive and disruptive jihads.

The counter-jihad has been especially evident among Sunni Muslims, who account for more than 80% of the Islamic world.

SUNNI VS. SHIA

At a more personal level however, Muslims seem increasingly to be searching to figure out how, if at all, either Sunni or Shia authority would make anything better – that is to make <u>real life and real things</u> better, like food, and homes, and jobs, and money, and health, and education and perhaps a decent old age. At this level, both branches of Islam seem to fail. Sunnis have in fact controlled most of the governments in the Muslim world, and thus, they are the ones that the people have come to hate. Shia leaders, equally disliked and distrusted, have risen to power in very few cases such as Iran (Persians) and Iran.

Almost every insurgent or terrorist group rising up in the Muslim world has been terrible, and when their leaders are asked how they would make the world better, the only answer from anybody is that Sharia Law would be installed and great world envisioned by Muhammad would miraculously return.

In the Muslim world, there are signs that the influence of the Mullahs is being more vigorously challenged. Even Saudi Arabia is toning down its unyielding support of the ultra conservative Wahhabi school of Sunni Islam. More drastic curtailments are seen. "Uzbekistan, Kazakhstan, Tajikistan are now using cameras to monitor the utterances of mullahs in the mosques. Kuwait has long installed tape recorders to monitor Friday sermons. Preachers in the UAE are required to read sermons from a text delivered to them each week by the government Department of Religious Affairs, which also pays their salaries. "Turkey has long maintained a close supervision of Islamic clerical activity through a government agency, the Diyanet, which employs more than 120,000 people and has an annual budget of $2.3 billion." Tunisia has restored strict state control of mosques. Morocco maintains a relatively tolerant version of the religion. "Its budget for training Imams, including a growing number of foreign students, has swollen ten fold in the past three years. The unspoken aim is to counter the spread of extreme Salafist ideas in places like Mali and northern Nigeria.

The Muslim world now appears to face three general options:

1. An ultra-conservative fundamentalist caliphate, driven by militant-terrorist interests.
2. A broad movement to change their world into one patterned on the West.
3. A new pattern somewhere in the middle: a repudiation of any form of oppressive regimes controlled by centrist elites, religious or otherwise, but a society and a government which is clearly and attractively Muslim in character.

In fact, it would seem perfectly possible to achieve a blend of 2 and 3. It must be emphasized that governance in the Muslim world must be designed and implemented by Muslims themselves; it cannot be simply some pale copy of some Western pattern. But having said that, think again about the nature of the opportunity! There are 21 nations that are Muslim countries by law and by reality. Far too many of these countries have invented horrible terrorist governments, and out of these same governments has arisen a shocking wave of vicious terrorist organizations, fed by irreconcilable schisms within the Muslim world and the failings of incompetent and oppressive governments. Is this another enormously important opportunity being missed? The answer is Yes.

The Muslim world is working its way toward some new versions of governance, but the pace is excruciatingly slow, with many gaps and stumbles. The "Arab Spring" seemed like a brilliant surge of pressure for reform, but sadly, it seems to be fading. So – the post WW II did not become of world of representative democratic governments, but instead it became a world of governance by authoritative centrist elites driven by State Socialism, and now by some conflict-ridden theological justifications of Islamic rule. As a result, these waves have preempted the possibilities of the emergence of democracy; closed down and limited the freedom of thought and action that should have been galvanizing the world; created governments that thought they had to right and even the duty to become dictators; and the almost inevitable triumph of greed and endless corruption.

COMMON CHARACTERISTICS OF MUSLIM GOVERNMENTS

There are 1.3 billion Muslims in the world. They are a majority in 57 countries, and have large populations in many other countries. 21 countries declare themselves to be Muslim governments by law or by predominant practice.

All Muslim governments without exception are highly centrist and power driven, and they are directed by a small centrist elite group of insiders -- some combination of a perceived strong leader, the military, and increasingly the intelligence apparatus acting as internal spies and enforcers. Far less significant are those agencies dealing with social services, public infrastructure, economic development or even religious affairs. Their psychology centers around the drive for power and its implacable retention in dictatorial patterns, supported staunchly by the military, the intelligence organizations. State ownership and control of major sectors of the economy, and a patronage system, often relying on family or tribal bonds enables absolute control of the economy. This system does not resist corruption – it utilizes it as lubrication and payoffs of reward and preferment.

The emergence of Islamic movements is heavily justified by the assertion of divine approval. These movements all, to some degree, say that they are directed by Divine Will, and thus can never be wrong, nor can they ever compromise. The Will of Allah is interpreted by the most zealous of religious leaders as fixed and immutable and not subject to change. Thus, no government, nor law nor policy can be permitted which conflicts with this sacred interpretation.

But this is an extraordinarily powerful example of the possibility of political interpretations that deny reality. In fact, almost all of the Muslim theology is open to substantial interpretation. The meaning of the Quran is generally said to be subject to five levels of interpretation:

1. There are many passages that are defined as the absolute word of Allah and as such, interpretation is regarded as sacrilege and never allowed.
2. Other portions of the Quran are said to be subject to further exploration and study, but only to assure that Allah's meaning is fully clear. But such assessments can only be undertaken by the wisest and most knowledgeable of Islamic scholars and even other scholars or religious leaders are not considered qualified.
3. There are passages of the Quran that are considered unclear and perhaps incomplete, and there is legitimate room to debate the full meanings. This kind of assessment extends to Islam's other holy documents, the Sunnah and the Hadith.
4. Other portions of these documents are also subject to considerable further interpretation, and there is in fact a vigorous intellectual interest in the Muslim community in doing just that. From this kind of analysis, there is a modest pattern of acceptable change in understanding.
5. In some parts of the Muslim world, there is a tolerance for the creation of a "new Islam", where philosophies and concepts outside of the traditional base are now being actively examined. Often, it is here on the edge of Muslim thought that the intersection between the Muslim and the secular is being worked out.

This is a crucial point. All but the most zealous of the ultra reactionary Imams and Mullahs recognize that the whole world, and thus also the Muslim world, is constantly changing. The ultra conservatives tend to tell themselves that the anchor of the Quran will not be submerged but will ultimately triumph. Most Muslims however believe that they must see this change not as a threat, but as an <u>opportunity.</u> Why? Because their world is, in the last analysis, the real world even if it is not theologically pure. Muslim people—like all other humans -- want food, a decent place to live, solid work, and a way to educate their children and protect them from harm. Theology does not provide transport, or electricity, or clean water or garbage collection, nor TV, or health care or protection for the elderly.

What do the 1.3 billion Muslims of the world really want? After decades of opinion polls and public utterance, the public wants are clear: a return to respect; jobs and stable income; physical safety; avoidance of cultural conflict; the ability to lead a devout, useful, honorable life. They want humanist laws based on the best religious principals. They want real and valuable equity and gender justice. They want decent governments that really care for the needs and interests of the people. They yearn for a world of fairness and equity. These are the most important of modern Muslim <u>opportunities.</u>

But there is a sense of serious failure often stemming from leadership policies that deliberately stirs up and exacerbates any disparities between segments of the population, whether it is ethnic or religious or clan, or geography: plus rich vs. poor, young vs. old, urban vs. rural, or native vs. foreign. The one conflict that is peculiar to the Muslim world is "Sunni vs. Shia". This has been a deep and abiding conflict, nurtured for almost 1400 years. This seemingly permanent urge for conflict is further extrapolated to sub sets of each of the two great streams of the Muslim world.

There is a further concern that once these centrist rulers achieve power, their grip is so strong that they have proved to be almost impossible to dislodge. The tenacity of leadership is amazing. Hosni Mubarak was president of Egypt for 28 years. In Tunisia, Zine al Abidine Ben Ali has been in office for 22 years. Ali Abdullah Saleh has been president of Yemen for more than 30 years. Jordan is still run by the Hashimite family, father and son, after 59 years; Morocco by the Alouite family since 1956; Saudi Arabia by the al-Sauds for more than 70 years. In Kuwait, the ancient al Sabah dynasty shared power with the British from 1899 to independence in 1961, and is still in power. Muammar Qaddafi ruled Libya for 40 years. Syria has been ruled by the al Assad family since 1970 (42 years), and the Sudan has been under the control of its Arab regime since 1956 (56 years). The government theocracy now running Iran came to power in 1979 (33 years).

MUSLIM GOVERNMENT FAILURES

As elsewhere in the world, the newly independent countries which chose state socialism as their governmental philosophy then suffered from its failures, largely because of its inability to stimulate sufficient economic growth. This in turn mandated a turn to more market based economies which were hampered by reluctance of the Old Guard to abandon the sacred writs of the Socialist past, some obsolete religious concepts, ever popular corruption and congenitally inefficient and repudiated government. In world terms, Muslim countries tend to be in the lower levels of country economic comparisons. In a number of areas, Muslim countries are not necessarily "bad", but may simply be late in coping, or slow to evolve, way behind the power curve.

These newly independent Muslim countries installed some of the key parts of with apparatus of governments: parliaments, independent judiciaries, constitutions, competent ministries, a formal civil service. But the reality seems to be that tyranny still trumped all. Governments don't know how to curb dictatorial power. Most governments are crude, unskilled and usually vastly corrupt. Most just preside; they don't really manage and are big on grand pronouncements and short of actual accomplishment.

Muslim governments have tended to cling together in two blocs; one led by Saudi Arabia and other mostly Arab countries; and another bloc seen as an implacable enemy, led by Iran and including Syria, Sudan, Hamas, Hezbollah in Lebanon, and countless terrorist and or insurrectionist organizations. This set of conflicts does not really reach the Far East, where some of the most populist Muslim nations are found.

The Middle East Arab/Muslim world is increasingly seen as stagnant and obsolete politically, and has failed with respect to the needs of youth or for general social welfare. The average age in Egypt is 24; in Algeria, 26; in Morocco, 26. On the other hand, the numbers of people 60 and older is < 7% (Economist; 25 July 2009). Arab leadership is now seen increasingly seen as arrogant, and inhibiting, including its staunch support of restrictive religious practices. Arabism has strong elements of longing for lost glory, the urge for new glory, a sense of oppression and fatalism, and a lot of guilt about "failure". But there is increasing disenchantment by other countries in dealing with governments that are so bad and discredited, and many of these foreign governments have jumped to support the Arab Spring. So now what? Its arch enemy, the "Iran bloc" is almost universally seen as far, far worse.

A very fundamental flaw in the governments and societies of the region is their inertia against change, but this inertia is overwhelmed by the great tide of change that represents reality in the world, whether wanted or not. But in fact, change is always a threat to some interests and a great boon to others, and the tides running in a given country are a fascinating blend of these pluses and minuses. In the Muslim world, the great believers in change are the people, but the great resisters to change tend to be the holders of power. Almost all regimes resist change because they see it as a potential loss of their own power. The more centrist and elitist a government, such as those that control the Muslim world, the greater will be their fear of loss. And in the Muslim world there is the special fear, even among advocates of change, that things will get out of hand and produce disaster – e. g. a government that is far worse rather than better, or one seized by some dreaded fundamentalist group such as the Taliban or ISIS.

But there seems to be a decline of two false theories: one, that Islam has strayed from the True Path and can advance only if they return to that path; and two, that everything bad can be blamed on Western colonialism and the "perversions" of western thought. Increasingly the compelling concept in the Muslim world is CHANGE, and the recognition that, in fact, the world has always been changing, usually for the better, and the ultraconservative leadership is increasingly perceived to be seriously and stubbornly wrong. But as modern societies and governments become more complex and interrelated, they tend to be better able to resist total upset, and to limit change to a rebalancing of forces within society. Such rebalancing is incremental, and it is often seen as enough. Governments can retreat as little and as slowly as possible, making concessions reluctantly. Those who seek change have a very hard time just creating any real organized leverage on a powerful regime. Many opposition groups are unskilled and poor at building coalitions and often, they end up fighting themselves.

Modernist Islamists tend to base themselves in mosques; communists favor labor unions; state socialists utilize government ministries; and intellectuals and students thrive in universities.

Government regimes in turn are very skilled in building up all possible conflicts between elements of society – religious, ethnic, political, regional, clans and tribes, economic levels, rural vs. urban, rich vs. poor, youth vs. the elders, and anything else they can think of. Regimes have learned to use their intelligence agencies for internal people-watching and information control. And finally, the police and the military are always available to prevent any pressures for change from getting out of hand. Some of the strongest institutions in truly open countries like the courts or legislatures are, in Muslim countries weak and subordinated and easily dominated by the centrist elite. It is also bitterly true that, for large numbers of the power elite, patronage and corruption are far more attractive and rewarding than efforts to provide "good government".

With one or two possible exceptions, all of these governments are held in contempt by most of the citizens of the country. They are seen as corrupt, incompetent, indifferent, and misguided. What people want most is not necessarily something called "democracy" but an end to UNFAIRNESS. They hate the insolence of office, and not having a voice.

Almost all governments are unable or unwilling to face up to problems. They don't seem to know how to negotiate or compromise or to mitigate conflict. In fact, there are endless examples of cases where the government itself has been the instigator or perpetuator of conflict. Mostly, they "preside" rather than lead or manage. City governments are weak, and under severe pressure. The whole of the Muslim world is moving toward increasing urbanization, and Muslim cities are not up to the task. In many case, there is little government provision of even vital social services, much of which is really supplied by an unplanned tangle of private organizations, mosque religious organizations, civic associations and trusts, and foreign NGOs.

Most countries have suffered from extremist attacks or have been forced to suppress them – often harshly. But this is an endless loser circle: government oppression breeds or justifies these attacks; the attacks are so vicious and menacing that the government must respond; the response is so harsh that it breeds further attacks.

Governments have widely neglected economic development. Foreign Direct Investment (FDI) is limited because potential investors do not trust the political leadership, or the environment for business. They see too much corruption, and too many bad laws. Economies are seen as "old fashioned" – not bad, but not keeping pace with the modern world. There is heavy government ownership of economic elements, and too much money is sucked out of the economy by the government. Private enterprise is taxed and regulated and is deliberately placed at many disadvantages compared to state enterprises.

Governments have been unwilling to accept responsibility for providing adequate social services, continuing to rely on older self reliance, or provision by religious charities, including waqfs – private trust organizations. There is an increasing and very embarrassing recognition that the "cradle to grave" social services commitments of Muslim Socialist governments was almost entirely mythological There has been increasing guilt about these failures, including lack of vital public infrastructure.

There is widespread disaffection about the power of elections. Who runs? Hand chosen candidates for the corrupt regime; equally incompetent opposition; religious militants; earnest innocents. The long term suppression of alternative political organizations has been highly damaging. What would a strong opposition effort do? Rise up on its political learning curve, gain practical experience in election campaigning and the rough and tumble of politics; honing of their public policy agenda, and the building of valuable alliances. But "out" parties seldom succeed.

Importantly, there is increasing public rejection or questioning of the false justifications offered by terrorist organizations, and the recognition that they stand for nothing, even Sharia law, and deliver nothing but pain. It must be recognized that most Muslim countries have suffered from severe and protracted conflict, from terrorist attacks, from insurgencies, or from outright civil war. Without debating the nature of these conflicts, it is certain that they have caused serious disruptions and destruction of assets and the provision of civil services, including medical facilities; and many educated professionals who have movable skills have been driven away. On the other side, few Muslim governments are entitled to claim that they have met the social services needs of their citizens. In fact, most of them would be considered to have failed. While civil servants continue to try and teach school or run hospitals or put out fires, the political leaders deem far too preoccupied with fighting each other, and nobody really runs many of these countries. These policy failures also lead to huge misallocations of funds; too much money for war and too little for social services.

There continues to be a vexing unwillingness to speak frankly about the real great schism in the Muslim world – that between Sunni and Shia. There is an unwillingness to admit it because it makes both forces seem wrong. There are no admissions about its corrosive consequences, and certainly no admissions that nobody have any idea of what to do about it – or even <u>whether.</u> Nearly all Arabs feel a sense of unity with other Arabs, and yet historically they have been among the most persistent antagonists of any segment of humanity in the world (Sunni vs. Shia). The Arab world is also broken up into hundreds of quarrelling sects and schisms, based on religion, religious aberrations, geography, history, culture, etc. The idea of a broader Pan-Arabism has been around for a long time, but has never really taken hold, in no small part because Arab nations have so often been ruled by egotistical tyrants.

Corruption is universally hated and condemned, but the truth is that it works. It is a set of recognized skills with well known successful techniques. In addition, it is not just the actions of an individual, but it is usually a refined management system, a conspiracy designed to reward all and protect and conceal all. Most developing countries with weak economies have almost ubiquitous deployment of corrupt practices among the rich and powerful, but thay also develop a huge "cottage" industry of small scale corruption, usually embedded in the informal economy. So what do young people learn? Corruption, drug dealing, thuggery, bribery and smuggling. What are the most serious arenas of corruption? Legislation, construction, land use, big development projects, customs, taxes, permits and licenses, foreign aid, inspections. Religion has little influence on corruption. The developed world believes in top down activity; the corruptors believe in bottom up activity. For example, the OECD has a "Convention Against Illicit Payments", and the UN has a "Convention Against Corruption" and both, while descending from heaven, are widely and safely ignored, with the exception of some tracking of corrupt bank accounts. Accusations of corruption are now a routine commonplace element of almost every election in developing countries – and unfortunately, they are often right. Corruption is so serious that is has become one of the key elements of resistance against ruling regimes. Some of the most notable of recent leaders have mounted major anti-corruption campaigns which seem not to have dented the problem: Fox in Mexico, da Silva in Brazil; Obasanjo in Nigeria; Toledo in Peru. Both Obasanjo and Lula blew their credibility by allegedly bribing member of parliaments.

But of course, Muslim countries are not alone. China has never seriously tried to curb corruption among the elite but they have prosecuted many local government officials. It is still estimated that 1.3 million party members (1/3 of total of official workers) are guilty of some form of graft. The Party secretary for Shanghai was dismissed (!) for misappropriating $700 million from the Social Security Fund and using the money for personal investments. The head of the drug approval agency was executed for sanctioning counterfeit drugs. The chairman of the China Construction Bank was sent to jail for 15 years for pocketing $ 500,000 in bribes. In December, 2009, an official national audit summary found that Chinese officials had embezzled or misused some $ 35 billion of government funds.

MUSLIM AGONIES

In the Muslim world, there is a pervasive sense of unrest and the need for conflict. There are high levels of motivation in general – somehow, every little thing seems portentous and threatening. There is huge and universal citizen dislike and even hatred for their self-selected leadership, who are seen as vicious, tyrannical, and grossly incompetent, but somehow can't be got rid of.

Islam wallows in self-denial. There seems to be a profound sense of greatness lost, and much of this feeling is misdirected. Muslims tend to feel that the world took unfair advantage of them in the form of European penetrations and colonial dominance, and yet Muslims tend not to mention their own thousand year long history of often brutal invasion and conquest. Muslim, mostly Arab invasions came in three great waves over more than a thousand years of history. The first wave occurred under the direction of the Umayyad Caliphate, beginning shortly after the death of the Prophet Muhammad in 632 and lasting until the middle of the 8th century. (See Appendix A). In a remarkable period of less than 150 years, Muslim forces invaded and conquered huge areas of what are the modern states of Syria, Palestine, Iraq, Egypt, Iran, the Maghreb, Transoxonia, the Arabian peninsula including Yemen and Oman, Lebanon, Libya, Tunesia and Morocco and even into parts of Spain and Portugal. In addition, conquests included Afghanistan, Uzbekistan, Turkmenistan, Byzantium, Azerbaijan, Crete and Sicily. The second great wave was the penetration of the Indian peninsula and conquest of the Sind valley and other parts of India.

What were the characteristics of this Muslim success in war? First, it was driven by religious zeal against countries where most governments/people believed in little or nothing at all. Arab armies were highly mobile and fast moving, and could usually live off of the lands they attacked. The Arabs developed a culture of warriors who trained for war, and fought against opponents who were not so fierce or trained. Usually, the countries attacked were oppressive and unpopular, and often incompetent. This created internal divisiveness that worked in favor of Muslim attackers, especially because these attackers used terror as a deliberate weapon. Thus, fast moving Arab armies were making lightning attacks on fixed targets guarded by smaller numbers of poorly trained local troops. When the Arabs took over, they usually retained local officials and government workers, but under strict control. Invasions were completed about 750.

The third wave of invasions and conquests occurred under the attacks of the Ottoman Empire beginning in the 13th Century and running of more than 300 years. (See Appendix B) Conquests included Hungary, Romania, Bulgaria, Greece, parts of Russia, Armenia, Croatia, Serbia, Macedonia, Kurdish lands and again the North African coast. Further incursions into Europe were only prevented by defeat of Muslim forces in central Spain and the successful resistance at the siege of Vienna in 1683 (after an earlier salvation in 1529).

These waves of invasion were aimed at permanent conquest and occupation. They were in large part motivated by religion and sought the Muslim conquest of "the infidel", and their conversion to the Muslim faith, by force if felt to be necessary. When modern Muslims yearn for the old "glory days" they all too often mean these periods of great conquest when Arabs were the "terror of the world".

Muslims have every right to see themselves as victims, but not to assign blame only to the outside world, and not to themselves or their rulers. Greatness must be earned, often by pushing through against odds. Where now is Islam great? Where are its great men? Will there ever be adequate encouragement of great Muslim women? Is Islam's only claim to fame its ability to nurture conflict and create terror? There is hatred of the West because it supported bad regimes, but it was Muslims themselves that created those horrible governments, and the Muslim population itself, country by country, that has been the main support of their own tyrannies. Who are the fat cats and corrupt officials who form these tyrannical elites? Whose sons become soldiers and police men and intelligence agents? Who offers the bribes, and who accepts them? Most Muslim media is under the control of governments and they too strengthen tyrants, and help to justify each new outrage. In most Muslim governments, the track record of the politicians is a disaster. They only know how to engage in sterile internal and external conflicts and feuds, and do not seem to understand the need for, and the skills of negotiation and compromise. Everything for them is negative in situations begging for intelligent initiatives. Muslim leaders have never forgiven the creation of Israel by Western powers. Even worse, they have never forgiven each other for the schism that eternally exists between Sunni and Shia, which has poisoned the Muslim world for 1400 years.

Even in religion, Muslims are experiencing ominous conflict. Islam is usually interpreted to mean a religion of peace and it prohibits the killing of innocents, and of suicide, and it calls for universal peace. But many Imams invent their own form of Islam, and especially in the Shia community, they are usually obeyed. Just as people distrust their political leadership, they are increasingly coming to believe they must beware of their own religious leadership. Radical religious elements are at war with the very idea of governments, or even individual nations. Instead, they envision the image of the umma – one all-encompassing international community of Muslim believers that would be guided (and controlled) by one set of religious beliefs as centrally defined by religious leaders and thus cannot be questioned.

But in fact, it seems that the general population rejects both the current political leadership and the more fundamentalist versions of religious leadership. They are beginning to believe that there is a middle ground. They are sick and tired of both incompetent tyrants and Jihadist/Fundamentalist extremism and violence. They wish for the emergence of moderate Islam, and they begin to see possibilities of a shift from fighting to politics, such as followed by the revamped PLO or, sometimes, the Muslim Brotherhood in Egypt or the Muslim parties in Morocco. At the same time, when confronted by Jihadist extremism, most governments fight back and many have won or are winning. Similarly, it is felt that, when confronted with Islamic movements that seek to impose strict Sharia law, most people will draw back. Almost all movements that seek to impose strict Sharia law and only Sharia law are seen as rejecting democracy, minority tolerance or "equality", women's rights, self determination, independence of thought (from religious leadership), secular laws, multiple political parties and much more. There is real concern that a fundamentalist government would not hesitate to use official terrorism to keep the population under control. And yet, the heart of Sharia law as moderately defined, is almost always positive and constructive, and its adoption would seldom present any serious problems even in tandem with a broader base of secular law. Most of the governments that are Muslim or have significant Muslim populations have already adopted some more moderate form a Sharia Law, usually along side forms of secular law. These countries include

Egypt, Turkey, Saudi Arabia, Morocco, Iran, Iraq, Afghanistan, Syria, Mali, Nigeria, Malaysia, Pakistan, Indonesia and Bangladesh. Here again, care must be taken in recognizing that many of the worst Islamic fundamentalists argue loudly for the adoption of "Sharia Law" of their own making to garner populist support, while reality is that Sharia Law and secular law regularly exist side by side.

So, if the general population feels tyrannized by their political leadership and distrustful of the motivations of much of the religious leadership, where do they turn? The United States and Europe and others tend to think – and hope – that eventually the Muslim world will turn to representative democracy, and that then two things will happen. First, countries will replace their dictators with duly elected governments which of course will be wise and efficient. Second, Muslim abandonment of government tightly controlled from the top because they have failed and it will be recognized that more effective market based economies will replace them and will generate enough new wealth that the wiser and nobler governments of the future will deploy this wealth to meet the people's real needs, as defined and insisted upon from the bottom up!

But there is a far greater likelihood that, for a substantial period of time, Muslim governments will experience a different pattern – one in which the tendency for top down centrist regimes will persist, but where the actions of these regimes can be mitigated by new pressures and perhaps new motives. Who really challenges Muslim state power? Mostly other Muslims: the political opposition, religious moderates, women's movements, even terrorists. Of the 21 Muslim governments, 13 are, or have been, centrist dictatorships, and most have built structures not for program effectiveness but for power retention. Muslim governments not only tend to avoid responsibility, but they show little interest or skill in resolving problems or settling differences The power base includes not only the military, but increasingly a growing intelligence apparatus, capable of dealing with the growing importance of social networking capabilities. In addition, the bureaucracy is usually loyal and favored, and arrogantly corrupt. The new pressures will probably come from both Islamic and secular sources, in some forms of political cooperation. Islamic forces probably feel that they can't displace powerful entrenched regimes, but they can be more effective by finding ways to penetrate the power system and moderate it is a few critical ways. Secular interests will undoubtedly press those arguments that center around the rapidly changing real world within which Muslim people must ultimately live. None of this is really about religion, even where regimes constantly cloak themselves in Koranic righteousness. This is not "Islam vs. the West"; it is "Islam vs. Itself". In essence, Islamic movements want to push themselves into some middle ground where they can portray themselves as a viable alternative to incompetent tyrants and excessive zealots. And yet, there is some growing feeling that the nature of terrorism is changing away from specific issues and demands for religious fervor toward a generalized rebellion against the modern world, where the terrorists feel themselves to be heroes saving the world from ----what? From itself?

It now seems to be recognized that Muslim governments are badly served when they cater excessively to the zealots of religious fundamentalism, and they had better avoid having their politics and political parties defined as this overly zealous fringe. Who must form the new definition of modern Islam? Certainly not the U. S. or the West, but Muslims themselves, country by country. Muslim governments have fought against radicals –Chechnya, the Palestinian Authority, in Egypt, in Indonesia, in Algeria, Saudi Arabia, Somalia, Yemen and in Afghanistan, and elsewhere. Initially, there was the fear that the "Arab Spring", which was really in opposition to tyrants, would open the flood gates for armed Islamic disruption, leaving affected countries in a state of turmoil for years. Said another way, moderate Muslim politics and governance would be more widely developed but for the inhibiting fear of fundamentalism. Muslims increasingly see fundamentalism not as religious movements, but as power struggles that can destroy but cannot create. The real hope seems to be in the reinforcement of moderate, liberal, secular and responsible elements of Muslim society country by country from the bottom up people level will be able to do much to mitigate the oppression from the top down political level.

Thus, the outside world should restrain itself from automatically deciding that, for the Muslim world representative democracy defined in Western concepts is the only legitimate solution, nor can it be assumed that if "moderate" Islamists emerge they will define themselves in Western terms. It is unfortunate that the terms "democracy" and "secular" have been stigmatized as the policies of aggressive American/European regimes. Concepts that do work well in the bottom up Muslim community are especially "justice" and "economic development" meaning more jobs and better pay. Other positive concepts of great influence in the Muslim community are such things as "good government" or "anti-corruption", or "law based society", or "rights of minorities" or "women's rights". Muslims are not against government; only bad government. Most would appear willing to accept an active government if it deals with the critical bottom up needs and does not get mired in poisonous political/military conflicts and power struggles. The most extreme of Muslim fundamentalist views rejects the very idea of governments because they believe all things must be decided and implemented in accordance with their limited interpretation of the holy documents. Yet few really believe their alternative: an all encompassing single international Muslim community of believers that would be guided (and controlled) by one set of religious beliefs that are centrally defined and cannot be questioned or defied. Increasingly, the Muslim world must redefine itself toward moderation, greater justice for all, more wealth and wealth distribution, and rejection of tyrants of whatever persuasion. According to endless public opinion polls, what Muslims want is what everybody else wants: respect, jobs and adequate income, stability and security, decent governments, avoidance of cultural and religious conflicts, and genuine gender justice. Muslims uniformly want the ability to live a devout, moderate life, with governance based on the core principles of their religion.

The future of the Muslim world does not lie with the West; it lies almost entirely within the Muslim world itself. Initially, one can expect to see the results of the Arab Spring mainly by a broader range of interests and organizations entering the power base itself, usually over the resistance of the old establishment. Even in "Muslim countries" not all citizens are Muslim, or are all Muslims the same. How can a Muslim citizen and family lead a devout Muslim life while still getting all of the advantages of a modern society and economy?

State Socialism failed this test; most current dictatorships failed this test. Increasingly there is the hope for something new.

Hopefully, there will be a gradual emergence in a more people oriented agenda – better elementary and secondary education, real health care, widely available and affordable, rational measures to expand and enrich the economy in each country, while avoiding the old patterns of the thieving rich and the rest of the population in poverty. Bottom up facilities such as food distribution centers, "store front" health clinics, vocational training centers, better sanitation, youth programs, and genuine anti-corruption attacks are relatively cheap and can be developed rapidly. There is a lot of potential help from the international community through government assistance, non-government organizations, and private sector investment. In fact, the U. S. and European nations could start up a new idea: a "war on social neglect" the equal of the current "war on terror." **The key should be the enhancement of a devout middle class supplemented by assistance for the poor an justice for all, especially women and youth.**

THE MUSLIM FUTURE

The key word in this emerging dialogue is **Comparability.**

If strict fundamentalism is ultimately a failure, and mere adoption of Western ways is ultimately unsatisfactory, what kind of government and society can be formed that somehow blends Islamic faith and desired secular forms of freedom and independence? The answer lies in the design of some form of government which uses the Islamic faith as its base, and adds secular thought and activities that are compatible with that faith. For example, most Muslim states have a combination of secular laws and policies, plus the partial use of Sharia law, primarily for religious and family matters. But it has been shown that secular laws can rather easily be designed to be highly consistent with Sharia law and the Hadith and the Quran. In a similar vein, it is now seen that democracy and Islam are not inconsistent, and often have a common moral and philosophical base.

It seems further to be a growing trend for modern Islamic thinkers to deny that Islam is fixed and immutable as it was defined in the 7th century, but that it is changing – and growing – through the interpretations of Muslims themselves. As this process quickens, it becomes possible to think about the future – not what Islam used to be, but what it can become. It is also true that this new freedom fits better into the realities of political action, which is heavily oriented toward, negotiation and compromise, and the acceptance of change and diversity, none if which is possible for fundamentalists.

If this shift continues, it will provide and new and more useful framework for the idea of Islamic political parties whereby Islamists can enter the power structure not by force but by election. Note that none of this is very challenging to U. S. or other western interests; it is only really threatening to other forms of Islam. "Today, we see multiple Islamist organizations across a broad range, both violent and peaceful, at work in Egypt, Turkey, Morocco, Algeria, Yemen, Indonesia, Pakistan, Kuwait and Palestine. But it is not clear that the conflict between schisms within the Muslim community are much less competitive and contentious. The great protagonists are

Sunni Saudi Arabia and Shia Iran. But there seems to be increasing recognition in the broader Muslim community that terrorism can destroy but it cannot create the way that popular uprisings and even military coups can. Terrorist groups have to morph into "national liberation" groups (Chechnya, Kashmir, the Philippines, Palestine) in order to have a chance for power.

When asked what they advocate, most Islamic organizations call for "Sharia Law", in a manner similar to Westerners who call for "democracy". But in truth, what already exists in all Muslim countries are legal systems that are blends of Sharia law, older common law and custom, and western secular law. The design of these legal systems and their interpretation is now the responsibility of formal governments, and this has meant the gradual decline the older tradition of religious scholars as the interpreters of the meaning of the law. There is every reason to believe that this trend will continue, and that it is a realistic refutation of those believe only in the pure, old Sharia law of a thousand years ago. In fact, today the following countries already have well developed systems of Sharia law, either compatible with or integrated into the national legal system, or in a parallel system compatible with the secular legal structure. Such compatible systems exist in:

* Egypt (since 1880)
* Turkey (a mixed system, since 1871)
* Morocco (based on the French code, but with substantial Sharia elements)
* Saudi Arabia (the most conservative of Muslim orthodoxy, but still able to blend Sharia law with secular law, which is judged "consistent with" the intent of Sharia law)
* Sudan (mostly about family law)
* Pakistan (a mix with heavy Sharia elements)
* Indonesia (mixed since 1970)
* Afghanistan
* Iran (Mostly Sharia law with secular elements that are "consistent with" Sharia law.)
* Iraq
* Malaysia
* Mali (if any law still exists)

* Nigeria (many northern provinces have what is essentially a Sharia law system)
* Syria (a mixed system, all of which his essentially useless now)

Thus, countries with a total population of more than 1.7 billion already use some form of Sharia law, and have found that it can be made compatible with other major elements drawn from Western legal systems. The key concept to grasp is that Sharia law can be, and usually is, judged to be "CONSISTENT WITH" secular law, and vice versa.

The fact is that there is no such thing as **"the"** Sharia Law. There are differing versions of many of its key elements, sometimes in direct conflict with each other. When terrorists advocate "Sharia Law" they mean the harshest and most oppressive elements such as whipping and mutilation. There are four major "schools of jurisprudence" for the Sunni interpretation of Sharia Law: Hanafi, Hanbali, Shafi, and Maliki. There are also at least two major schools of jurisprudence for the Shia interpretation, the Ismaili and the Ashari.

But it does not seem that the rise to power of top down Islamist regimes is the answer either. Take the example of Sudan, where only the second Islamist regime in the world (after Iran) came to power (by military coup). Once in power, the Arab Islamist regime turned totally autocratic, closing down political freedom, extending the scope of domestic intelligence forces, and reducing civil freedoms. This was done not only in the Christian/animist South, but among Muslims in the North and the use of "janajaweed" gangs of terrorists against the black citizens of Darfur in the west. It is interesting to note that many Sudanese leaders are not narrow-minded religious zealots, but are a far more sophisticated elite, many of whom have advanced degrees from American or European universities. Yet this cadre entered into a long, vicious destructive war in the South, and sponsorship or terrorist gangs in Darfur, alienating more moderate people even in the Arab North, and alienating all of its neighbors, including its sponsor, Saudi Arabia. The war in the South ended in stalemate, and ultimately, the independence of S. Sudan, forced on the ruling regime which is still fighting the outcome. Meanwhile, Sudan itself is one of the least developed countries in the world, suffering from poor governance, widespread poverty, heavy foreign debt and reliance on foreign aid, poor to non-existent social services, high inflation, and lots of enemies.

In a blog in 1996, an observer (Kenneth Abeywickrama) describes Khartoum/Omdurman in 1996 as a gigantic slum, dilapidated, dusty, filled with camels and donkey carts. But then, reports that, by 2007, "the country had been transformed". GDP was up by more than 5 times. A massive construction program was under way in the North, the South had succeeded in breaking off into a separate South Sudan, and the end of the war lifted a heavy burden, although war continued in Darfur. In addition, oil exports had risen and this is the main source of funding. FDI has increased, and GDP is up 9-10% each year. But other reports are far less sanguine, and behind it all, **Sudan ranked 176ᵗʰ out of 180 countries in Transparency International's Corruption Perceptions Index for 2009!** It is extremely difficult to argue the case for Islamic morality in the face of such assessments.

Muslim governments are now belatedly being more seriously pressed to provide adequate social services and public infrastructure, but they conceal the fact that they can't afford them, largely because of the huge sums spent on the military and intelligence services, the money wasted in supporting outside terrorist ventures, and the huge amount of corruption losses. There may be a crisis looming – a crisis of unmet expectations.

Meanwhile, what do Muslim people really want? Justice, honesty, jobs, respect, an honest and just government, cooperation and participation, not conflict and oppression; an end to "the insolence of office".

What is also urgently needed is some better ways to attack universal pervasive corruption: There have been hundreds of anti-corruption efforts, but most have withered. An effective anti-corruption campaign must be holistic and should include, at a minimum: stricter laws on campaign finance and political fund raising; a strict clampdown on all forms of petty corruption generated by the delivery of public services (police protection, health care, tax collection, licenses and permits; inspections, etc. In addition, there should be a focused campaign against organized crime; a root-and-branch reform of the procurement system; a reform of land allocation; the establishment of an effective judicial dispute resolution system; full disclosure of the value of public assets; careful monitoring of banks; control of money flight." Sadly, making the list is easy, but it is often merely political wishful thinking.

VI

GOVERNMENTS AGAINST THEMSELVES

THE POWER OF GOVERNMENTS TO REGULATE

Regulation is theoretically intended to protect the public from abuse. At the same time however, regulations are the application of government control, and many are designed to force people and institutions to change the way they act. But it is very hard to decide when such enforcement goes beyond reason, and in oppressive governments, regulation tends to become an end in itself. There is such a thing as the regulatory mind which has a tendency to push regulatory authority broader and deeper, frequently beyond need or reason, and into second and third levels of detail, often as unwarranted extrapolations of what began as a sound basic statute.

Why do Governments regulate? There are, of course many legitimate reasons. In economic terms, regulations are used to moderate and control economic activity, to preserve market competition, to prevent excess profits, or to prevent actions damaging to the economy or to individuals. But regulations can give governments the ability to control entry into a market place by controlling the issuance of licenses to do business. This has proved a powerful means to reward friends and punish enemies. They have been used to protect monopolies, especially in energy, public utilities and banking, and to control the allocation of scarce resources including land and valuable mineral resources.

Then there is a whole second arena of regulation aimed at a nation's social services and public infrastructure. Social regulations may used for the following purposes:

1. To provide national or specific standards to assure equity, fairness and equality in issues of race, gender, ethnicity, cultural beliefs.
2. To preserve and enforce public/private rights (i.e. voting, civil rights, health and safety protections).
3. To prevent injustice (e.g. cheating, misrepresentation, failure to perform under contracts, freedom from civic or government abuse of authority, etc.).
4. To prevent or control anti-social behavior (e.g. sexual harassment).

It is unsettling but illuminating to recognize that each regulatory power can be made either pathological or corrupt or both. Regulation has become one of the most powerful tools by which governments enforce their will. The power to regulate can be given to almost every government agency at all levels, and it is used to redirect institutional and individual behavior by defining what is prohibited and what is "allowed". The proliferation of regulations is so great in some countries that nobody, including those who write them and enforce them understands them all, much less understanding their consequences, which can be enormous.

To quote Bhagwati: "Few outside of India can appreciate in full measure the extent and nature of India's controls until recently. The Indian planners and bureaucrats sought to regulate both domestic entry and import competition, to eliminate product diversification beyond what was licensed, to penalize unauthorized expansion of capacity, to allocate and prevent the reallocation of imported inputs, and indeed to define and delineate virtually all aspects of investment and production through a maze of Kafkaesque controls.

"Swedish economist Gunnar Myrdal found that India's social system and attitudes were important causes of its low productivity, primitive production techniques, and low levels of living. According to Myrdal, poor work discipline, contempt for manual work, lack of punctuality, lack of alertness and ambition, low aptitude for cooperation, and superstition were frequent attitudes. Additional inhibitors are the cast system, a debilitating land ownership and land tenure system, low standards of efficiency and integrity in public administration, weak participation of the people in local and cultural affairs, and a rigid and unequal social structure, beyond caste."

In some countries, regulations have been used to force organizations to pay their workers more money, or grant greater benefits, or simply to employ large numbers of redundant employees, regardless of the economic consequences. For example, wages may be forced so high for perverse political motives that many smaller businesses are driven out of business or forced into the informal economy. Labor standards may require such exceedingly expensive compensation for released workers that companies avoid hiring them in the first place. In one African country for instance, night and weekend work is forbidden, and the minimum wage is 82% of the average value-added per worker. To discharge an employee an employer must first retrain him, place him in another job and pay him a lump sum equivalent to a year and one half of his regular wages (XX).

Similarly, bureaucratic complexity makes the creation of new businesses extraordinarily costly and time consuming. According to the Economist: "In Congo it takes 215 days, costs close to nine times the average annual income per person, and firms must start with a minimum paid-up capital of more than a third of that preposterous fee. These rules are generally regarded as stupid and pointless." [ii]

Governments have proved universally and notoriously unable to regulate themselves. State owned enterprises and other government monopolies are far greater threats to public wellbeing than private monopolies ever were, and many are deliberately exempt from regulatory controls. Laws intended to protect the public are often drawn too broadly, giving too much room for perverse interpretation, and the abuse of power. Political leaders can and do violate even well defined regulations. Many regulations contain the power to allocate valuable resources, and this has proved to be an enormous source of corruption. (Bingman, "Why Governments Go Wrong")

PROBLEMS OF REGULATORY EXCESS

There are no effective policy, political, or even intellectual limits on the theoretical power of governments to regulate, and there is a tendency of regulators to expand and extrapolate the range and depth of their regulations. Abuses of regulatory power have created a growing feeling that governments can and do go too far, and there are no effective means to limit the expansion of such power. Regulation is intensely bureaucratic: regulations are complicated, technically hard to understand, and often lacking adequate justification for their creation. Enforcement is usually costly and time consuming, requiring long time delays, and excessive paperwork. And regulations, once imposed can prove to be highly rigid, difficult to change, and almost immortal. Even worse, the whole massive complexity of regulatory authorities has created the ideal breeding ground for oppression and equally massive corruption. Regulated industries learn to play "the game" better than their government supervisors, and in effect, they capture the regulatory apparatus by fair means or foul. Then, regulations can be softened or avoided, enforcement can be fended off, oversight can be made friendlier, and price or cost control regulations mysteriously turned to the advantage of the regulated.

But most of the time, the power of the government is so strong that a pathological regime can easily use regulation as a form of tyranny designed deliberately to enhance the power of an authoritarian regime, providing the basis for reward of one's friends and punishment of one's enemies. It is also possible to avoid the consequences of regulations that would quash corruption such as prohibitions against bribery, influence peddling, money laundering, concealment of assets, extortion, malfeasance, misfeasance, and others. This has led to a new interest in what effective alternatives to regulation could be used, including the following:

1. Societies may want deliberately to decide more carefully that there should be some functions in society that need not be regulated (religion, personal privacy?). The basic question is whether there are elements of society that can be trusted to conduct their activities with only general community

oversight and not official government regulatory oversight. The answer of the authoritarian regime? We trust nobody.

2. The public can be protected by public education instead of, or in partial implementation of situations needing control. Voluntary controls are feasible in many areas and should be tried before government application of controls. Most corporations exercise voluntary controls through the use of independent auditors to provide public assurance of legality and probity as a vital element of business conduct.

3. Professional standards are a widely used and highly effective means of assuring publicly acceptable outcomes. Doctors are strongly motivated to observe professional ethics in the treatment of patients. Professional engineers are motivated to build bridges or dams that will not collapse. Teachers and university professors usually want to teach the truth. Professional managers have personal reputations at stake, and in many cases, managerial experience and judgment are superior to hard regulatory mandates.

4. Instruments other than regulation may be employed. The tax system can be used to design rewards or penalties to achieve acceptable outcomes in lieu of regulation. There may also be rewards/penalties available through fiscal allocation.

Regulations are tough to deal with because they are so complicated and technical. This means that there is little public understanding of them. In fact, in places like Egypt, which has more than 400,000 regulations in force, not even the people who created them or enforce them understand what they all mean. At best, public ignorance can be mitigated by careful public education and explanation. At worst, public ignorance is deliberate and highly prized by the holders of power. Governments can select from an almost unlimited variety of tools in the regulatory tool kit: price regulation, import/export limitations; quotas, tariffs; granting or withholding of licenses and permits; health and safety regulations for every segment of the economy; franchising and licensing; controls for anti-trust, anti-monopoly and anti-cartel mechanisms; and control of the right to do business. It can be seen that regulations -- limitless in their scope, obscure in their technical detail, open to extrapolation and interpretation, and selective in their application -- are the ideal tools for government centrists, whether they be democratic representatives, socialists, dictators, or tyrants.

Regulatory statutes when enacted are usually followed by a "lock-in" of clientele interests, and regulatory statutes are enormously difficult to change -- especially if change involves a shift in power. Thus, a regulation may be "forever." This should suggest that regulatory statutes should be carefully drawn, but many are not. The attitude of most politicians seems to be the urge to draft a vague general law conveying sweeping powers but with no definition of limitations. This then provides a platform for forcing everyone to come to some element of government to negotiate the consequences. The results of these protracted negotiations are then "sealed" into the basic law, which tends to accrete endless immutable detail.

In most governments, the tendency in regulation is highly centrist. That is, where there are regional and municipal governments, it is their desire to have some regulatory authority of their own, to accommodate regulation to local circumstances. But the centrist government argues "if it is right to enforce a regulation, it is right that it be enforced all over the country with little latitude for variation." It has long been reasoned that the political capital is best expended in passing a single national law, than in permitting regulatory variations to exist at lower levels of government. In the United States for example, advocates lobby for one controlling national law, as opposed to attempts to have to deal with 50 states, or hundreds of cities.

REGULATION OF SOCIAL RISKS

Social services regulations tend to have high public acceptance and support, and are relatively free of corrupt practices. But there are many nations, mostly developing countries, where these protections are not nearly adequate. In part, this is due to the fact that many of the developing countries are barely surviving, and have trouble finding funds for more than the bare essentials of life. In part, social services themselves tend to lag behind the demands of economic development that preoccupy poorer countries. There is a significant correlation between national wealth and the ability to afford social services programs. Where a country is marginally able for example, to afford an adequate national health care capability, it is marginally able to enforce laws mandating universal health care or regulations that seek to enforce levels of service that cannot be afforded. Environmental protections are often neglected not only because of their costs and the complexities of their enforcement but because they are regarded as creating negative inhibitions to some form of industrial or commercial development. But industrial waste may be dumped into lakes and rivers because it is deemed too expensive to dispose of them properly. Power companies pollute the air with effluents from their smoke stacks because they do not want to bear the costs of cleaner but more expensive fuels, and because corrupt government enforcers are paid to ignore problems.

It is not unusual therefore to find that implementation of the legal or regulatory base that is handsomely enunciated in broad fine sounding commitments falls far short of achieving such promises. Socialist/communist countries in particular undertook a "cradle to grave" philosophy which placed an almost impossible burden on the State. Thus, when governments were unable or unwilling to live up to these commitments, loss of confidence in the government was inevitable. Each regulation requires often very complex and expensive enforcement which has seldom been fully achieved, since it is far easier to write a regulation than it is to see to it that it is enforced. In some countries, the political and bureaucratic thrill of creating regulatory mandates has produced absolutely ridiculous situation where thousands of detailed regulations are on the books. This allows those in charge to "select" those regulations they choose to enforce, an opportunity seldom missed by the corrupt. Even where government ministries are trying to act responsibly, they have often lacked the numbers of trained staff to reach all of the people and institutions required to live under regulatory mandates, and it has proved relatively easy to ignore such mandates, or to get around them.

The lack of adequate staff is often pathological in the sense that the shortage is deliberate in order to limit the effectiveness of enforcement.

Many regulations written for political visibility prove impossible to implement. Others are so poorly drafted that getting around them has become a cottage industry. For example, the simply obtaining a license to start a new business can be so difficult and protracted that it actively discourages new starts, or causes small business owners to operate in the informal economy with no license. The alternative of course is to resort to bribery. Inspectors, who are generally underpaid and overworked, often find it easier to decide when and how to enforce by the simple process of soliciting bribes to assure inaction. "Speed bribes" are paid to overworked officials in order to get approvals or clearances put at the head of the queue. There are thousands of cases where construction inspectors are bribed to turn a blind eye to serious violations of construction standards, and often buildings, roads, or bridges collapse as a consequence. Doctors in state hospitals may face hopeless patient loads, and decide to provide medical service first to those who are willing and able to pay extra. Corporations that build facilities in places where they can take advantage of cheap labor often collude with governments to keep the cost of labor down. This may lead to neglect in the development of health and safety protections in the work place, or the ever popular "selective" enforcement of such regulations.

So in the end, almost nothing in society and life is unregulated, and nobody can say where regulation should stop and at what level. The basic questions are the hardest to answer: how safe is safe? How safe is safe enough? What, in society should be left essentially unregulated? When and why does regulation become excessive and pathological? How far should the needs of governance be permitted to overpower the rights of individuals and of institutions? Most people favor control of improperly performing private sector institutions but are often not aware of how their own individual rights are also constrained. But who can regulate the government regulators?

GOVERNMENT INTERNAL DILEMMAS

The almost universal form of government in the world centers around the concept of centrist power held by an elite group. Such governments seek to gather power into their control against the desires of the people, the private sector, and even against local governments. These governments are elitist in that they are specifically designed to keep power in the hands of a limited number of power holders who are kept together in a number of ways. Most notably, control is maintained by the functioning of the key elements of the government: the law, government regulation; the government tax system, and the government budget. When force is needed, the elite will employ the military and central intelligence forces, the police, and the court system. Americans are used to thinking of these government organizations as delivering the democratic will. People in more than a hundred countries around the world know differently.

It is likely that the key set of relationships in a country will be those of special interest politics. Governments want money, support and backing. Special interests can be corporations, state owned enterprises, civic groups, unions, and others. Especially important are special interests representing energy, transport, banking and trade.

After WWII, it seemed that many governments around the world had found the solution in the form of State Socialism where governments made themselves all powerful and thus supposedly the "protector" of the public from these special interests. But in reality, State Socialism became the ideal format for special interest politics. State Owned Enterprises (SOE) were often the instruments chosen by governments to control the major elements of the economy, often as total monopolies, only to come to realize that these SOEs had become very powerful special interests in themselves. The new independence of many countries in the period from 1950 to 1990 led to a wave of pro-democracy hope. Instead, most countries got a local "big man" version of centrist elitist power.

What is the option? First, a democratically *elected* government; then a democratically *designed* regime; then a democratically *functioning* regime; then a democratically *motivated and driven* government. But "democratization" often simply meant the reform of the political system in terms of how to divvy up the spoils. In Somalia, Bosnia, Liberia, Afghanistan, S. Sudan, Haiti, and many others the institutions of the central government were always so weak that they could not really govern or assure safety or security. In many newly independent states of Africa and East Asia, the states never had the talent or experience to govern, and many were not economically viable. Many have never overcome these blocks. Countries still lack not only democratic political institutions by also skilled operational public management, and influential civil organizations and private enterprise leadership. But one of the continuing power bases, even in the modern world, are clans, tribes, regions, ethnic brotherhoods and religious affiliations. Regional politics are a relatively safe place to build counter forces to the incumbent government.

What do people really want? Not necessarily to be rich, but they want safety, security, reasonable income, and FAIRNESS. One of the greatest objections to governments is that they are UNFAIR! Stability and safety are so important that the urge for them may cause people to accept the centrist oppressive government that seems to produce them. Yet governments seem inherently the source of much of the conflict in a country, especially when ruled by a dominant dictator. An all-encompassing public sector, and a small, weak private sector means that there are few opportunities outside of government, thus giving the government added power and money control. Unfortunately, building resistance to the regime in power usually heightens conflict and destruction in a country. Unrest over social problems is destabilizing. Political parties are "special interests". **Power comes before democracy.**

But so does state failure. Consider some of the most evidence of such failure:

* when the government favored and enforced a closed economic system.
* when social indicators such as infant mortality rates were high
* when states were widely and deliberately undemocratic.
* when inflation is out of control and the currency becomes devalued
* when domestic investment dries up through investor loss of confidence
* when government responses are incompetent or non-existent.
* when smuggling, tax evasion, and criminal activity surge.

State failure is largely man made and not accidental. Sometimes, it is because the government is congenitally unable to deal with its problems. Sometimes it is because the ruling elite protect themselves only by a complete and sophisticated destruction of opposition and independence, which feeds a downward spiral of support for the state. There seems to be a pattern where really bad governments really don't understand how wrong they are and thus are not inclined to "correct" anything. But the control of the elitist top-down state is so great that people are driven to the belief that the only way to get rid of the tyrants is through some form of violence.

IRAQ: DUMB AND DUMBER

Iraq has made very bad choices of government since the American-led invasion, including the first Prime Minister Nouri al-Maliki, who was heavily biased toward the Shia population and generated outrage and hatred from both the Sunni and the Kurds. The current PM is better but has still proved unable to provide adequate public services, and a repaired public infrastructure. In addition, his regime is notoriously corrupt even by Iraqi standards. This has led to further divisions in the country beyond the Shia/Sunni/Kurd conflicts. Militias have partly taken the place of an undertrained, badly led, and fearful military; the Iranian backed Asaib Ahl al-Haq is perhaps the most disciplined military in the country, and is now meddling heavily in politics. There are other militia groups, backed by both Shia and Sunni powers. There are even supporters of former PM Maliki despite his horrible reputation. Now, there are huge public protests by everybody of all persuasions asking why there still is not an effective and reliable power system, enough food, and adequate provision of critical social services of education, health care and housing. People fear that they are not secure from ISIS and other terrorist organizations. The economy, which was weak and in poor shape under Hussein, remains largely a shambles, and there is little hope for the creation of an adequate number of jobs. Even government economists predict a budget deficit of more than $30 billion this year, and worse to follow. In short, Iraq has been going from bad to bad to bad for 35 years. As a result of these enormous stupidities, Iraq has lost 2.4 million refugees, another 4.5 million people internally displaced, and a further 8.2 million seriously at risk. At least 150,000 people had been killed by 2014, and current numbers may be much greater.

CHINA'S ONE CHILD POLICY: AN EXAMPLE

In 1979, China initiated a policy that, with certain exceptions, limited every Chinese family to one child. In order to enforce this policy, a huge government bureaucracy was created at the national, township and village levels. At its peak, this bureaucracy had 400,000 officials at the township level and more than one million at the village level. In addition, neighborhood "snoops" were employed to rat out their neighbors. The State Planning Commission had absolute authority to set quotas for the numbers of children allowed at the township and village levels, and local governments were given unbridled power to enforce these quotas, often by brutal and expensive means.

In the early 80's, a Chinese peasant named Chen and some of his friends had become outraged by the local consequences of this one child policy, and had done a survey in their city of Linyi and its surroundings. They discovered that 7,000 mothers with two children each had been forcibly sterilized during the past three months, and that several hundred others had been forced to undergo abortions, even though they were eight months pregnant. The city's hospital staff admitted that, under orders, they had immersed fetuses in boiling water to make sure they did not survive. This became known as "the Linyi incident."

Chen, who was blind, and his wife went to Beijing to report their findings to an appeals commission. The police intercepted and arrested him despite the fact that his intended complaint was perfectly legal, but the Linyi incident became a famous example of the terrorist capabilities of the Chinese government. The incident became famous in part just because it became known, and in part because of the extreme official brutality it revealed. The municipal authorities had indeed published an official order directing that forced sterilizations and abortions should be carried out. According to Guy Sorman "As this became known, terrified pregnant mothers who could do so fled the city to hide out with relatives. The Linyi police, with the full knowledge of the family planning commission, used hired thugs to track down these pregnant women and other women with two children. Parents and neighbors who failed to report them were jailed, beaten, and fined a hundred yuan a day. Entire neighboring villages then found themselves besieged, cut off from the rest of the world until they handed over the accused. Husbands who resisted their wives kidnapping were badly beaten. Herded into a hospital like sheep, the hapless women were summarily anesthetized and operated on, often in far from hygienic conditions. The Party cadres heaved a sigh of relief; their jobs were safe."

MYANMAR: MILITARY VS. THE PEOPLE

Intractable ethnic conflict has marked the recent history of Myanmar (formerly Burma). The country's tribes were unified by a treaty signed in 1947, as part of independence from Great Britain, but as in so many other cases, the government that was created was neither democratic nor rational, but a military dictatorship of overwhelming brutality. It is faced some of the heaviest fighting in years against the Kokang, and Han Chinese people in the north of the country. Fighting also continues against the Palaung forces, a non-Khmer people also in the north, and against the Kachin Independence Army in Kachin state. These rebel groups tend to reinforce each other seeking a government based on "democratic and federal principles." But these groups have a very complex set of interests. Some are true democrats; some are hoping force a redistribution of wealth in the county; others would like to become eligible for some flows of government money. Others want to get into the national power base. But all stand on the same ground: the power of ethnic solidarity in the face of oppressive government. In an election in 2015, the military regime lost control, and is now facing challenges to its grip on power. The very popular Aung San Sun Kyi is semi-officially the national president while the legislature considers some fundamental constitutional amendments to reduce the power of the military. One of Kyi's major priorities will be the mitigation of intense national prejudice along religious lines: Muslims vs. Buddhists, with serious concern about the state of the large Rohinga community, after decades of military oppression.

NIGER: THE POLITICAL ROLLER COASTER

What has particularly distinguished Niger has been the extraordinary turbulence and the dramatic swings in a decade-long political roller coaster ride. A count of the decade's major events reads like a litany of chaos: four republics, and hence four constitutions with presidential or semi-presidential regimes; three transitions of six, nine, and eighteen months; one National Conference and a Committee on Fundamental Texts; one Forum for Democratic Renewal; one Technical Constitutional Committee; a consultative Council of Elders; three constitutional referenda and eight other national elections; four heads of state and one President of a High Council of the Republic; four National Assemblies; nine prime ministers; at least one hundred and fifty ministers; one civilian coup d'etat; two military coups d'etat; one electoral boycott; one strike by the president and one strike by parliamentarians; one campaign of civil disobedience; and one dissolution of the National Assembly. All of this has taken place against the background of armed rebellions and communal and rural conflicts.

THE DEMOCRATIC REPUBLIC OF CONGO: LOST IN A SEA OF TERROR

Horrible war in Rwanda and Uganda between the Tutsis and the Hutu tribal groups not only terrorized Rwanda, but overflowed into other countries, notably the DRC. In part, it centered around refugee camps for both groups in the DRC, which unfortunately became a recruiting ground for insurgent groups to support their war in Rwanda, but also to build a serious attack on the government of the DRC, in alliance with the DRC's native insurgency groups. From 1994 on, conflict raged, running up a death toll of 3.3 million people.

As part of the tragedy, the DRC is really a very rich country and could be healthy and prosperous if its national resources could be utilized and converted into productive economic activity. But most of these assets have been undeveloped for almost 50 years since national liberation, and the DRC has stupidly been allowed to become one of the poorest nations in the world. The country is a total shambles; failed education, health care, transport, finance, pensions, and justice for citizens. The only people who seem to prosper in the country are the crooks. The whole border regions of Congo, Rwanda, Burundi and Uganda remain a sea of vicious ethnic militias with no comprehensible agenda, wildly killing people and destroying property. The UN has had a "mission" in Congo for 13 years, but it has never come close to clamping down the horror.

ARGENTINA: THE SHRINKING GIANT

The former president, Cristina Fernandez de Kirchner tended to continue Juan Peron's leftist policies and populist subsidies. She forced companies to repatriate profits and pay higher taxes on imported materials, reducing trade and interrupting vital supply channels. Since 2008, she has nationalized airlines, public pensions, and the largest oil company, YPF. The nationalization of YPF caused major convulsions in the economy and scared off potential investors who also remember the disasters of a 2002 default on the government's debts. In addition, some of the biggest beneficiaries of these policies have been the crooks: there has been a positively overwhelming revitalization of piracy, smuggling, illegal importing and exporting of everything from computers and electrical equipment to pharmaceuticals to CDs and canned goods. More than half of Argentina's population – some 40 million people – live below the poverty line in a country that used to be rich. Even the labor unions, which have long been ardent socialist/communist supporters of Peron and those who followed, are unhappy, and despite some wage increases and a relatively low unemployment rate, they mounted more work stoppages and street demonstrations because they recognized that the policies meant to stimulate the economy had failed, creating just the opposite effect. What is increasing is smuggling, tax evasion, loss of quality control, a rise of the informal economy and the high skills of bribery, theft and widening corruption. In many cases, this corruption has been shown to reach to the very top of the government; two former presidents have been formally charged with accepting huge bribes from contractors.

Crime is the biggest concern for many of the government's critics. 81% of the public believe that their government is ineffective in fighting crime. 60% of the public believe that they can bribe a police officer or official. Newspapers and television programs provide a daily diet of stories about increasingly bold home robberies in which armed bands sieze families and force them to pay ransom. The vast majority of crimes are never solved, and the death toll is rising. And while the government says that annual inflation is "just" around 10%, private economists say that prices are rising at about three times faster than that.

A companion to crime is corruption, for which Argentina is justly infamous. An Argentine court sentenced former president Carlos Menem on Tuesday to 4 ½ years in prison for embezzlement. The judicial news agency said the court also sentenced former economy minister Domingo Cavallo to 3 ½ years for his role in illegal payments to staffers that were authorized by Menem during his 1989-1999 presidency. Menem and Cavallo were part of a scheme to overpay certain officials and then split the illegal take. However, Menem is now a senator, and is thus protected against being imprisoned. (Washington Post, Nov. 30, 2015).

In December of 2015, Kirchner and her party lost an election, finally revealing how fed up people had become with their miserable governments. But in the muddled world of Argentine politicians, it is not yet clear what will happen. New Argentine President Maurico Macri faces "a daunting legacy: an economy paralyzed by exchange controls, deprived of foreign investment, and stricken by inflation of more than 25%; institutions compromised by political interference, including a weakened judiciary and press; and a foreign policy that has left the country closer to Iran and Venezuela than the United States and other democracies. (Washington Post Jan. 2016). Macri has lifted exchange controls, abolished taxes on agricultural exports, and opened up negotiations with government creditors to settle old debts. He has plans for increases in subsidized power rates that have generated chronic power shortages in the country, and he is planning to revamp the government's official statistics agency which has been falsifying inflation data. He has also begun to back away from de Kirchner's questionable relationships with Venezuela and Iran. Argentina remains a classic example of how an arrogant, ignorant and oppressive government can all but ruin a rich and proud country.

BRAZIL: SUPER SCANDAL, SUPER CATASTROPHE

"Brazil's bubble seems to have burst. The economy is mired in a deepening recession, thanks to a drop in oil and other commodity prices. The state owned oil company Petrobras has triggered the biggest scandal in the country's history, with dozens of businesspeople and more than 50 members of Congress and dozens of government officials have been implicated in some $ 2 billion in kickbacks. Investments in vaunted new oil fields have been cut back, even as Brazilians fume over the billions spent on new sports stadiums. With Brazilian credit ratings in danger, Ms. Rousseff was forced to impose the same austerity measures typically favored by the IMF, including cuts in energy subsidies." (Washington Post, June 28, 2015).

Meanwhile, allegations of corruption involving government funds are pending against dozens of Ms. Rousseff's party, including its treasurer, who is also connected to the huge scandal involving Petrobras, the giant state controlled oil enterprise. The heads of two huge construction firms, including the largest in Latin America, have been accused of paying enormous bribes to the ruling Workers Party and its friends and they were arrested in June of 2015. Her national popularity ratings are a pitiful 10%, and she is in constant conflict with Congress, which has acted to strip away some of her executive powers, and has diluted some of her austerity measures, and has now voted to enable her impeachment trial.

"The state of the economy continues to worsen: too many unprofitable state owned enterprises; too much anti private sector government meddling and regulation; loose questionable government budgets;

declining wages; rising prices; lack of investor confidence; loss of 500,000 jobs; government bonds classified as "junk" – all have caused a near collapse of the Gross National Product, and worse seems destined to follow. Largely as the result of her fiscal and monetary policies, and regulatory interventions, confidence in the economy has sagged, GDP shrank for the last three consecutive quarters, and is down a scary 4.5% from the same period last year, and inflation is pushing 10%." (Economist, Sept. 19, 2015)

Increasingly, health care has risen in importance in election campaigns because Brazilian political leadership has long been disgracefully neglectful and indifferent. Assessments point out the lack of adequate funding but also the poor performance of many elements of the system including squandering of scarce funds, questionable deals with drug manufacturers, and lack of necessary staff and equipment. There is a growing movement for the private sector to step up their competition with the governments near monopoly, with new lower cost health insurance plans, cheaper X-ray and lab services, and services extended to rural and urban slum areas. Other elements of Brazil's social services system are also badly neglected.

EGYPT: A SUCCESSION OF POWER ELITES

The government that might have been. The "Arab Spring" unseated Egyptian president Hosni Mubarak, and in the following months, opened up the opportunity for a new and modern and more moderate government. But the very organized Muslim Brotherhood (MB) managed to win the ensuing presidential election, putting Mohamad Morsi of the MB into office, despite the acknowledged suspicion and opposition of a large majority of the Egyptian public. The Muslim Brotherhood was founded in 1928 by Hasan al-Banna, and it began largely as a social assistance organization, dealing with the problems of the poor, the sick, the oppressed and unemployed youth. Gradually, it broadened its base to introduce new "product lines" such as political agitation, political candidacy, and ultimately the conduct or support of terrorist activity.

Egypt declared its independence from Great Britain in 1952, and it has been ruled ever since its independence by three dictators: Gamel Abdel Nasser, 1954 to his death in 1970; Anwar Sadat from 1971 to his assassination in 1981; and Hosni Mubarak from 1981 to 2011 when he was ousted from office be a huge upsurge of popular outrage. None of these three rulers ever managed to create a truly democratic government or an adequate and stable economy. The Nasser government was a loser. The regime was officially Socialist, and pursued most of the Socialist economic policies formulated in the USSR and in Europe. But Socialism failed both as economic and social deliverers. The national economy remained weak, the people were neglected by the governing elite, and social services never managed to reach the whole population. Nasser tried to create a "Pan Arab" combination with Syria, but nothing really took hold. Nasser was succeeded by Sadat, who was assassinated in 1981; Sadat was followed by Mubarak who ran a corrupt, oppressive government with a continued weak economy and economic stagnation.

The Muslim Brotherhood was almost always well organized, even when officially banned. This paid off after the Arab Spring, because they succeeded in electing Mohamad Morsi when the real majority of people did not really back the MB. But Morsi overplayed his hand, and obtained modifications to the Constitution granting the president much greater power, and putting a Muslim slant on public policy. This produced a strong counter reaction by the military, which overthrew the Morsi regime and installed Gen. al-Sissi as the new president. At that point, the public generally had dark suspicions about the MB, and generally thought that the military had done the right thing.

Morsi was always in major trouble of his own making. "More than half of his score of official advisors abandoned him, along with his vice president, his Minister of Justice, and many senior officials. His senior legal advisor, when resigning, said that Morsi "a lack of vision; failure to achieve revolutionary goals or to empower Egyptian youth, failure to accommodate or even to consult political opponents, and the overweening influence of Morsi's fellow Muslim Brothers in devising policy." And Morsi has been accused of "pandering dangerously to the Islamic Republic of Iran, allowing an "infiltration" of Iranian money and influence." (Economist, May 4, 2013).

"Among Sunnis, the influence of Saudi-style puritanism has risen. Salifist parties fiercely reject anything alien to the "pure" faith of Islam's founding fathers, including Sufi mysticism, or Shia veneration of imams or descendents of the Prophet Muhammad. The irony is that such displays of Sunni chauvinism cause deep discomfort to the Muslim Brotherhood, the most successful Sunni champions of political Islam." Egypt is 90% Muslim and has always been solidly Sunni, and people are very confused about why their government would deal with the Shia Iranian enemy.

But unfortunately, the new regime, installed by the military has, in its turn, overplayed its hand as well. When a mob assault murdered 14 policemen, the government reacted with overwhelming oppression and questionable tactics. Hundreds of MB officials and backers have been seized and jailed, and the motives and decisions of both prosecutors and judges seem highly questionable. Now, "To many Egyptians, such justice seems geared to punish those who dare to challenge the State, and to rebuild the near impunity enjoyed by officials in Mubarak's time." "Egypt's government has of late clamped unprecedented controls. In January, it decreed that all Friday sermons in Muslim mosques must adhere to a weekly theme set by the Ministry of Religious Affairs, and establish a hot line to allow worshippers to denounce preachers daring to voice political dissent. Further decrees have required all preachers to be government-licensed, imposed a code of ethics forbidding the discussion of politics in mosques and banning smaller prayer halls from holding Friday prayers. The Ministry fired 12,000 preachers and now allows only those trained in government approved institutes to deliver sermons. The MB has been allowed to run more than 7,000 mosques, but now the government has announced its intent to take over those mosques as well.

In summary, Egypt never produced "the government that might have been". Egyptian recent efforts to devise an effective government were fatally wrong three times: first, the tyrant Mubarak; second, the conniver Morsi; third, the new tyrant al-Sissi. Both Morsi and al-Sissi had opportunities to design and install a real an effective new government. Both failed miserably.

VENEZUELA: STATE SOCIALISM AS FATAL FANTASY

When Hugo Chavez died in 2003, his successor Nicolas Maduro continued his policies. But the fear is that the badly declining national Socialist economy is deteriorating to the extent that it threatens the collapse of the economy and the end of public subsidies, and the unseating of the Maduro regime.

One of the issues assuming new prominence is the long term relationship with Cuba. Venezuela has sent large amounts of oil to Cuba either free or at subsidized prices. In exchange, Cuba has supplied doctors, medical care in Cuba for Venezuelan citizens, researchers and technology experts and even sports coaches. But the deterioration of the Venezuelan economy (down 5% in the first half of 2015 alone), and the inability of the regime to cut expensive subsidies for housing, food, electricity and much else means that Venezuela will be hard pressed to continue its Cuban subsidy program at its past levels. Venezuelan citizens now realize that the State Socialist civil society is also deteriorating. More than one third of consumer goods have disappeared from store shelves, or are in very short supply, and the government has been forcing store owners to sell their goods at a loss, which not only further wounds the general economy but is seen as so obviously unfair and destructive. The government continues to lie about the situation; for example, the official rate of conversion to the dollar is less than one third of the actual rate.

The collectives which the government created throughout the country are uniformly incompetent and they interfere with the official leadership of local governments. There were 25,000 murders in the country in 2014 – the second highest in the world. Venezuela has become a major part of the shipment of cocaine, and this traffic, often abetted by the police and military, and many of the new collectives, has generated new levels of other types of criminal activity. Chavez and his successor Maduro have bragged about the triumph of Socialist

149

Democracy. What in fact they have produced is Socialist tyranny and failure. It would not be far from the truth to say that Venezuela is about to become a failed state in horribly destructive ways.

RUSSIA: LEARNING TO LOVE A TYRANT

In the late 1990s, Vladimir Putin had a choice: he could install a government which righted the flaws of the old USSR, based on market competition, the rule of law, social services, and democratic participation. Instead he built a government of patronage, corruption, the suppression of dissent, and a badly distorted economy. Why? He is now facing the result: an economy far too heavily based on the one economic sector of energy. The regime has failed to diversify the economy and point it toward economic competition, nor has it been able to create an expansion in the consumer economy to meet general public needs. In addition his actions in the Crimea and in the support of the Assad regime in Syria have precipitated severe sanctions opposed by other nations that have further choked the economy. People are poor, the economy fails to produce what people need, inflation is running wild, public services are still wholly inadequate, and resistance to the will of the government is severely punished. "The collapse of the ruble is directly caused by Vladimir Putin and the corrupt elite that support his belligerence, greed and paranoia." (20/12/14) Why did this repressive regime emerge? An even worse question is why is Putin still very supported?

Modern Russia is a perfect example of the failure to seize the opportunity to create a good new government. After the breakup of the USSR, Russia had a golden opportunity to develop a new government based on the best and most productive principles and policies. Instead, it invented another brutal, centrist dictatorship. What seems to have happened is that the worst people quickly pushed to the fore, outhustled and outflanked the best of national interests, and stole the economy of the country. Russia has now perfected what is surely the worst government in Europe, and one of the worst in the world. (Economist, 18/4/15)

President Putin has emerged as the head of a regime that has proved to be horrible; the center and anchor of a universally greedy and corrupt elite controlling the country, skilled at the fine arts of public disinformation, and blaming everything on America, and its lackeys in Europe. All of the faults of his government are blamed on the US – the "unleashing of a military-political adventure" in the Ukraine; support of the extreme nationalists in eastern Ukraine, wanting and attempting to ruin Russia, accusing the E.U. of having precipitated the collapse of the Soviet Union; and blaming Europe for the Russian economic disasters. (Economist, 13/12/14) Sanctions are not about the Ukraine, but the US desire to weaken Russia. The U.S. has supported Chechen insurgents. The U. S. staged a coup in Ukraine to install the current government. The U. S. is arming Russia's neighboring countries with evil intent. Etc. etc. etc.

Russians saw a period of relative prosperity and growth during the last decade, and then saw the beginnings of this very ominous spiral of decline. This is increasingly hitting home with the people, and a growing resistance to government policy is trying to emerge. Protests have been driven mainly by Russia's middle class, frustrated by their lack of prospects. After a decade of rapid income growth, priorities shifted to such aspirations as better justice, education and health care that the Putin regime either cannot or will not provide. In fact, spending on health care and public infrastructure has been cut from what were obviously inadequate starting points. Hopefully, Putin is increasingly being seen as a symbol of stagnation and corruption, rather than as the provider of stability. The sense of restoration of national pride which has been so important to Putin is now seen as not enough; people want a better life for themselves, and a yearning for Russia, somehow, to get modern and honest. A war in Ukraine is increasingly less attractive against the lack of social services.

Meanwhile, Russia is nearing a real economic crisis with the fall in the value of the ruble, eroding living standards, increasing shortages of consumer goods, increasing food prices, and declining public hope. The economy is far too reliant on oil, and no Russian government has really pressed effectively for the diversification of the economy. While Russia has reserves in excess of $370 billion, it has foreign-currency debts of more than $600 billion. Manufacturing and technology industries remain far behind international competition. Putin is busy severing economic links with the West, and trying to cultivate ties with China and Iran. The result in the short run has, remarkably, been to enhance Putin's popularity, because of his strong appeal to nationalism and "a return to past glory".

Russia has become the premier practitioner of a new form of government foreign policy: the Misinformation War. In the past, governments have been perfectly willing to "spin" facts, to publish misinformation, or to hide bad news. Then, they went farther: lying became a fully accepted tool of government. The reasoning was that the collective wellbeing of the masses, as defined by the government, far exceeded the condition of individual citizens, therefore, the State was entitled – in fact obliged – to protect and defend the government's position by any means. Thus, lying, or cheating, or stealing are perfectly acceptable elements of government policy and operations.

But now, Russia and other governments have taken information management to another level. Internally, the government will use lies or misinformation deliberately to attack its opponents. "The Kremlin's propaganda machine has been a key component of the "hybrid warfare" that Russia has waged in the Ukraine, and has helped shore up Putin's support at home. But it spreads much farther. It spills into European countries via huge television "services" provided by Russian sources where gullible or needy editors unknowingly reproduce Russian misinformation and fake news. Meanwhile, Russian operatives deliberately and persistently poison online discussion forums and social networks.

As European governments and private interests become more aware of this "war", there is a growing struggle over what to do about it, and the issue is different in different countries. Media regulators should be more alert to the most brazen lies, and prevent their repetition. Opponents should grow in strength and outreach, and in their ability to cooperate quickly. More effort must be made to expose Russian lies. But misinformation is a murky world, and much is very difficult to prove or disprove.

But the real test is beginning to unfold. Putin's war and growing isolation are confusing people. Over the past nine months, opinion polls find that support for the presence of Russian troops in the Ukraine has fallen from 74% to 23%. Other polls show that the persistent view that the state is corrupt and uninterested in the people. Potential investors, both domestic and foreign, are getting increasingly hesitant because the Putin regime is not trusted to be rational. The jury is still out.

CUBA: THE SLEEPER AWAKES

Reflecting the hopes engendered by the removal of most U. S. sanctions, the Cuban government has initated a guarded retreat from some of it long term Socialist "cradle to grave" social policies. The government is beginning to shut down free cafeterias and canteens for government ministries, which used some $350 milliion in imported food last year. There are said to be 24,700 free canteens in workplaces, and it is expected that most of them will be shut down as an economy measure. Their importance lies in the fact that they are seen as a crucial part of the Socialist guarantee of social services. Further, this seems to reinforce speculation that the government is quietly moving toward other eliminations or serious retrenchments of free monthly rations for food, housing, health, education, transport and power. Socialist theory required that individuals sacrifice their individual rights in favor of "all-embracing social provision". But the government failed in its ability to provide all theses social services at an acceptable level. The public's view has become the certainty that the government cannot deliver, and a growing realization of the need for greater self-reliance. Yet the government continues not only to control most of the means of production, but it dictates what consumers can buy, and how much. Agricultural production is controlled, and the governent has a monopoly over both purchase and sales of agricultural products. Wages and salaries are rediculously low, based on the premise that great value is provided in government subsidies. But as subsidies are reduced, can wages and salaries somehow miraculously be increased?

Cuba, in terms of its government and its economy is close to bankruptcy, and the Soviets won't be available to bail them out as they did in the past. Foreign investors are gun-shy after a brief period for better times with Raul Castro, and many want to get their money out of Cuba, but must wait for government approval to transfer their funds. The government has been forced to slash approved imports by 30%, and it has cut funds to both ministries and SOEs, despite earlier efforts to give SOEs more flexibility. The government says it wants to increase the number of small businesses, but as part of the economic crackdown, the number of small business licenses has shrunk from 360K to about 200K. Public infrastructure has not been upgraded and in fact is deteriorating, especially in transport and power.

Cuba does have the reputation of genuine free education, and a reasonably high level of health care. Yet wages are still less than **50%** of what they were in 1989! The government is being forced to consider the abandonment of the free subsidies policy, which, far from guaranteeing equity is now seen as a contributor to inequity – the government as allocator of scarcity, where everybody is becoming poor together. One option is to turn instead to a policy of more targeted social policies, and more priority setting.

MALI: THE LAND OF AZAWAD

Mali has long had a large and coherent traditional region for the largely nomadic Taureg tribes, and the Tauregs have long opposed the central government and sought independence. More recently, for many years, the Gaddifi regime in Libya recruited young Taureg men to fight in his army. As a consequence, when these men returned home, they bring back a lot of battle experience and a whole lot of very dangerous weaponry. Thus, they now pose a more formidable opposition than in the past.

In truth, the central government is widely hated for its incompetence, lack of humanity, and unbridled corruption. These failings have stimulated the formation of many insurgent groups in the country, in addition to the Tauregs, who have formed the National Movement for the Liberation of Azawad (MNLA)– the name of an ancient version of a Taureg nation. The MNLA has pushed an undermanned and largely incompetent Mali army out of whole regions in the northwest of the country and it has established the country of Azawad and fought off government efforts to recapture the terrain. Note that the MNLA is Taureg and not Muslim.

In addition, a real Islamic group has been established in the form of the Ansar Dine, a fundamentalist group seeking to seize the whole country and to convert it into an Islamist State, including the imposition of a very stringent version of Sharia law. Then, there is the Movement for Unity and Jihad, which is loosely linked to al Qaeda in the Magreb (AQIM), which is supposedly led by a notorious smuggler of drugs and guns. Finally, there is AQIM itself which sees Mali as a valuable base for meddling in the entire region.

The formal government of Mali continues to exist, but its grip on most of the country is very tenuous, not only because of these insurgent groups, but also its own evil reputation. This led to a military coup d'etat in 2012, by a very junior group of officers. They in turn were ousted by another coup in 2014. So Mali has virtually no legitimate government in the South; it provides only endless, pointless bickering and infighting. In 2002, an election was held for 147 deputies out of 1,103 candidates, registered on 387 lists presented by parties, coalitions, and independent candidates. This pattern of fragmentation was happily supported by the ruling elite. Also, it proved to be almost impossible to understand what any of these parties stand for, and how they significantly differ. It is easier to design structure and put it in place, than to define its real intended purpose or objectives. People lack knowledge of what "democratic government" really means or how it should operate. In fact, true democratic governance is very complex and sophisticated, and requires a far broader base of support than found in most countries.

The military can't seem to fight, and the government has solicited and received help from neighboring countries who fear that this whole mess will spill in over their borders. As these countries were going about the establishment of some sort of intervention group, the insurgents beat them to the punch, invading the South and threatening the capital. While they were held off, the whole situation is still poised in mid-air.

Meanwhile, poor social services and public infrastructure have gone from worse to much worse. The whole mess has left the country back at a medieval level: nothing works, nobody has a clue, conflict is invulnerable to solution, and the only thing that anybody seems to understand is hatred and combat. Muslim organizations could have stayed out; instead, they hastened to attack – in the name of the Muslim religion.

NIGERIA: FROM WRONG TO WRONG

Everything in Nigeria seems to be broken. Nigeria has the largest population of any nation in Africa, just under 175 million. It is a land of great beauty and a lot of natural resources, especially oil. Yet almost nothing goes right. The country must contend with a serious difference between the largely Christian and relatively well-off south, and a mainly Muslim and largely poor north of the country. While previous governments have made efforts to reconcile differences, including allowing most of the Muslim north to follow Islamic Sharia law, somehow the differences persist and cause endless forms of conflict. These conflicts however have been enormously exacerbated by the stupid, highly corrupt relationship between key political figures and the management of the huge Nigerian National Petroleum Corporation (NNPC). Control Risks Ltd., a London consulting firm, says that billions of dollars worth of operating contracts have been let without bidding, leading to a massive looting of the public treasury, to the tune of more than $8 billion. But somehow, the citizens of Nigeria never seemed to benefit, and the level of dissatisfaction reached hatred. Gangs of people punctured NNPC pipelines and stole oil for sale or their own use. In addition, such groups became terrorists, blowing up government facilities and pipelines, kidnapping government and contractor employees, and fighting the police. "Lagos has a lousy reputation. The mere mention of Nigeria's commercial center, conjures images of crime, corruption and motionless traffic. The bodies of people run over in car accidents can be left in the streets for hours, and commuters in even the poshest parts of town are sometimes caught in shoot-outs between robbers and policemen. In the ranking of "livability" in 140 cities cited by the Economist Intelligence Unit, Lagos sits in the bottom five, almost tied with Damascus!" (Economist, July 4, 2015)

In the north of the country, the situation has become even more terrifying. Boko Haram, an Islamic terrorist group, has invaded many villages and towns, killed thousands of people, destroyed hundreds of homes, businesses, and schools, and assaulted police and military outposts in Nigeria, Niger, Chad and Cameroon. In Borno province alone, 30% of health facilities and 70% of the fresh water supply are ruined or seriously damaged. According to a recent UNICEF report, more than 1.4 million people are now displaced within the country, and as many as 50,000 children are in danger of dying if they do not receive both food and medical assistance very soon. International aid organizations are trying to respond, but they are simply overwhelmed by the enormity of the problems.

In short, Boko Haram has created one of the worst human disasters in the world, and the Nigerian government seems hopelessly unable to protect the country. In the old saying, "nothing is so bad that it cannot become worse", the Nigerian Army has been revealed as under equipped, virtually untrained, under motivated, stupidly led, and deprived of necessary arms and supplies. The whole service was and is badly mismanaged, especially since many of the generals are busy embezzling army funds.

SYRIA: OPPRESSION RUNS IN THE FAMILY

Syria is another example of a government that deliberately fomented conflict among national groups. Syria contained Hashamites, the clan of the current rulers; other Muslims; Christians; Kurds; and Druze Christians. The French deliberately played each group against the others. Then, when the al-Assads came to power, they gave widespread preferment to their Hashamite clan, deliberately over the others.

The al-Assad regime of the 70s to date has been very bad. In addition to its inherent unfairness, the economy was weak and outdated and shrinking; the government was widely corrupt, and the secret police – the MAKHABRAT – were infamous, even by Middle East standards. There was a major war in the 60's involving the Muslim Brotherhood, and the government slaughtered 25 thousand people in a series of major massacres. This horrible history has culminated in a serious revolution against the regime, but even this has become horribly screwed up.

Syrian leadership has proved disastrous for more than 60 years. (Economist, 8 Jan. 2011). Syria suffered from the usual failures of planned socialist economies, and it economy, even before the civil war, was obsolete, inadeqate, neglected and poorly managed. Efforts for reform were modest, and the government was in a constant muddle about when and where to try reform. There was an effort to balance the national budget by mandating big cuts in public subsidies: fuel, electricity, water, transport, food, and there was some reduction in government mandating of prices, restricting itself to controlling three things – cotton, sugar beet, and wheat. But domestic production of food products is very low and inefficient, and imports are more expensive, and freeing up some segments of the market place resulted in many price increases, which, while necessary, hit consumers very hard. Local businesses are so weak that they tend to lose out to foreign competition. Some weak efforts were made to control property speculation and inflation, but failure of these efforts simply emphasized how miserable things have become. The whole elementary and secondary education system is inadequate and inferior, and health care is just as bad. Before the civil war, the government was thinking of removing some of its subsidies which would have been catastrophic, but the civil war has simply destroyed much of what little existed.

It was this horrible record of inadequacy, oppression and failure, and the closed options of the Alawite regime that were instrumental in creating the surge leading to the current civil war. There was a total loss of confidence in Bashar al Assad, even when he was making his few feeble efforts for reform, because people saw the fifty years of family failure, and in the end, Bashar al Assad has simply proved to be more of the same. By 2015, almost half of the pre war population of 22 million were either refugees to other countries, displaced persons in Syria, or in serious distress at home. The war has produced more than 400,000 killed, four million refugees, and more than seven and a half million internally displaced persons. It has now drawn the intervention of Iran, via its own troops, militias from Hezbollah. ISIS too has intervened, claiming both Iraq and Syria for itself. And finally, in 2015, Russia put its military on the ground to prop up the Assad regime. There is no end in sight for the war, but no matter how the war turns out, Syria will be a country in ruins, and it will need decades to recover.

MEXICO: THE WRONG SKILLS

Almost since its creation, Mexico and its government has been famous for its mastery of the skills and arts of corruption. The ruling parties – currently the PRI, have become skilled at how to buy votes, fix elections, corrupt the army, exploit the media, loot the economy, buy off the criminals and beat off or absorb the opposition. There has always been a ruling class which permanently "owns" the instruments of power to maintain absolute authority. The system is not democratic, but rather centrist and elitist, based on patronage, nepotism, preferment, influence peddling, protectionism and bribery. These are not even especially considered crimes but rather ways of doing business. The many monopolies and government controlled state owned enterprises are not really so much business interests as they are instruments for controlling more and more in the hands of the elite. Official attitudes are excuses: "Everybody does it"; "it could have been worse"; "it's not me"; or "others are worse than me."

Also, in the last four years,more than 1200 municipal employees, including hundreds of police officers, have been killed across Mexicos states where criminal organizations dominate and terrorize everybody. The central government seems unable to cope – or does not want to. Criminals have heavy political influence and are seriously involved in politics of the most corrupt nature.

Here is a whole country which, when given independence and the opportunity to produce a decent and effective government seems enthusiastically to have cultivated the worst government in the hemisphere, built on all of the wrong and distructive things.

PAKISTAN: THE MILITARY VS. THE GOVERNMENT

Within Pakistan, any government moderation in relationships with India, especially over Kashmir is undermined by the separate force of the ISI – the Interservices Intelligence department of the Pakistani Army. ISI is a negative meddler in the whole area, and it has allied itself from time to time with the Pakistani Taliban and the Afghanistani Taliban, to the great disadvantage of the country. National leaders has failed to oppose the extremists, in part because they commanded a good deal of public support. The media in turn refused to speak out. But the resulting arrogant assaults by Taliban and allied forces against the Pakistani government and people have finally forced the government to order the Army to destroy them, despite the ISI. During the Russian invasion of Afghanistan, the ISI dangerously allied itself with various terrorist organizations in the area including al-Qaeda, the Afghan Taliban, and the Haqqani network. Often, the ISI acted secretly, even from its own army and national government leadership. These unwise relationships have now come back to haunt the country. The Afghan Taliban is now the implacable enemy of Pakistan, and Pakistan has evolved its own Taliban "Tehreek-e-Taliban", or Pakistani Taliban (TTP) now vigorously attacking targets in the country. "On December 16th seven heavily armed Taliban gunmen scaled the outer wall of an army run school in Peshawar, and began shooting indiscriminately. Before order could be restored, 141 people, most of them teenagers and younger children had been killed, and many others were injured. This is the deadliest terrorist attack in Pakistan's history.

The army (ISI) and previous governments must take much of the responsibility for the violence the country has suffered. Since 2007, the annual toll of murders by jihadists has never dropped below 2,000 and in 2012 and 2013 it was not far off 4,000. The growth of

TTP is a direct consequence of a neurotic fear of encirclement by India which is widespread in Pakistan's ruling class, and has led to the disastrous policy of exploiting and encouraging jihadist terror in Kashmir – territories disputed by India and Pakistan (and hated by the people of Kashmir), and in Afghanistan. Thus, Pakistan has created, and suffered from a horrible group of terrorist organizations : the Pakistan Taliban, the Afghan Taliban, the Haqqani network in the border areas of both countries. It is inexplicable why the ISI stupidly supported and partnered with such groups. The Taliban have long had a history of destroying schools and colleges and killing students, arguing that only strict fundamentalist teachings by radical mullahs are acceptable to Allah.

With the attack on the school, the new President, Nawaz Sharif is finally able to face up to terrorist threats. Normally politics are hysterical, unthinking, and vicious. There are eight main political parties engaged in knock down-drag out conflict: always "anti" and never "pro". But because of the attack on the school, there has been general backing of lukewarm assaults on the insurgents. Since June of 2013 the army has finally been carrying out a serious offensive against the militants, largely in the province of North Waziristan, and have ceased to protect the Haqqani network. The governments of the two countries are finally working together to seal the border. All of these terrorist groups have cloaked themselves in Islamic piety while committing the most vicious and murderous acts. Why has Pakistan been so feckless for so long? Why do so many people in both countries still buy this nonsense?

But Pakistan remains a hugely important nation of 180 million people, highly intelligent, generally well educated, highly emotional and often almost hysterical, and very conflict ridden. It has a mediocre record in both economic and social terms. It was not until 2013 that the first-ever handoff from one civilian government to another occurred. Far too much of the economy is in government hands, and attempts to push toward privatization are constantly foundering. It has trouble keeping up with its population growth, and constantly experiences shortages of power, water, sanitation, urban facilities, highways and roads, ports, etc. There is persistent unemployment and under employment; the average wage is just $1,500 per year, and nearly a quarter of the population are below the poverty line. Social services are not only in short supply, but they are heavily slanted to serve the urban middle class in certain key cities, and the rest of the country is knowingly neglected. Such things as child care and child nutrition are sadly neglected. The real tragedy is the fact that, with proper leadership, Pakistan could be highly successful.

COLUMBIA: MORE OF THE SAME

Colombia has been increasingly trying to come to some form of accommodation with its all-powerful drug cartels. Peace talks are now more than two years on the road, but they are dealing with the embedded and intractable conflicts of the longest armed revolt in South America, lasting more than 60 years. Oppositon strongly resists the idea that some form of immunity from past outrages must be given to FARC rebels. Others have benefitted from the drug cartel businesses, and fear a loss of revenues. The whole process is also slowly revealing to a horrified public exactly how extensively the cartels have penetrated the governments at both national and local levels, especially the "public defenders" of the police and the military, who, in their ineffective thrasings around, have killed far too many citizens themselves. Neverthless, FARC has been set back seriously, and raids, murders, kidnappings and extortions have been noticably reduced. As in Mexico, there is a culture of acceptance of tyrannical government and vast universal corruption as "a way of life", the norm in the country for decades. But huge amounts of government funds designated for urban development, health care, and education seem always to get "lost" by public officials who inflate the cost of programs and pocket the differences. Impunity is common for the elite and their allies, who seldom pay their taxes and are never caught. Meanwhile, the average citizen gets little benefit, and the poor are in serious shape.

Hopefully, common sense is breaking out and governments are beginning to realize that the needs for social services are so great that all elements of society both public and private must be marshaled to address them. Innovation is needed in the creation of a total revenue package for social services involving continued central government fund transfers, new taxing powers, private sector responsibilities, intergovernmental cost sharing, and freedom to reallocate funds as judged against local government priorities. In many developing countries, local governments are so weak and inexperienced that whole new programs of capacity building must be generated. There is a growing realization of how technologically obsolete the old systems have been and how far each social service has to go in making remedial improvements to reach even basic adequacy. There are enormous unfunded costs involved in expanding social service to adequate levels for the majority of citizens. In addition, professional knowledge, new equipment, major repairs and renovations to obsolete physical plant all must be brought closer to current international standards. In failed or failing states everything seems to have slumped into a state of decay and governments in these countries are faced with excruciatingly difficult decisions on how to set priorities for severely limited funds. Finally, since the old regimes have failed to protect the public, whole new sets of regulatory protections are needed. Literally hundreds of important public regulations must be created for a social services system that is still in flux. And if the eternal civil war is really finally being ended, there is a whole enormous problem of reincorporating the rebel forces into civil society.

VII

ECONOMIC DEVELOPMENT: TOP DOWN AND BOTTOM UP

The United Nations, the World Bank, the International Monetary Fund and many other international organizations are eager players in the economic world. In 2000, the UN developed and enunciated the following **Millennium Development Goals:**

1. Eradicate extreme poverty and hunger.
2. Achieve universal primary education.
3. Promote gender equality and empower women.
4. Reduce child mortality.
5. Improve maternal health.
6. Combat HIV/AIDS, malaria, and other diseases.
7. Ensure environmental sustainability.
8. Develop a global partnership for development.

These goals include 18 sub-targets, measured by 54 indicators.

Then, in 2015, it issued an upgraded version of these goals as "**THE NEW SUSTAINABLE DEVELOPMENT GOALS (SDGs):**

1. No poverty
2. Zero hunger
3. Good health and wellbeing
4. Quality education
5. Gender equality
6. Clean water and sanitation
7. Affordable and clean energy

8. Decent work and economic growth
9. Industry innovation and infrastructure
10. Reduced inequalities
11. Sustainable cities and communities
12. Responsible production and consumption
13. Climate action
14. Life below water
15. Life on land
16. Peace and justice, strong institutions
17. Partnerships for the goals.

REALITY: THE WORLD IS TORN BY IMPLACABLE ARMED CONFLICT

At any given time, reality is that there are a dozen major wars in action. Consider current and recent history:

1. "The Great African World War", involving Rwanda, Burundi, Democratic Republic of the Congo and the horrible conflicts between the Hutu and Tutsi ethnic groups.
2. The war between Ethiopia and Eritrea, and the war between Ethiopia and Somalia.
3. Sudan – the ethnic Muslim north vs. the Christian/Animist south, and the Darfur in the west. This conflict was so bad that it led to a major revolt by the Christian people of the south of the country which ended in separation and the creation of the new nation of South Sudan. Then, tragically, two conflicting groups were formed in South Sudan that entered into a horrible murderous war of their own.
4. Nigeria vs. Boko Haram. Boko Haram is a fundamentalist Islamic sect bent on creating some kind of dark homeland. In the process, they have destroyed whole villages, murdered thousands of people, and burned or torn down huge numbers of both public and private enterprises. Their reign of terror has been extended to neighboring Niger, Chad and Camaroon.
5. Lebanon and its long term conflicts between Christians, Muslims and Druze

6. South Ossetia/Abkhazia vs. Georgia.
7. Spain vs. its Basque separatists.
8. Sri Lanka and thirty years of war against the Tamil Tigers separatists.
9. Philippines and Muslim rebels on its southern islands, supported in part by assistance from Iran.
10. Algeria, attacked by ISIS and al-Qaeda terrorists.
11. Nepal vs. rebel Maoists.
12. India vs. Pakistan over Kashnir; India vs. its own Naxilite rebels.
13. Israel, confronted by Fattah and Hamas.
14. Mali and the revolt of its Taureg tribes, seeking independence and the creation of a Muslim country of Azawad.
15. Iran vs. Iraq, culminating on one of the most damaging wars in the 20th Century.
16. US involvement, over 50 years, in Korea, Vietnam, Afghanistan and Iraq.
17. Turkey vs. its Kurdish minority, seeking either more freedom or actual independence, and maintaining an active terrorist group attacking Turkish targets.
18. Libya is now torn by a conflict of two terrorist groups seeking control.
19. Yemen, the revolt of the native Houthis, and Saudi intervention.
20. Indonesia vs. it province of Timor-Leste.
21. Also, internal convulsions in Thailand, Colombia, Guatemala and Burundi.

Then, consider also some of the great traditional and intractable conflicts: Sunni vs. Shia, developing countries vs. "colonialist" countries; tribal hatreds, ancient enemies, and even rural vs. urban conflict. Russia, China, N. Korea and others are said to have "weaponized" information. Reality is concealed by a pattern of denials, misinformation and lies. Social media systems have become deliberate vehicles for a blizzard of misinformation and propaganda. It should be emphasized that misinformation and denial of reality are now <u>official policies!</u> Governments such as the "big three liars", Russia, China and N. Korea, flatly state that if misinformation serves the needs of the State, then it is justified and in fact mandated. The "truth" has ceased to be a definer of anything governmental.

THEN: ADD THE DISASTERS OF INFERIOR NATIONAL ECONOMIES

Every government has its share of bad economic policies, economic cul de sacs, failed investments, or just plain incompetence. The socialist tendency for economic centralism is replete with lessons learned (or not yet learned) about how economies go wrong. The experience of the U. S. S. R. and in most of the "Soviet style" governments of Eastern Europe showed declines in something like the following pattern:

First, there was a general decline and pervasive stagnation of the economy, even in the face of growing national needs. State controlled economies proved especially unable to grow and improve enough even to deal with growing populations. Ambitions for improved social services and "quality of life" were generally abandoned because they never had been realistic and because the ruling elite had placed them at the bottom of their priority lists. The promises of socialism with respect to social services declined. The general population recognized this, and was increasingly disenchanted with their governments.

There was a withering of investment both from internal sources and from potential foreign investors. There is a world-wide shortage of capital investment money, and attracting capital is a competitive situation where "command and control" socialist countries could not or would not address. The Soviet Union, for most of its life, maintained a "closed border" policy which actively prevented foreign involvements in domestic Soviet economic affairs because the real motive of the government was to favor the SOEs that they had created and to protect them from formidable foreign competition which they could not match. But this cut off huge amounts of money that might have been attracted, and contributed mightily to the stagnation of the economy. Investments in the USSR looked far less attractive than options available to investors almost any place else. This failed program was repeated in many of the Socialist states.

Socialist governments and their state owned enterprises never quite figured out the opportunities available to them to move low value elements of the economy upscale to higher value added levels. Modern technology and new models of entrepreneurship are on a rapid upward power curve. Manufacturing is now benefitting heavily from automation, driving down prices for their products. Small entrepreneurs from "the bottom up" make it possible for consumers to buy marvelous new home products and services, some of which did not even exist 20 years ago. If the government would work harder to diversify the economy, they could create whole new sources of wealth and worker employment opportunities at higher levels of pay. Even in agriculture which is still the economic base for huge numbers of people, there are cheap, widely available upgrades of seeds, fertilizers, insecticides and animal breeding that can produce remarkable upgrades of agricultural productivity

Wages and salaries too became stagnant. There was little understanding about the relationship between productivity and management efficiency and the ability to increase wages as a consequence. Wage increases were most often granted for political reasons. The motives of the regime were mainly to buy loyalty, or at least to mitigate labor unrest as workers suffered from the consequences of an incompetent economy. Such increases almost always proved inflationary, and produced high discontent among other workers because the real motives of both management and workers was to conceal the failures of these structural mistakes. In fact, despite government efforts, unemployment – real or hidden – went up. Worker redundancy (i. e. workers without real jobs) was as high as 40% in some industries occurred because workers and political leaders combined to keep it that way.

The pressures of stagnation caused governments to fail to deal encourage entrepreneurship, modernization and new technology potentials that might have improved productivity. Funds for modernization simply were not available, and even maintenance of current production facilities was neglected, leading to further declines in efficiency. In many cases, the state tried to cover up these problems in the short run by lying about them, or by running larger deficits, jacking up taxes, skewing bank lending practices, restricting of worker mobility, and a broad agenda of excessive regulation as control, and a improperly shifting resources between parts of the economy.

Concentration on salvaging huge loss-making SOEs seems to have so preoccupied the attention and resources of governments that they neglected opportunities they might have seized to foster and assist small businesses. Many small businesses are the kind that can use the services of the less skilled and less educated in such arenas as light manufacturing, construction, consumer services, and transaction oriented activities such as handling payments, generating information material, or processing paperwork. This entrepreneurial potential is especially important in developing countries that lack an advanced education system for large numbers of people, such as India where elementary and secondary education was, foolishly, not compulsory.

Economic development is never easy; financial resources are limited and competitive around the world. Economic development must compete with urgent priorities for the provision of social services and the mitigation of poverty. When economic development is interrupted for any reason, it may stop or even collapse. India's 25 years of lack luster socialist economics was a cul de sac from which India must now spend further years in withdrawing. The total collapse of the Soviet style of command and control economics has left Russia and perhaps 30 other nations with the enormous task of reinventing their economic institutions. Tyrannies such as that of Saddam Hussein in Iraq, or Robert Mugabe in Zimbabwe, forcefully pursuing false motives, produced economies in protracted decline over 15-20 years – ground that may never be made up. Wars, rebellions, warlords, tribal feuds, terrorism, all interrupt any serious prospect of vigorous economic development.

ECONOMIC DEVELOPMENT FROM THE BOTTOM UP

OBJECTIVES OF ECONOMIC REFORM

It would be to the great advantage of any nation if it can get the three critical elements of their economies – the people, the government and the private sector - to stop their conflicts and concentrate on coordinated efforts for stimulation of the critical elements of their national economy. First and foremost, every effort and every effort must be committed to making the economy grow and become more "value added". This is absolutely fundamental and critical. In almost every country, the population is rapidly growing, and this is particularly true in developing countries. More wealth must be generated to take care of more people. In addition, for the first time, more people are living in urban areas than in the countryside, and enormous amounts of money must be invested to make these urban areas capable of dealing with the huge and unstoppable surge of people to the cities. Finally, it is simply human for people to want to make their lives better: for higher wages, more benefits, a higher standard of living and a better future for their children. The message for economies from the bottom up – grow, grow, grow!

The funds for such growth in developing countries were seriously constrained by bad socialist policy, but now almost every socialist country is reluctantly abandoning their failed policies and moving to new economies that are more market based, more competitive, less subsidized, more developed and productive and much more profitable. This change has had the collateral effect of loosening up sources of investment funds. Business executives are guardedly more willing to put their money on the line without fear of government suppression. International donors and investors now have more confidence in the prospects for effective investment. Individuals are far more willing to risk their own scarce funds in bottom up business enterprises. And slowly, as these valuable new economic investments take hold, the government is likely to receive more revenue from its taxes and fees, and thus they will be better able to afford the urban development, the revitalization of public infrastructure, and the upgrading of social services that will move their country forward. One example of the changes being implemented is the general abandonment of old policies blocking imports of goods and services on the premise that this would protect and development of local providers, particularly state owned enterprises. As this policy has been abandoned, miraculously, citizens are gaining access to better products, for less money. Similarly, when the government stops forcing banks to make subsidized loans to loser customers, banks began to be able to place loans where they really did the most economic good. Gradually, the possibility has been created to get control of inflation, and get a grip on runaway public debt, and to restore some greater rationality in the allocation of funds in the public budget.

Most of this new wave of economic reform is very popular. People are sick and tired of governments which are unable to do anything but fight each other and run dictatorships. There is more vigorous pressure for governments to seriously step up their priorities to create and maintain adequate facilities for the poor, the hungry, the dispossessed, the refugees and the displaced. This is not only the moral thing to do, but it is the best way to restore some degree of public confidence in the government. It is generally understood that these changes will require more self reliance, and may lead to the abandonment or retrenchment of previous political subsidies on things like gasoline, or food, or housing in favor of more rational use of scarce public funds.

Another critical change that needs to happen is the release of constraints on social cohesion. Regimes have often seen any social combination as threatening, no matter what its real purpose. Now, governments must let people freely develop social relationships and self help organizations, including economic cooperation, and begin to encourage the education and upgrading of peoples skills. Finally, people urgently want two additional changes: the provision of genuine public safety and security, and not crooked cops; and an all out attack on rampant public corruption, often from the top down.

THE INFORMAL ECONOMY

One of the most important elements for bottom up economic activity and an alternative for social development is the existence of what is called "the informal economy". The informal economy is defined by De Soto as "the refuge of individuals who find that the costs of abiding by existing laws in the pursuit of legitimate economic objectives exceeds the benefits." But informal economies have become vitally important in country after country where the so-called formal economy has failed to develop in magnitude and strength sufficiently to provide enough jobs, or enough economic wealth to afford adequate public services. "It is essential that the state remember that before it can distribute the nation's wealth, the nation must *produce* wealth. And that in order to produce wealth, it is necessary that the state's actions not obstruct the actions of its citizens, who, after all, know better than anyone what they want and what they have to do. The state must restore to its citizens the right to take on productive tasks, a right it has been usurping and obstructing. The state must limit itself to functioning in those necessary areas in which private industry cannot function. This does not mean that the state will wither away and die."(De Soto) The dumbest of governments think that the informal economy is illegal and a bad thing because it avoids taxes and bypasses regulations, and these governments try to close it down, even though it is obvious that it provides employment, income and social grounding that the formal economy has failed to provide.

The most likely kinds of workers found in informal economies are service people: taxi drivers, construction workers, custodial personnel, trash collectors, porters, delivery people, servants and child care providers, restaurant workers and all kinds of street vendors. An examination of these informal economies shows things that are quite astonishing. The World Bank did studies in 2000 which showed that, in developing countries, the informal economy employed between one third and one half of the national workforce, and created up to 40% of some national gross domestic product. In Zimbabwe for example, the GDP impact has been measured at around 70%, and it clearly reflected the damage caused by the horrible Mugabe government. Other countries such as Turkey, Brazil, Egypt, and the new Russia register averages of from to 40% to 60%. Even the developed countries average informal economies of around 18-20%.

"The informal economy is the masses' bottom up response to the system, which has traditionally made them victims of a kind of legal and economic apartheid. The system invents laws to frustrate the legitimate desires of the people to hold jobs and have a roof over their heads." Informals are not chaotic: they have clear and specific interests and a level of organization and sets of rules that have been spontaneously developed to replace those which the state has failed to provide.

Typically the following types of work grow well in the informal economy:

1. Small scale manufacturing
2. Crafts: carpenters, plumbers, masons, electricians, auto mechanics, tailors, etc.
3. Personal services: servants, janitors, trash collectors, porters, messengers, errand runners, delivery people, car washers, street vendors, etc., etc.
4. Casual laborers in areas of physical labor
5. Transport furnishers
6. Small retailers
7. Small construction.
8. Money lending

The informal economy is not chaotic; it has its own set of rules and prohibitions and they are enforced. It is also marked by high innovation and entrepreneurship. There are no barriers to entry, but also there is little job security, often unstable and fluctuating incomes, and big wage variations. Capital requirements are low, but there is little ability to protect resources or operations. One of its great advantages is that it employs many women and young people, giving them an opportunity to learn vital skills and hopefully pass on up to better conditions. Its exact size is very difficult to estimate, since in many places it is largely illegal. But World Bank estimates that, in many LDC's, it is between one third to one half of the labor force.

Specific country estimates:

Egypt	41-43%
United Arab Republic	70%
Morocco	57%
Turkey	36%
Iran	35%

In most of the LDC's there are three main sources of employment: the public sector, the private formal sector, and the private informal sector. In most cases, there is a continuing shift from the rural areas of the country to the cities; the "entry level" for these rural workers is usually into the informal economy. The growing trend for the employment of women is largely a phenomenon of entry into the informal sector.

The public sector is the usual starting point for educated young men. Where is a vigorous public sector, the flow may be from the government to the private sector. The public sector is also the "employer of last resort" in many cases. Thus, government staffs are usually stable groups of relatively well paid professionals plus large numbers of poorly educated and trained people as supporting or even redundant workers. In almost every instance, it would be wiser for governments to encourage their informal economies instead of opposing and harassing them, especially since they offer some of the best opportunities for economic accomplishment for women and young people. Most of the growth of the economies of developing countries comes not from massive SOEs but from **the bottom up – from small entrepreneurs, and by individual initiative.**

Economic liberalization has almost always led to greater economic development. The greater wealth produced can/should be plowed back into education, health care, elder care, mother/infant care, clean water, sanitation. Foreign direct investment is heavily responsive to political liberalization because the public sector leadership has never trusted the policies and motivations of socialist or tyrannical leadership. So the more that the government moves toward a market based competitive economy, the greater is the willingness to invest.

Centralism has almost always led to oppression. Oppressive governments tend to bloat their bureaucracies. Arrogant bureaucrats turn to corruption, allied with subsidized SOEs, and state overregulation. Time and time and time again: it is easy to say something, but far harder to actually do it, especially if you don't really want to try.

When developing countries fall into economic trouble, it almost always involves short term international debt, and the loss of fiscal control. But increasingly, external lending institutions have been bringing pressure to bear to force longer term economic solutions. This has been given the general term "structural adjustment". This means generally that it is perceived that the current structure of a country's economy is seriously unbalanced, or is too weak in certain areas to produce adequate economic results. For example, there may be too much concentration in low value agriculture or primary natural resources development, and too little strength in manufacturing; or there may be too much investment in heavy industry and too little development in the service sector.

The following represent the most important motivations—good and bad—for undertaking major transformations of a national economy:

1. Move up from an agrarian economy.
2. Force the pace of economic development.
3. Diversify the economy. Often, this has meant denying the agriculture sector needed resources in order to fuel ISI strategies elsewhere in the economy.
4. Break down class structures; create a larger more powerful middle class.
5. Build national strength and military support. This usually involves creation of a form of "military-industrial complex" which gives the military greater leverage over elements of the economy, and generally exempts it from full accountability and even civilian scrutiny.
6. Break free from external "colonialism"
7. Protect/develop infant industries.
8. Constrain improper actions of the private sector by control or regulation.

9. Fill gaps in the economy left by the normal evolution of the private sector.
10. Share—or assume—the large investment costs when the private sector cannot.
11. Use SOEs as a source of political patronage, jobs, graft, etc.
12. Greater control of productive resources as a source of public revenue.
13. Doctrinal resistance to the investment of foreign capital. In some cases, the nationalization of foreign properties led to creation of SOEs.
14. Use of parastatal institutions to provide "business management" of public infrastructure and services (i.e. insurance, health care, etc.)
15. Gain control of development financing.
16. Provide guaranteed financial backing (i.e. "full faith and credit") for international loans. Use external capital to finance industrial expansion at a greater (usually excessive) rate, while using domestic revenues for social programs.
17. Take over failed private enterprises.
18. Create competition for monopolistic private sector situations.
19. Stem capital flight.
20. Reallocate investments by sector.
21. Build up workforce intensive industry; avoid "exportation" of jobs. But there is a nasty track record of excessive redundancy, low labor productivity, large inflationary wage settlements, politically powerful unions, etc.

In summary, the socialists in many countries stressed income redistribution, job creation, industry at any cost, and containment of the private sector, and especially the dominance of the economy by the public sector, largely through state owned enterprises. The conservatives emphasized fiscal restraint, productivity and profits, and the need to stimulate private initiative. In many countries, these two philosophies exist side by side, often with a good deal of acceptance of the State as orchestrater of all aspects of the development process. Over time, socialism has declined, the conservatives have gained ascendancy and they have begun the process of neoclassical economic transformation. What governments seem slow in learning is that the deliberate, enthusiastic promotion of needed forms of structural adjustment is far more effective in developing national economies than constriction and limitation. Despite shortages of development capital and the desire to limit imports, it is important to facilitate the kinds of imports (i.e. machine tools, or raw materials) that enhance domestic production capacity, especially for new small entrepreneurs. Instead of regulations that are oppressive, regulations or policy controls can be used to encourage individual savings so that these funds can be invested in development. Also, governments must resist the political temptation to subsidize parts of the economy through subsidized loans, loan guarantees, artificially low taxes, tax incentives and waivers. Such preference almost always goes to large and powerful special economic interests, and seldom to the small business interests.

Further, in low quality economies, the tax system is more likely to be putrid. Economies that are primarily low value added are notoriously hard to tax. Rudimentary economies tend to tax the hell out of farmers and small town residents to generate the funds to develop the cities. Most centrist governments are prone to distorting both the collection and the distribution of revenues.

The top down vs. bottom up competition has also now entered the arena of the provision of external economic involvement. International organizations such as the United Nations or the World Bank, and the governments of many countries have, since the end of WW II, been strongly motivated to provide funds to newly emerging developing countries, and most of these motivations are very positive. Why do donors donate? First and foremost, they want to help newly independent countries to stabilize and to begin to develop their own governance. Then, donors have proved more than willing to support and assist in the evolution of vital elements of these new countries: social services like education and health care; or elements of a program of economic development; or to build up civil society; or to build up a friendly and supportive military and police; or to help deal with emergencies and humane crises, such as the enormous problems now being experienced with millions of refugees and displaced persons. These reasons are more compelling for developing countries that are friendly or at least neutral. They are less compelling for Socialist states where the state is so totally dominant and insist on controlling their own problems.

But there is a "down side" even for these noble efforts. Many countries come to rely far too heavily on external donor support. In some cases, donations and loans are more than 40% of certain kinds of public programs such as education or health care, and local governments cravenly decide that they need make no efforts of their own for these services if they can get foreigners to continue to pick up the check. Banks are an integral part of the borrower business, and they can be especially important as sources of funds for struggling "bottom up" new business efforts. But in most countries, the banking system is a crucial form of power for the top down ruling elite. Retail banking for the small saver or investor is on the bottom of the priority list. At the top is the use of the banks to aid the friends of the regime, and to punish its enemies, and often (as in Greece) they are artificially propped up by foreign lending. Some governments are perfectly capable of cynically borrowing to fund their banks, then forcing the banks into patterns of subsidy lending, such that they become unable (or unwilling) to repay their foreign loans. The World Bank, the IMF and other similar international organizations, usually impose requirements on borrowing nations aimed at forcing prudence and austerity to get their national finances in shape. But borrower nations are notorious for either not being able or not being willing to carry out these mandates. This creates a dilemma for the lenders, again ala Greece. Do they close down on loans and thus seem dictatorial and heartless, or do they cut the ties so that they do not have to tell their own voters that there tax money has been squandered. In addition, if Greece is allowed to get away with avoiding repayment, what next? Spain? Portugal? Italy? Etc. etc.

Even aside from the issues of repayment, many borrower nations simply squander the money on waste, mismanagement, corruption and plain old theft. This infuriates the tax payers of lender nations. Even when borrower nations are trying to do right, they may be so bumbling and incompetent that they are hopeless. Increasingly, aid money is being directed to independent NGOs rather than to government officials. Also, loans have often been used to prop up tyrants and dictators, much to the disgust of the citizens of the lending countries. Why for example, is the world paying to support Hamas in the Gaza Strip?

But there is a new bottom up tide that is running. Increasingly, private donors are willing to form organizations that specialize in lending – outside of the formal banking system – to small investors for bottom up business development. At to the great surprise of pompous central bankers, it has proved to be true that these small borrowers have a remarkably good record, not only for effective use of the money, but for the proper repayment of such loans. They are often better and more honest at it than the big time buddies of the ruling elite. As a result, more countries appear to be willing to restructure the major banking system to provide more retail banking and small loan facilitation.

EXPORT PROMOTION VS. EXPORT RESTRICTION

One of the great policy mistakes of Socialist regimes, from the Soviet Union on down, was the belief that the domestic economy had to be "protected" from foreign competition, and that it was the responsibility of the government to control the national borders, to keep out ominous foreign imports to avoid undesirable competiton with domestic sources. Even foreign money was somehow viewed with the darkest suspicion because investment in domestic enterprises was seen as a form of invasion and loss of control.

But very often,the critical element in a poor developing country is exactly that: some form of alliance with outside private sector organizations, which provides investment funds not available locally, provides access to new vital equipment and services, provides access to new techology, and helps to upgrade manager and worker skills. Often, it has been a relatively small "catalyst" that has made just enough difference. A key element is often skill transfers. In many developing courtries, their initial economic advantage was in the existence of a work force willing to work for very low wages, but increasingly, it has become far more important – for everybody – to provide training of local people, not just in processing, but in management skills; supervision, efficiency, planning, input outreach, output marketing, financial control, change management, quality control, and productivity enhancement. In other words, capital seems not to be the only major constraint for development of new light manufacturing or commercial businesses. Know-how and networking are far more important and once a good reputation is earned, small investment capital sources become available. And increasingly, these lending sources are "global".

In many cases, the key to success has been the identification of market opportunities, and for bottom up small businesses, this might involve new "niche" markets of the kind not dominated by hugh top down SOEs, and where the existing competition is not so tough. Marketing now truly seems to be global. One of the most successful private sector institutions has been the trading company; which become international marketing and networking operations available to serve small companies in ways that they could not directly afford.

PUBLIC SECTOR ELEMENTS OF ECONOMIC DEVELOPMENT

There is a pattern of success by less developed countries in the use of special incentives for exporting. These include:

1. Waivers of taxes on income earned by exports
2. Special subsidized loans for equipment, marketing, etc. for the purposes of exporting. This can include the establishment of special export banks.
3. Setting up a government ministry or state enterprise as a facilitator. These seem to have proved that relatively small increments of assistance can produce very successful results. In some cases, governments have set up joint public/private corporations to promote export industries. In many cases, when the government is a "player" it magically reduces the bureaucratic red tape that hinders the straight private sector companies.

4. Governments have to ease limits on entry of foreign capital and even on foreign companies into their domestic economy. Often these limitations are imposed out of some doctrinal mind sets (self sufficiency; anti-colonialism, anti-capitalism) where public policy skews market reality.

5. Note also that many small business/light industry initiatives offer exceptional opportunities for the employment of women. For example, the emergence of floral export industry in Colombia now employs 70,000 people including 50,000 women; and it has generated many related small support companies which also employ women.

6. LDCs are finding out that local industries that have strong export elements are better protected against recessions or economic hard times in the domestic economy.

7. In some cases, governments have tried to "leapfrog" from low value to high technology industry; examples; the Hungarian government promotion of independent efforts to develop a domestic computer software industry; Japanese government support of research and development in expensive technological arenas; the Australian government multi-purpose technology development institute.

VIII

Destructive Universal Corruption

Lots of people have invented lots of excuses to "justify" corruption, or explain it away. Here are some of the most popular.

1. "Corruption is a way of life; it has been 'built in' to the culture." Some countries/cultures are victimized by such widespread corruption that it is interpreted to be part of the culture, and therefore somehow acceptable. But in a deeper sense, it is clear that no society in history has really endorsed corruption; all consider it wrong; every religion or secular philosophy condemns it; and the laws of most countries make it specifically illegal. So the "way of life" argument is merely a feeble rationalization when tested by these broader societal views.

2. "Everybody does it; how can you stop 'everybody'"? But it is not true that everybody does it. Most people are remarkably honest, hate corruption, oppose it where possible, hate to be its victims, and will support anti-corruption efforts.

3. "Corruption has its advantages". This kind of argument has been advanced by both political scientists and corporations. The corporations argue (especially around tax time) that bribery is a necessary business tool to avoid bureaucratic constraints and help to gain business. Corruption is often seen as cheaper than complying with laws and regulations and business people argue that "if we don't bribe corrupt officials, our competition will." Political scientists may have given up, decided that corruption in inevitable and therefore is justified to get the bureaucratic apparatus to perform. But the wheels do not have to be greased; most government programs can

and do function well without the grease of corruption, and accepting and using corruption simply encourages more of it.

4. "<u>Fighting corruption is too expensive and difficult</u>". Where corruption is widespread and systematic, the means to eliminate or reduce it become so difficult and expensive that governments begin to believe that they cannot afford to eradicate it. But the <u>cost</u> of corruption exceeds the cost of reduction many times over; a corrupt government is never a "cost-effective" government, nor is it serving the public interest. Desperately scarce public funds are diverted into the bank accounts of cynical crooks, and vital public programs see their money stolen.

5. "<u>In a truly representative government, democratic practices will cause corruption to disappear</u>". Corruption can exist even in a truly democratic government. Hopefully, one of the adjuncts of a truly democratic government will be openness, transparency, lots of watchers, and managerial measures to fight corruption. But these means must be deliberately cultivated and will not happen spontaneously because a government has the democratic apparatus.

6. "<u>In a truly market based economy, the forces of the market place will cause corruption to wither and die</u>". Corruption is perfectly capable of flourishing in a market economy because a market economy can contain pathological forces which find corruption useful and profitable -- just as it does with straight crime, or "cheating." When corruption becomes a means for the allocation of business/resources, it ceases to be a "market" economy, and becomes something else. Bribery provides a way to beat competitors who may have better skills or lower costs. The costs of the bribes becomes built into tax deductible business expenses, and is another form of tax on citizens, while being essentially free for the corruptors. Currently, only the U. S. makes bribery of foreign officials a crime.

7. "<u>It is not clear exactly what 'corruption' means</u>". This suggests that governments can't really take full measures to oppose corruption because there may be grey areas or areas of legal uncertainty as to what is wrong and what is not. But in most cases, what is corrupt/pathological in government is much the

same as what is seen as corrupt/pathological in society and there is a broad range of known corrupt practices that can be attacked immediately without waiting for the perfect legal certainty. If it is not certain whether some kinds of activities are corrupt or not, then specific legal actions are available to make that determination if there is the guts to do so.

Few people realize the extent to which corruption has become a universal instrument of government. Corruption is more than just a form of robbery; it is a form of control, especially over the flow of money. It is very important to recognize the direct connection of highly centrist governance, driven by special interest politics and the overwhelming urge of centrist governments to regulate/control, as the perfect home for universal corruption. In some countries, corruption has become a second stream of governance, a system attached to, and growing out of the official government structure. It is almost always true that, when the top people in an organization are corrupt, people at lower levels feel "entitled" to be corrupt as well. When the big guys are stealing big, the little guys are stealing small, and it is to their mutual advantage to develop elaborate systems for mutual concealment.

It is sadly true that, in many cases, the bad guys are smarter and/ or better organized than the good guys. Corruption remains highly popular because it is hugely successful. The small group of controlling elites turn the system to their own advantage, and they neutralize those defenses that the formal governments employ – the responsibilities of managers, the auditors, the inspectors, the investigators, and those "anti-corruption" committees. Government regulations designed to protect the system or the public seem to end up instead as instruments of top down control. And lying, always popular, has now become an official government policy. For example, China and N. Korea, Russia and many others have large government agencies devoted to generation of lies, misinformation, false statistics, false accusations, and endless "spin" about government policies and actions. Truth is not the basis for judgment; every thing that strengthens or protects the ruling regime is defined as "good". Any small thing that resists or questions government actions is "bad" and must be suppressed.

In all truly scandalous governments, corruption is not just ignored, it is organized and encouraged. Even where the apparatus for controlling corruption exists, it may be ignored or neutered. What the public deserves and wants to see is that the corruptors are caught and removed, and that corrupt acts receive serious punishment. For situations of entrenched corruption in agencies, it may be impossible for the organization to purge itself from the inside and the only alternative may be the creation of external anti-corruption campaigns mounted and enforced from outside of the agency. Thus, it is vital that there exist a forceful government-wide posture against corruption and a set of instruments by which this posture can be carried out. But, for example, when the authoritarian and highly corrupt government of Viktor Yanukovich was overthrown in the Ukraine, the promises of the new government to wipe out corruption have been useless and corrupt systems and networks have comfortably survived untouched. Most countries have various forms of oversight agencies: Inspectors General, government-wide auditing and evaluation agencies, a government-wide budget review organization, and often, a contract review and oversight board. There is a growing tendency too to create a special anti-corruption agency with strong independent powers.

Every country produces a high level of corruption, and developing countries are the worst because weakness allows easy seizure of control; such leaders then prove very venal, and the defense against corruption are usually weak, and often <u>deliberately</u> made weaker. The "most wanted" targets for crooks are government contracting, land control and allocation, taxes, rules and regulations, authorizations, customs control of imports and exports and any other government activity that uses real money.

It is disturbing how few political organizations have a real agenda. Most are empty "anti", or "us vs. them", and "ins vs. outs". Look at insurgency movements: how many ever are able to say what they stand for? For example, Muslim insurgents say they want "Sharia Law". But this is an essentially meaningless position since there are many variations and interpretations of Sharia Law, most of them perfectly moderate and desirable.

Aid to governments has been stolen or misspent so often that the voters of donor nations are increasingly condemning their governments for their failures. Money has lavishly been supplied to regimes that are obvious oppressors and human rights violators, and people are asking why they should be supported. In many cases, donors have initiated funds to support key social services such as elementary/secondary education only to realize that the recipient governments expect such aid to go on forever. As a consequence of this version of top down failure, many donors are now assisting from the bottom up. Funds are given, not to government agencies, but to Non Government Organizations (NGO) which may be either government sponsored or entirely independent, but which have a far better record for the effective delivery of assistance. Even China now has as many as 400,000 of such organizations at work, often despite the government.

TRANSPARENCY INTERNATIONAL RANKINGS
OF GOVERNMENT CORRUPTION

Canada	8
United States	19
Qatar	22
United Arab Emirates	30
Brunei	39
Oman	39
Bahrain	46
Jordan	49
Turkey	61
Saudi Arabia	63
Tunisia	65
Kuwait	66
Romania	66
South Africa	69
Brazil	69
Bulgaria	75
China	79
Peru	83
India	84
Morocco	89
Colombia	94
Argentina	102
Bolovia	105
Mali	105
Philippines	105
Mexico	105
Egypt	111
Indonesia	111
Djibouti	111

Algeria	111
Guatamala	113
Syria	126
Nigeria	130
Libya	130
Bangladesh	139
Kenya	139
Yemen	154
Haiti	168
Iran	168
Cambodia	167
Turkmenistan	174
Uzbekistan	174
Chad	175
Sudan	176
Iraq	176
Burma	178
Afghanistan	179
Somalia	180

A COMPENDIUM OF THE MANY FORMS OF CORRUPTION

Whole books can be written about the thousands of forms of corruption and the means by which corruption is undertaken. Here is a modest listing of the most useful and popular arenas for corrupt activity, starting with the old standards that have worked since the age of the Pharoahs: bribery, kickbacks, theft, blackmail, extortion, embezzlement, misappropriation, nepotism, preferment, or the tolerance of mere bumbling incompetence. Then add these more specific corruption arenas:

A. POLITICAL CORRUPTION

Avoidance of responsibility
Populist bribery and subsidy
Stolen elections
Preferment, nepotism, favoritism in political appointments
Deliberate racism, bigotry
Perverse special interest concessions: the "influence peddler"
Lying and misrepresentation for many reasons
Phony promises, never intended to be fulfilled
Creating deliberate conflicts; religions, tribes, clans, locations, age, etc.
Tyranny and oppression
Corrupt practices against individuals
Corrupt practices against institutions
Corrupt laws – perversion of the "rule of law"
Government links to criminals
Fake elections as political cover (Iran, Iraq, Pakistan, Lebanon, Vietnam, Myanmar, Sudan, Ethiopia, China, etc.)
Arming internal rival militias
Letting criminals into government; use of criminals for political harassment

B. FAILURES OF THE RULE OF LAW

Laws that are themselves perverted
Laws that are vaguely stated
Laws that are selectively enforced

C. POLICE CORRUPTION

Petty bribery, extortion
Police perverted as a political tool
Transport related extortions
Illegal arrests, imprisonments
Labor camps for unconvicted
Threats by police against citizens
Murder
Assassinations
Kidnapping
Intimidation
Theft of property
False accusations
Illegal search
False arrest
Bribery for release
Bribery for bail

D. CORRUPT COURTS

Courts that are not free; court packing
Politically dictated verdicts
Selling verdicts
Crooked brokers and intermediaries
Domination by the police
Separate military courts, often corrupt
Lack of enforcement of court rulings
Elites escaping punishment

E. CORRUPTION IN STATE OWNED ENTERPRISES

See discussion of SOEs in Chapter VIII.

F. MACRO ECONOMIC POLICY CORRUPTION

Patronage
Special interests dominance
Rent seeking
Slanted price controls
Rigged exchange rates
Closed borders; corruption of import/export controls
Busted budgets
Failures of structural adjustment

G. CORRUPT BANKING AND FINANCIAL MANAGEMENT

Corrupt practices of banking SOEs, for and against the government
Wretched excess; the culture of greed
Lies, secrecy
Shelter for crooks, dictators, cheaters
Computer vulnerability – i. e. no protection
"Wealth management" perversions
Disappearing money
Corrupt currency manipulation

H. CORRUPT REGULATION

Excessive numbers of regulations
Excessive regulatory control and restriction
Deliberate complexity
Confusing and conflicting types of regulations, licenses, permits, etc.
Deliberate lack of enforcement
Improper enforcement

Concessions for use of public land, resources

I. CORRUPT INTERGOVERNMENTAL RELATIONS

Perverse motivations – in both directions
Corrupt purposes for money transfers
Unfunded mandates
Suction
Misappropriation
Tribalism: anti-central government sectarian outrages, massacres.
Ethnic cleansing
Bribery contests
Buyouts and sellouts
Centrists vs. local control
Concessions of critical functions to outsiders: emergencies, critical
infrastructure, health care, mother/child care, education, refugees,
deficit spending.
Central government protection for crooks and corrupters.

J. PERVERSIONS OF THE TAX SYSTEM

Special interest domination
Perverse tax expenditures
Overtaxing
Under taxing
Failures to collect
Tax cheating; tax avoidance
Deliberate complexity

K. CORRUPT INTERNATIONAL RELATIONS

Power grabs
The outsider urge to meddle; blundering around
Doctrinal conflicts, deliberate and inadvertent

Seizure of assets
Border disputes, controls
Need definition of what is "acceptable"
Corrupt use of donor funds
Western leverage and meddling – or lack of involvement
Western use of NGOs.
Support of corrupt regimes

L. ENVIRONMENTAL SINS

Misuse of land, water, natural resources
Theft of property by government
Theft of property from the government
Confiscations, seizures by government, agents
Special interest preferment.
Neglect of serious environmental problems
Theft, diversion of income
Theft, diversion of useful funds
Illegal mining, etc.

M. CORRUPTION IN GOVERNMENT SERVICE DELIVERY

Stealing from public contracts
Cheating on contract competitions
Perverse contract requirement
Ghost companies, workers, tasks, purchases, equipment, facilities
Cheating on performance: quality, safety
Corruption in education
Corruption in health care
Corruption in public infrastructure
Robbing the poor

N. CORRUPT LABOR RELATIONS

As political support; campaigns, marches, voter turnouts
Forced union membership
Theft of union funds
As political opposition vs. the ruling elite
Forced worker redundancy

O. CORRUPTION INVOLVING RELIGION

Deliberate manipulation of religious beliefs
Creating environments of hate, prejudice, exclusion, fear
Making religions the justification for wars, terrorism, violence
Deliberately false religious interpretations
False prophets
Using religious fronts to conceal illegal, immoral actions
Perverse accusations of apostasy; often, heavy punishment for so-called apostasy.
Religion vs. the State: Iran, Egypt, Sudan, Nigeria, Mali, Somalia, India/Pakistan, Lebanon.

P. CORRUPT MILITARY

Deliberate over statement of national threats to justify money, equipment
Lack of financial constraint
Inveterate meddling in power struggles
Corrupt relationships with politicians
Corrupt relationships with contractors
The fact that counterinsurgency is inevitably brutal and hurts the civilian population. This is a failure of leadership, since it could be carefully pursued.

SOMALIA: CORRUPTION EQUALS COLLAPSE

"Twenty years later (1969- 1989), Siad Barre (Somalia) had succeeded in wrecking any semblance of national governmental legitimacy. Backed first by the Soviet Union and then by the United States, Siad Barre destroyed institutions of government and democracy, abused his citizens' human rights, channeled as many of the resources of the state as possible into his own and his sub clan's hands, and at the end of the Cold War, deprived everyone else of what was left of the spoils of Somali supreme rule. All of the major clans and sub clans other than Barres's own became alienated. His shock troops perpetuated one outrage after another against fellow citizens. By the onset of civil war in 1991, the Somali state had long since failed. The civil war destroyed what was left, and Somalia collapsed onto itself." (Rotberg, p. 112).

MOBUTU IN ZAIRE: ME FIRST; ME ONLY

"Mobutu used analogous tactics in the patrimony of Zaire. As his people's self-proclaimed *guide,* or as the personalized embodiment of national leadership during the Cold War, he deployed the largess of his American and other Western patrons to enhance his personal wealth, to heighten his control over his countrymen, and to weave a tightly manipulated web of loyalties with the army and into all aspects of Zaire's society. Every proper political and democratic institution was an obstacle to the edifice that he created. So was civil society, politics itself in the broad sense, and economic development. He rebuffed the rise of a real bourgeoisie, and fed his people puffery and false glories instead of real substance and per capita growth, and accentuated his own power, wealth, and importance.

FIGHTING CORRUPTION: FIND THE WILL

Given the will, there are many ways in which, for example, management corruption can be prevented or mitigated. Some involve broad government-wide management policies which can be mandated in law or implemented through individual agency adoption. Perhaps the most important is the use of maximum feasible competition in all government activities that allocate resources – systems such as awards of contracts, grants, loans, or the use of public lands or facilities. This may also include careful control of licenses for valuable assets such as broadcasting wavelengths or the allocation of access to airport gates.

It is also vitally important to require internal transparency of agency operations. The processes by which agencies carry out their programs should be clearly defined, made as simple and understandable as possible, and widely published for all employees who can then know what is acceptable and what is not. This transparency must also extend to the outside through published summaries of agency authority and operating procedures. This can and should be accompanied by some form of public review and comment <u>before</u> important decisions are made, or key processes changed. Special emphasis, often neglected, should be placed on making visible which official makes key decisions and why.

No public official, including political leadership should be authorized to have what are generally known as "slush funds"; that is, funds that are available without controls or justifications or audits. Somewhat more problematically, it may be vital to develop some forms of protection for career officials from the unwarranted intervention of political leadership into decisions that should rest on merit or competition. Obviously, political leadership is necessary but what should be restricted is the tendency o politicians to meddle in management decisions such as contract awards.

In addition to these broad policies, there are many measures to increase the likelihood of detection and prevention of corrupt practices. Inspectors General should be legislatively mandated, with strong independent powers of investigation and discovery. Either independently or as a part of an Office of Inspector General, a skilled corps of auditors should be authorized to insist on the examination of all agency records and actions. Every program manager should be charged with the responsibility of assuring that each program is free of corruption or mismanagement even before the auditors arrive.

There is an old axiom for auditors and inspectors: "follow the money". Special attention should be given to the creation and enforcement of close controls over financial flows from initial collection of revenue by the government to the authorization by legislatures of funds for expenditure by the agencies. Within each agency, authority should be limited as to the numbers of officials who can authorize the commitment of expenditures – the fewer the better. A second internal control should be maintained through the use of separate officials who can approve the actual disbursement of funds. Then, there should be management reviews and post-audits of whether the funds were actually used properly and for the purposes for which they were authorized.

Experience shows that perhaps the best "auditors" of agency actions are not necessarily official auditors, but the general public and sometimes employees of an agency who have inside knowledge of what is happening. Good confidential methods should be available for the public to lodge complaints or report corruption. The best intelligence about government corruption often comes from its victims. Those agencies that operate hotlines are often amazed and gratified by the numbers and sharpness of public responses. Internal agency whistleblowers may also be remarkably valuable but this often is punished by agency officials who have something to conceal, even if it is only their own mismanagement. Whistle blowing is a term coined to highlight the fact that agency employees who witness corrupt practices are motivated to try and stop them. The key problem is for the employee or a member of the public is the fear of reprisal. There needs to be a safe place to go with this kind of knowledge, and the sense that there will be some protection to justify the risk.

In a corrupt or pathological organization, the employees may become victims. They must be protected in some way from the arbitrary and capricious acts on the part of agency leadership, including unwarranted firings, transfers, or demotions. Most employees probably want to be honest, but they can't be if they are subject to threats, coercion and intimidation, or if they are ordered to carry out what are clearly illegal or improper orders. Often, it is actually bureaucracy that protects them. If policies and authorized procedures within an agency are clearly defined in some detail, the employee then has a basis for resisting or fending off an order is improper or illegal.

In addition to the fight against management corruption, it is also necessary to attack it at the political level, and for this it is of critical importance to engage the participation of the national legislative body. It was argued earlier that the rule of law can become perverse if the laws themselves are pathological and this is a sin laid at the door of parliaments and congresses. The fact that such legislative bodies can be dominated and perverted by tyrants does not relieve them of the ultimate responsibility of maintaining the integrity of the base of national laws and fiscal appropriations. Part of this responsibility involves the oversight of the executive agencies of the government, and these agencies can be aided and abetted in preventing corruption if the laws themselves make it clear exactly what practices are defined as illegal or improper. Further, anti-corruption controls can be deliberately incorporated into laws and mandated in more detailed government regulations. Legislatures can and should maintain their own forms of transparency and openness to public comment, review, complaint and education. Legislation can even be created that mitigates the worst forms of political patronage, both within the civil service and among top political appointments. It is even possible, if not likely, that the opportunities for corruption may be substantially reduced by the elimination of useless or wasteful public programs and activities. Every public official at senior levels should be required to disclose the state of their personal finances; however, a mistake often made is not to extend this requirement to politicians.

In an extreme environment of embedded and institutionalized corruption, some governments have turned to a promising new approach – popularly called a "watch dog agency". These agencies are not designed for routine auditing or inspection but have the single purpose of mounting government-wide anti- corruption attacks, and they are equipped with special and very strong legal and police powers. The record of watch dog agencies is mixed, with some such as that in Singapore cited as highly effective while others are all but useless.

Robert K. Noble, the Secretary General of Interpol, the international police organization, discusses corruption linked to organized crime. He notes, for example, how very easy it is to rob a bank electronically these days -- no mask and gun needed. Organized criminal groups will go online and steal small amounts of one or two thousand from medium sized accounts. They might do this in bank A for a month, then shift to bank B. Each theft is seen as too small to be cost-effective to pursue. Thefts are cross border, expensive to investigate, difficult to track, and confused by many jurisdictions. Over time, huge sums are are quietly liberated by highly mobile crooks. Interpol now has 20 million stolen or lost passports and visas in their data base. In 2009, they did 300 million searches. "In 2009, there were over 500 million international arrivals where passports were **not** checked against the Interpol data base. Says Noble, "We have the technology to identify false passports being used by war criminals, terrorists, assassins, drug traffikers and fraudsters." But there are only about 40 countries that do routinely screen passports. Where countries do real screening, crooks simply tend to shift their activity elsewhere." Every time somebody is arrested for any form of terrorist or narcotics violation, his/her fingerprints, photos and DNA is taken." Noble has a wish list of what needs to be done. It is in every country's best interest to make sure their borders are monitored 24 hours a day, seven days a week. All countries should screen passports of all international air arrivals against Interpol data bases. All prison escapees, known terrorists or other dangerous people should be reported to Interpol. Like it or not, governments must identify and track corrupt officials, especially in law enforcement, and then have the courage to close them down.

What are the most corruption ridden sectors of the economy? Energy: oil, gas, coal, electricity production and distribution, construction, transport, customs, granters of licenses, inspectors. Where do the bribes go? The favorites are government officials who authorize the expenditure of money -- officials of SOEs, government supervisors of contractors, inspectors, customs officers, and tax officials. The cleanest countries are the richest; the poorest are the dirtiest. The worst are N. Korea, Somalia, India, China, Mexico, and even prosperous countries like Brazil or Egypt. Corruption has grown more sophisticated; technology has created whole new fascinating ways to cheat.

CHINA: POST MAOIST ERA CORRUPTION REFORMS

Corruption is an ancient Chinese skill and therefore it was not surprising that while the Maoist Revolution was destroying much of the nation's economy and society, the thieves and crooks were looting everything not nailed down, and under Mao, <u>nothing</u> was nailed down. The normal forms of governance were in total chaos, replaced by a miserable disastrous mélange of cooperatives, communes, work groups and "struggle" groups. Money was forcibly seized from farmers and other elements of the economy and convulsively squandered on foolish Communist Party programs, or simply made to disappear. Mao was the great destroyer and, while spouting noble Communist philosophy, he created what should be regarded as the worst government in the world.

After Mao's death in 1976, his successors had to move urgently to restore some sanity to Mao's crazy world, and a vital part of this reform was a program to get a grip on corruption. How this task was undertaken contains valuable lessons for other governments.

The Chinese Communist Party (CCP) was well aware that its fate rested on its ability to do two things: first, to reform and expand the obsolete, unrealistic and horribly inefficient economy; and second, to beat back the universal sins of corruption, most of which flourished within the government itself. Without doubt, the most important, absolutely critical decision that the CCP had to make was this: to abandon major sacred elements of Communist theology requiring absolute control of the national economy, and to make major shifts toward some level of market based economic privatization, including even the conversion of thousands of State Owned Enterprises (SOE) into private entities – or extinction.

As the CCP began to face up to this choice, it realized that the whole structure and operations of all levels of government in the country was totally incapable of rational direction and control of such a sophisticated role. So, the first need became a change in political policy. Then, there had to be major reforms of government structure, a "redesign" of agencies, the quiet dumping of the communes and a big move back to some more effective capacity of local governments to function effectively. This redesign had to get a grip on the delivery of public services, and the management of government finances. This in turn made vital the more effective education of a new wave of serious professionals, both as managers and technical experts to take over as the old corrupt and incompetent leaders were, hopefully, pushed out.

Along with everything else, existing anti-corruption policies and methods were feeble or non-existent, and for perverse political reasons, the leadership wanted it that way, because they did not want to get caught, or forced to admit their own monumental mistakes. Internal anti-corruption efforts thus were most often aimed at the small fry, and the top fish managed to protect themselves. Reform therefore meant that the top officials had to be made vulnerable to examination, and indeed should realistically be made the first and prime targets.

But here again, the government had a hard time getting real. The CCP created a series of high profile actions against a few top Party officials in a deliberate "spin" program to regain public confidence. But the era of automatic public acceptance had passed, and neither the show trials nor the pompous, self serving Party pronouncements had the old impact. As the century turned, for the first time, the public increasingly began to think for itself and to demand real action. And slowly, some real changes began to appear. New protective mechanisms against corruption were created at all government levels and in all government agencies. Much of the reform effort was aimed at the provincial and municipal level, even as they struggled to dump the old Maoist mess of communes and cooperatives, and recreate a competent civil service. There was a forceful integration of important oversight and watchdog organizations from the top down. For example, city audit officers were accountable not only to their own bosses, but upward to audit offices at the provincial level. Provincial audit offices were in turn accountable to a national government audit organization.

The absolutely most crucial reform centered around the urgent need to get control of government finances, both incomes and expenditures. Under Mao, absolutely nobody had any real control over anything. Local communes and collectives dreamed up their own forms of tax and fee collection and they spent irrationally and wastefully. Local governments also created their own taxes, maintained their own bank accounts, spent recklessly and often foolishly, and stole enthusiastically. The central government usually assigned program operations to local governments, but refused to provide funds for them. SOEs that failed at the national level were cynically dumped on provinces and cities. Local governments created a whole "second government" of Township and Village Enterprises (TVE) and a "third government" of Public Service Units (PSE) all of which were allowed and expected to pry their funding out of the Chinese public.

Not surprisingly, with literally more then two million government related enterprises of all kinds running their own activities, the financial chaos was unbelievable. At the best pace possible, the government began the long term processes of elimination of large numbers of organizations that were improper, illegal, obsolete or merely fatally incompetent. In other cases, organizations were folded into the more formal structure of local governments. Separate unauthorized taxes, fees or charges were eliminated. All revenues were forced into a single official agency budget. The purposes for which funds could be expended were reduced and brought under control, and the number of officials who were authorized to approve expenditures were more strictly limited. For the first time, governments moved to create sound accounting structures and to demand that all funds had to be adequately accounted for. Accounting, finance and budget offices were strengthened and their employees trained to be more professional.

One of the most reluctant reform decisions having to be made by the CCP was to "regularize" the national banking system. The banks had become a key element of political control of the economy. Banks themselves were SOEs. They were often forced to lend to meet political motivations, most of which were economically corrosive. Banks were forced to lend to the supporters and friends of the regime, and to ignore their opponents. They were forced to lend at subsidized rates to SOEs which were known to operating at perennial loses, and it was politically "understood" that many of these loans would never be repaid. Local governments created many semi-official economic development agencies which have borrowed heavily from banks and state insurance companies, and lent it in turn to local enterprises for transportation, energy, water, urban infrastructure and public housing. Suddenly, the national government became aware of the fact that these entities had piled up debts in excess of 11.4 trillion yuan ($1.7 trillion) and had further commitments totaling a further 12.7 trillion yuan. Because of a long past history of debt abandonment, it is estimated that as much as 25% of local investment company loans will go bad – then state banks and insurance companies will be in trouble – and the bad debt will once again descend on the central government. And unfortunately, bad politics forced banks to allow a wide variety of fake name accounts, nameless accounts, and a pattern of "ghost" borrowing. Government reform efforts now include forbidding such accounts, and making depositors and borrowers prove their real identity. This kind of control has also been extended to stock market accounts, purchasers of government bonds, and to contractors doing business with government agencies. In many cases, contract corruption was so overpowering that the central government has taken over control of payments by local governments. A policy is now being implemented for direct payments for major public projects such as the Three Gorges Dam system or the South-to-North Water Program.

This program is perhaps the most ambitious reform program in modern history, simply because there was so much that needed reforming. Has this program eliminated corruption? No. It has reduced corruption and made it more difficult, but corruption is still very widespread, and it still involves people at the top. The next real attack against corruption will come from the bottom up.

IX

THE NEGLECT OF GOVERNMENT OPERATIONS

Every politician ever born sees the world of government from the top down, because they are the "top". Political systems are designed and intended to be the ultimate decision makers in a contentious world. Some political leaders attempt to cling to the concept that the precursor to decision making is consultation, negotiation and compromise. Most simply move directly to the reality of top down command and control. Meanwhile, the people look at the world from the bottom up. What they want is not political parties or theories of government, but the satisfaction of their own human needs, especially since, ultimately, they are paying for them. Truly, the very best governments are those that can and will effectively meet these needs. Part of that reality is the fundamental requirement that individual people should be able to take care of themselves. But it has also been true that people operate at two additional levels: one is personal responsibility, and the other is the voluntary associations that people form among themselves – from tribes and clans and villages, to religions, down to charitable organizations and Little League Baseball.

But the world has become greatly more populous and infinitely more complex and contentious. Thus, governments have become an absolutely vital level of human association, and their greatest value is not in producing arrogant politicians, but in producing the programs that governments are supposed to deliver: education, health care, public infrastructure, national security and police services, protection of resources, right on down the list to the rescue of the world from garbage. These programs are managed and delivered by armies of public workers, and while they function under the direction of political leadership, they have their own particular varieties of sins of omission and commission.

For the purposes of this discussion, the delivery of vital public programs is considered as an enormous set of opportunities. How well do the pubic services in 200 countries meet these opportunities? When and how do they fail?

To begin with, governments almost always face dissention between politics and management because the two groups think differently and have different motives. The basics of management have evolved into one of the most highly sophisticated forms of human endeavor and have produced a class of professional executives and managers at a level of skill comparable to any other in society. Management has it own professional culture, disciplines, techniques, standards for success, and ethical ground rules. Management skills are not just used in business. Housewives manage their homes – they plan, schedule, budget and (try to) manage and direct their children's development. Individuals plan and manage their education, careers and finances. Churches, law offices, medical clinics and even kindergartens all seek to avoid chaos and incompetence through use of managerial skills. In short, management has become an essential in any modern society. On the other hand, politicians yearn for political popularity, and are often willing to buy it by funding programs that are popular but of low value. Career managers may find themselves running politically mandated programs that they know are useless, obsolete, misdirected, wrongly targeted or of very low payoff.

THE NEGLECT OF PROGRAM EVALUATION

Every government is supposedly responsible for the provision of a whole range of public programs: education, health care, public transportation, national security, taxation, foreign policy, economic development, and many others. Each of these programs will contain many related activities and projects, and all are complex, difficult to administer, and not guaranteed to succeed. It would therefore seem sensible and logical to develop the means to evaluate each activity and project to determine whether it is being done well or poorly, and is achieving its stated purposes. Yet managers and politicians may take radically different views on how to evaluate programs – or whether to evaluate them at all. The managerial attitude about program evaluation is generally straightforward; of course you evaluate your program. You must know what is working or failing so that failures can be eliminated and performance results enhanced. Evaluation is both a part of the professional ethics of management, and the route to greater success. Even managers who are making mistakes and might wish to cover them up in the short run know that eventually their mistakes will be found out and they will be made to pay for them

On the other hand, politicians tend not like program evaluation even if they do it themselves. Their concern is this: what if the evaluation shows that the program is (a) useless; (b) too expensive; (c) poorly designed; (d) poorly managed; (e) corrupt; or (f) all of the above? This "exposure" is seen and negative and destructive since it can lead to client and constituent disappointment – with politicians. Politicians who visibly backed failing programs fear that people will blame them. This is especially true since the political opposition will happily point out these failures as often as possible.

Professional program evaluation is therefore seen as a management tool, based on management principles and practices. Politicians find this approach uncomfortable, since dispassion is not valued or even believed in. Obviously, corrupt officials will automatically oppose and sabotage any evaluation of their performance.

Even among professional managers however, evaluation is often viewed darkly. Many managers reject it simply because the results may be negative, and their reputations may suffer, or that people may actually expect them to do something about perceived negative results. In governments, there is the added negative that managers may believe that poor evaluations will either be ignored by politicians, and are thus a waste of time; or that they will get the manager in trouble at the political level, and are thus better off not attempted.

LOOTING PUBLIC FINANCES

One of the things that governments do best is to get into debt. Of the more than 100 governments discussed here as in serious trouble, more than 20 are essentially permanently broke, and another ten survive mainly be incurring very heavy debt, much of it owed to foreign lenders. The world is being treated now to several classic examples of massive and probably incurable examples including Puerto Rico, Greece, Venezuela, Malawi, Myanmar, and even resource rich countries such as Argentina and Brazil.

The two main attributes of debt management are of course, the nature of income, and the nature of budget expenditures. The key to the state of national finances lies in the size, the vigor and the profitability of the national economy. A larger and more profitable economy provides the wealth that can be tapped to generate more government revenue. But national tax systems are extraordinarily complex, sophisticated and gamed to favor the governments that collect them. There are income taxes: licenses and fees; taxes on private investment; taxes on business income; land taxes; import/export fees; asset seizures; user fees; harvesting the income from SOEs; income from banking; income from corporate investment; foreign investment; foreign loans; income from the sale of government assets, and perhaps another couple of hundred lesser examples.

One of the most popular approaches for incurring public debt is to borrow from foreigners, thus using OPM: other people's money. Why do lenders and donors provide money? For at least the following reasons:

* To provide emergency help, for humanitarian motives
* On the expectation of some ultimate advantage or profit
* To provide short term assistance to stimulate long term economic development
* To exert some form of control or manipulation
* To capture assets: e. g. mines, airports, power grids, etc.
* To protect some existing asset or investment
* To create useful alliances

Over many years, there is a growing perception that foreign money, either by loan or gift, is being badly wasted, for three main reasons. First, it is being used to prop up dictators and tyrants. Second, that it is not effective and does not produce adequate reforms or improvements. Third, that it is easily and enthusiastically stolen, especially by government officials. Greece is a highly publicized current example of such scandalous misuse. As partial cause of the huge debt is the excessive cost of pensions, which in Greece is at the level of 17.5% of GDP, compared to the rest of Europe at 12.3% These "little" numbers are in fact a huge difference. And the "replacement rate" (the percentage of pension income compared to the last earned wage) has been at a lavish 96%, the second highest in the OECD, which is now finally being reduced to 54%. Greeks are notorious for not working; the employment rate among 55-65 year olds is a mere 36%. In Germany, the US, the Netherlands, Japan and Sweden, that number is greater than 60%. The arrogance of the situation is outrageous; the public in many OECD countries is angry that their money has been going to subsidize "Mediterranean spendthrifts".

PERVERSE GOVERNMENT BUDGET MANAGEMENT

With the exception of national tax systems, the most important instrument for pathological governance is the central government budget system. The tax system supposedly identifies and captures all forms of government revenue, from taxes to customs fees, land and equipment rents, fees for services, property taxes, social security and unemployment compensation systems revenues, gas taxes and hundreds of smaller sums from every conceivable source.

The budget in turn is supposed to identify and analyze all demands for money to finance hundreds of authorized public programs. The concept of "authorization" here is very important. In theory at least, no government agency or program is allowed to obtain public funds unless it is created, designed and legally authorized by a specific law. Also, in theory the amount of money made available for all government programs is also specifically stated in a separate law called an appropriation. As each program proceeds, funds will be spent only for its authorized purposes, and these expenditures are, at least in theory, carefully controlled before they are disbursed. Only certain senior officials should be authorized to approve any expenditure, and the purpose of each expenditure should be specifically stated and related back to the appropriation that enabled it.

Every government budget will contain hundreds, and even thousands of "line items" – one for each program or activity. What is authorized and how much money is authorized is the culmination of a complex, often fascinating, and often corrupt set of maneuvers, each of which is an art form. Programs may range from vital to mythological, so in order to understand the budget, one must start with the nature of the programs and activities they supposedly represent.

To begin with, almost every public program is both a political manifestation and a genuine managerial responsibility. Budget estimates may be inaccurate simply because they rest on difficult and hard to predict future realities and decisions; or they may reflect political and managerial distortions and a corrupt strategy of some kind. Perhaps the ultimate and most popular pathological technique guiding budget preparation might be the <u>values of overestimation.</u> Take for example the purchase of a military weapon system. Realistically, the people who control the purchase of the weapon will probably know the true cost of manufacture, but this is not necessarily the cost estimate to be used. It would be in the interest of the seller to overstate the cost for the purchase, and the buyer/seller relationship can take one of three possible courses, two of which are pathological. One result is that the buyer is too dumb to recognize the excessive price, and will approve it. The second result might be that the buyer and the seller will collude to approve the corrupt purchase and the buyer will share the illegal profits with the seller. The third option should be that the government rejects the improper price and insists on a more honest estimate ---- or some other seller.

Consider then the next step in the budget process. Assume that the price for the weapons purchase, however arrived at, it $100 million dollars. Is that the number that is placed in the agency budget request? Maybe, maybe not. Here again, the government agency making the purchase has three options. One is to use the $100 million number and let the budget process advance it. The second choice might be to understate the cost estimate to make the politicians who approve the budget request happy. This has been done since the construction of the pyramids, and it still works. The secret of this approach is that the unrealistically low cost estimate, when approved, can easily be pumped back up over successive periods to its corrupt illegal level.

Option three is simply another form of political hypocrisy. The cost of the weapons purchase in the budget can be seriously overstated, knowing that the chief executive and the legislature will cut the number so that they can brag about how fiscally prudent they are. Thus, the $100 million could be budgeted for, say, $120 million. When it is cut back to $100 million, everybody will brag that they have "saved" $20 million. This marvelous technique leaves everybody happy! Options two and three are both pathologically corrupt. At the very least, they are organized lies, designed to delude the public. At worst, option two is designed by thieves, and it can go on for years. This example illustrates another of the key pathologies of public budgeting – the triumph of special interest politics.

In almost every country, the pathologies of program budgeting start with what gets authorized in law. Enabling statutes or executive direction can and will be designed to lock in special advantages for some interest groups, often to the detriment of the general public. In other words, the program is designed to reflect political value and not program excellence or necessity, or cost effectiveness. Most public programs run forever and once special interest preferment is locked into statute, it becomes almost impossible to change. The pathology goes on forever, stoutly defended and embellished by its fortunate beneficiaries.

It is impossible to overestimate the power and impact of this special interest politics. It is true that much of it is perfectly responsible and acceptable. Worthy programs are legally supported along with those that are unworthy or improper, and it is hard to know which is which. But it is clear that, for many programs, at some point special interest pressure can become dysfunctional, unrealistic, or overly expensive. This is not really old fashioned corruption; it is a pathology of a more sophisticated kind, enabled by skewed laws, backed by perverse politics, nurtured by political cowardice, and powered by cold organized greed. It is pursued, knowing that much may act against the general public good.

There are other perverse motivations that sully the public budget process. In the normal course of events in complex governments, many programs prove to be of low value or even unnecessary, and yet the realities of budget politics simply crushes any attempts to cut these losses. There are hundreds of examples in every government – every government – of programs that are obsolete, low payoff, dysfunctional, overly expensive, or simply horribly mismanaged. This is true despite the fact that there supposedly protective mechanisms such as auditors or investigators, and credible outside views that identify these failures. Serious evaluation of such poor program performance is avoided or ignored. In many countries, no legislative oversight is allowed, and the real actions taken are by key officials of legislative committees on how to share the loot.

THE PRIME TARGET: GOVERNMENT CONTRACTING

Most governments enter into contracts. The role of the manager is to contract for the right things, at the right price, and a satisfactory level of performance. Yet there is a vastly disturbing record of the mismanagement of such contracts and the failure to contract with the best bidding company. Then, once under contract, the government can be billed for things not really delivered; for goods and services that are overpriced; for "ghost" workers and activities; for services never delivered; and for plain old fashioned lying and cheating. Both politicians and managers are guilty of these sins.

There are, unfortunately, many good reasons for the phrase "petty bureaucracy", which frequently means "petty corruption". Every law, regulation and government process must be enforced – or maybe not. Many of these bureaucracies involve large numbers of untrained and underpaid workers, locked in a tightly frozen structure with little room for thinking or initiative. And in these underdeveloped countries, chances are that the inferior and stagnant world is the deliberate product of a leadership that is itself corrupt and disdainful. In case after case, when the big people at the top are stealing big, the lesser people at the bottom are stealing small, and all of the players formulate highly successful hidden networks and self protection mechanisms to conceal their real world. And the people or organizations that are supposedly to prevent them are usually part of the corrupt alliance. Truly, it is disturbing how often the bad guys are smarter and quicker than the good guys. Thus, in this world, "opportunity" has a pernicious meaning where acting badly is very richly rewarded.

While the use of contracting is vital in the work of most governments, it is also perhaps the single most important source of corruption and perverse policies and operations. Every element of contracting from the initial decision to contract down to detailed operations is highly vulnerable despite government protective mechanisms. Many governments have corruptly contracted for things that they do not really need as a perverse way to pay off certain companies or as the source of bribe seeking by government officials. A good example is the purchase of expensive military hardware even though there is little military threat. Even where the need for a contract is justified, there may be rules for determining who is eligible to bid which are perverse. For example, eligibility may be limited to domestic companies, even where it is clear that foreign companies might offer better capabilities. Bids may be confined to state owned enterprises in recognition of their monopoly position. Eligibility criteria may be skewed to give unfair advantage to a single company – often one that is willing to pay for the privilege. A "sole source" decision may be driven by the prospects of later payoffs.

The whole process of soliciting bids and evaluating them to determine which company will receive the contract is highly sensitive. Legitimate bids may be rejected for many technical reasons so that "friends" of the regime may win the bid. One of the major sources of fraud is called "bid rigging" where bidders and public officials collude to fix the outcome of the competition in advance. Often, such bid rigging arrangements are organized by industry associations to share the wealth among its members. Public officials can and do provide insider information (at a price) to their favored companies to make sure that they win. Another form of corruption is called "bidding in" – a deliberate understatement by a bidder of the expected cost of the contract in order to win the bid. The contractor relies on the high potential of raising costs once they have the contract. Many so-called contract cost overruns are the inevitable and plotted outcome of bidding in the first place. The whole bidding process may have been a false front to mask the fact that the winner has already been selected by the public officials involved. A bidder may simply offer a bribe to the selecting official. Even where some formal process of bid evaluation is used, the selecting official may have the authority to ignore the technical evaluation of bidder's competence and make a prejudiced selection.

Once a contractor begins work under the contract, whole new forms of corruption become possible. The work itself can be pathological: shoddy work, substandard materials, failure to perform required work, unwarranted expenses, overstated costs, deliberate cost overruns, and many more failures. Cost may be overstated. The government may be billed "phantom charges" for work or supplies not actually provided. The workforce may be overstated and phantom wages and benefits billed to the government. Work delays may be deliberately created to pump up costs. Management salaries or overhead costs may be excessive. Unfortunately the contractor may feel that the quality of government oversight is so poor that such illegalities will never be caught. In other cases kickbacks are simply made to public officials to turn a blind eye to such cheating. Government managers and inspectors may not be competent, or may be too few to cover all contracts. Performance is not evaluated, costs are not verified, goods are "lost" or stolen, and accounts are not audited. Where a contractor is caught in an illegal or improper act, the overseeing government official may be bribed or coerced to ignore the fact. Even the protections of auditors or inspectors may be frustrated through bribes or political pressure.

ANOTHER PRIME TARGET: BANKING AND MONEY MANAGEMENT

In many countries, banks have lost their individuality, and their interest in individual borrowers. They want to become players in huge powerful international systems. All banks now seem to be locked into this world system especially for money movement and "money management". But increasingly, banks have instead become instruments of the State, and governments demand the right to exert heavy control of the national banking system: bank reserves; capital size; control of interest rates; forced lending; forced ownership of government debt; subsidies for political friends – closed doors for political foes; forced loan forgiveness. In many countries the government actually owns the whole banking system as SOEs, or it owns a few of the very largest banks; or it allows banks to operate independently only on a small scale. The middle ground would be to have a banking system that is primarily independent and free of regulation that inhibits their ability to maximize lending decisions. Banking regulation would then be confined to those measures needed to protect the public interest.

There are good arguments that suggest greater support for alternatives: credit unions, investment companies, mortgage lending, access for foreign banks.

There also has to be some form of protection for the small, poor borrowers, either individuals or small businesses. There is a growing record of remarkably good repayment levels by small borrowers. (Think FINCA).

There is a special situation with respect to banking under Muslim Sharia law. Under Sharia law, speculation is forbidden, charging interest is prohibited, and returns are based on schemes for profit sharing. (Economist, Jan. 5, 2013). But Malaysia has become a world center of expertise about Sharia banking. About 25% of the national banking system is Sharia compliant; the average for Muslim countries is more like 12%, and often a lot less. For example, Indonesia which has the largest Muslim population in the world, only 4% of the banking system is Sharia compliant. But Malaysia proves that Sharia banking can be accommodated into more modern systems of banking.

WORKFORCE MANAGEMENT

Under most forms of state socialism, the government was urgently motivated to control the workforce and especially unions, because they were capable of marshaling their membership into disciplined action, and the political leadership wanted to make sure that actions favored them and not opposing interests. For more than one hundred years, unions were worker oriented and usually well regarded; now they are all too often political units and creatures of, or allies of the government.

At the same time, the whole nature of employment needs have changed. There has been a general decline in the relative value of manufacturing and a great surge of employment in commercial activities such as retailing, banking and insurance, communications, education and governments. These changes have happened most extensively in developed countries which have the sophistication in meeting workplace demands requiring more education and personal skill. Manufacturing jobs meanwhile have shifted to developing countries were there are cheaper workers, and governments that must urgently expand their national economies. But in almost all cases, governments in turn urgently feel the need to control the unions through subsidies and other forms of preferment. Many unions, especially in Socialist or Muslim states are simply the mouthpieces for the government. And especially in Socialist countries, governments have imposed serious controls on worker mobility. People were made to work where the government wanted them to work, and they were not free to make their own choices. But eventually, even devout Communist/Socialist dictators finally had to admit that this policy, along with many others, was a demonstrated failure. In recent years therefore, major relaxations of control have been made in China and Russia, and a little bit in Vietnam. But much of the job mobility involves skilled workers simply leaving the country, whether the government wants it or not, and many of the leavers are those having the most critical skills, like doctors, nurses, engineers and managers.

Another facet of State Socialist workforce management has been tight control of wages and benefits but these policies have almost always proved to be abject failures and have seriously harmed many economies. Parts of this "strategy" have been the deliberate suppression of salaries and benefits; denial of workplace training or upgrading; worker redundancy for political reasons, and freezing employees into politically important workplaces.

In all too many countries, all of this is moot. Countries are destroyed by conflict, both internal and external. People are killed, injured and displaced, either in their own country or as refugees to another country. Houses, which are the most important asset of most people, are destroyed or seriously damaged. Businesses and public facilities are similarly destroyed and badly damaged. Large numbers of people lose their jobs, and no new jobs are being created. People's life savings are stolen or dissipated. Nobody wants to risk their meager resources, and neither individuals nor businesses want to invest. Vital supply channels such as those for food, or water, or fuel, or electric power are disturbed or destroyed. Farmers are driven of their land and do not plant their crops.

Almost always, these internal conflicts exacerbate latent conflicts that become overblown. Many governments stupidly think that creating or encouraging the heightening of internal conflicts (racial, religious, ethnic, tribal, age, urban vs. rural, etc.) strengthens their political position. But then, insurrection destroys everybody, friend and foe alike. As the elements of governments that are supposed to provide stability and safety weaken, the crooks and the thugs and the smugglers and the drug traffikers gain strength. Population growth is often terminated or substantially reduced, as in Afghanistan, Angola, Burundi, Cambodia, El Salvador, Ethiopia, Eritrea, Guatemala, Lebanon, Liberia, Nicaragua, Rwanda, Sierra Leone, Sudan, S. Sudan, Tajikistan and Uganda.

REFORMS FOR HUMAN RESOURCES

Every country's government will present a full array of organizations ostensibly to provide programs to protect and assist the nation's people. This human resource management can be interpreted narrowly as dealing with workforce management, or very broadly, to include elementary and secondary, and college levels of education, the whole health care system, a wide range of welfare services, and the formal legal system defining the role of unions and of labor-management relationships. There are now other means of government activity that are more "bottom up" and interactive, since they deal not just with people relationships with the government, but also with people relationships with each other and with their neighbors and communities.

In a very general sense, these relationships can be examined at three levels: first, the very broad demanding dealings controlled by the central national government; second, the more direct service delivery relationships provided by local governments; and third, the relationships centering around people's ability to be self reliant, plus their more structured relationships with each other ranging from churches, unions and organized advocacy groups down to Little League sports. Now, increasingly, there are the astonishing new relationships arising from the enormous attractions of social media outlets. At the extremes are the fading validity of the "cradle to grave" mentality vs. the increasing perceptions of the virtue of self reliance, letting the government stay clear. But in fact, no country is either/or. Every country and every government is a complex confusing, often bumbling and always fascinating mixture of all three. In the last analysis, no matter how powerful and oppressive a government, the real world will exist within the individual, and the ultimate strength will be from the bottom up, no matter how long it takes and how difficult the journey.

What the people want from government centers around the need for safety and security, help for the helpless, the provision and facilitation of all vital forms of social services and public facilities. Even where many such needs could be met by the people themselves, governments are capable of meeting them more effectively. In most countries, it is naturally expected that the elderly will be taken care of by their children and their families, but effective government programs make meeting these needs a great deal more effective. People skills can be upgraded by education. The private sector is capable of providing all levels of schools, but the system is more extensive and more productive when governments play a constructive role. Informal elements of the economy can be supported and assisted by governments instead of opposed and criminalized, and millions of new work opportunities can be made more secure and profitable.

Safety and security are vital human needs. Every government is entitled to maintain a military establishment to defend the nation. Every government is entitled to maintain police forces to serve and protect citizens, subject to legitimate supervision of their great power. Every government is entitled to develop a body of laws and regulations – hopefully to protect against public enemies and not to oppress. But it should be noted yet again that many of the most disturbing threats to public safety and security in the modern era are posed by the governments themselves.

PATTERNS OF LEADERSHIP AND MANAGEMENT FAILURE

Not too long ago, the world was applauding the BRIC: the dynamic new economies of Brazil, Russia, India and China. Now, Russia's economy is suffering from the unbalanced policies of its dictator, a heavy recession, and neglect of social services and consumer goods. Brazil suffers from a stagnant economy and blatant apparently uncontrollable corruption. China is beginning to feel the slow down of its overstressed and heavily indebted economy. India now seems to be the one in the BRIC group which still shows signs of economic dynamics. Here are some depressing examples of the failures of government management around the world.

BRAZIL: RIDING A ROLLER COASTER

Over the last decade or more, Brazil has been touted as a shining example of the growth and increasing strength of developing countries, and it has been linked with Russia, India and China as the BRIC – leaders in positive economic development.

But the latest assessment of Brazil's public infrastructure finds that it is seriously lacking, shabby and run down. The World Economic Forum ranks it as 120th out of 144 in overall quality. The worst seems to be roads and airports, but the rail system is far too small for the size of the country. Why? Apparently, the general economy is inadequate. There is a congenital big budget deficit, a large public debt, and high borrowing costs for a suspect and widely distrustedgovernment. Foreign investment is waning, in part because of the past left-wing and anti-private sector attitudes of the president, Dilma Rousseff. Investment has fallen off from $40 billion in 2014 to an estimated $25 billion this year. And this is in spite of a fairly drastic weakening of the currency. Local firms are seeing declines in profits because of lower sales and higher expenses and higher taxes. The tax increases are part of the government's effort, along with budget reductions to cut the budget deficit.

Many of the country's problems are directly attributed to the government. There is widespread concern that problems are beyond the capacity of government officials who are seen as lacking managerial skills, and being overwhelmed by their responsibilities. The government lacks key skills for engineering, IT and high tech programs, and the bureaucracy is widely seen as not capable of being professional and merit based. Projects are all too often fumbled, mismanaged, wasteful, over budget, plagued by mysterious delays, hampered by excessive red tape and painfully slow to respond. Major sectors of public service carry nasty reputations: poor health care, poor primary education, lack of clean water and treated sewage. Public assets are sold cheap; illegal logging is a monster industry, the whole legal systems is seen as slow, incompetent, vastly overburdened with useless actions, and widely corrupt. The labor market has two levels: the well protected, union dominated upper level, and a vast informal economy, especially in the cities. In fact, the informal economy is said to be almost 40% of GDP, despite being relatively inefficient. Special interest politics is rampant.

Far too many items in the public budget are earmarks and special advantages for the business friends of the government. Yet, in general, corporate taxes are seen as too high, and potential investors are scared off by a combination of the tax system, harsh government regulation, rules favoring unions over employers, and general vulnerability to law suits which tend to run on expensively forever. And now, President Dilma Rousseff is being tried by Parliament leading to her forced removal from office because of egregious scandals involving the misallocation of public funds, and suspicion of involvement in the huge and almost unbelievable scandal involving the state owned energy enterprise PETROBRAS. Even if Rousseff escapes this threat, literally hundreds of public officials of her administration will end up in jail. In sum, it is extremely frustrating for Brazilians in a country of vast natural and human resources to be living under a government that is increasingly unreal, ineffective and blatantly and arrogantly corrupt.

CONTRACTING IN PUERTO RICO

"For a case study in how to run a company into the ground, look no further that the Puerto Rico Electric Power Authority (PREPA). The island's government-owned electric utility has $9 billion in debt, falling sales, and rising costs. Its electricity rates for consumers run 2 ½ times the industry average, and higher than any U. S. state except Hawaii. All that money has purchased precious little. The utility's power plants, with a median age of 44 years, lack pollution controls and violate EPA mercury limits. Power plants burn dirty residual fuel and diesel oil to generate about two-thirds of the island's power. And thanks to aging infrastructure, frequent and costly power failures plague customers. A recent IMF study stated that "PREPA is an inefficient and overstaffed public enterprise using technologies decades out of date. Three quarters of the their trucks are obsolete and often out of service. The workforce payroll is twice as large as utilities on the main land. The calls of customers bold enough to phone the utility to complain about service are dropped more than 50 percent of the time. Now, however, PREPA is running out of cash and its creditors,-- including the major bond funds Oppenheimer and Franklin Templeton – can't be put on hold. (WP)

Meanwhile, the country faces a mounting financial crisis, of which the abject failure of PREPA is only a part. The governor looks at the country's $73 billion in debts, and calls it "unpayable". PREPA's excessively high costs for power have been a serious drag on the whole economy and its competitiveness.

In addition, power service is maddeningly intermittent, and many businesses are forced to close down intermittently.

Nor can all of the blame be placed on PREPA's management. "Both of the island's political parties have been complicit: they have padded the payrolls with loyalists in equal number as part of an unwritten pact to feed off the utility's revenues. How much an employee works, and what authority they hold is a function of which party is in power. And the utility company has arrogantly ignored regulations dealing with air and water quality, storage tanks leakage control, chemical spills, and worker safety in general. In addition, there has been a pattern of subsidies for political friends, and punishments for enemies. Many friendly banks, hotels, and businesses have failed to pay their utility bills for years. When forced to make deals for the installation of wind or solar sources, PREPA signs contracts, but then does nothing.

If there is any good news in this government created mess, it is this: The new president has been forced to appoint a reform commission. If it really works this time, the potential for savings could be enormous – enough not only to bail out PEPA but also to provide money to plough back into general economic development.

CUBA: BACK TO THE FUTURE

The Cuban Revolution has always benefitted from exceptional public support, even when the performance of the government does not seem to warrant it. The recent easing of relationships with the United States has begun to seem to the Cuban people as an OPPORTUNITY! What do they want? In a sense, what the want of an upgraded version of what Cuba used to have before the Revolution. And the government seems to be promising to make that happen. But retrenchment from the Cuban version of State Socialism inevitably poses the threat of the loss of many of the ways in which the government delivered on its "cradle to grave" philosophy, as it contemplates a movement at some pace from elimination or serious retrenchment of free monthly food rations, government housing, free education, public transport and electric power at highly subsidized rates.

Socialist theory required that individuals sacrifice their individual rights in favor of "all-embracing social provision". But the government failed over the long haul in its ability to deliver all social services at an adequate level, and increasingly, the public view became the certainty that the government could never deliver, and greater self-reliance became an increasing necessity. But this shift is taking place in a world where both social and economic thinking and policy is stuck back in the 1950's. Despite the government's slow and half hearted movement away from total socialist thinking, it continues to control prices, much of the means of production, limits on what people can by and at what price, and much more. Agriculture especially is almost Soviet: the government has a state monopoly over agriculture and dictates what can be grown, and what can be sold, and what can be bought and at what price.

But instead of being the allocator of wealth, the government has had to become the allocator of scarcity. Cuba, in terms of its economy and its government policies, has been brought to the brink of bankruptcy, and the Soviets are no longer available to bail them out as they have done in the past. Foreign investors are gun-shy after a brief period of hopes of better times from American accommodation. Many are actually trying to retrench or escape, but the government forbids the movement of money and assets out of the country. The government has been forced to put limits on imports, and it is cutting its subsidy funding to its inefficient SOEs, and its popular public subsidies. While trying to increase the number of small businesses, the number has actually shrunk from 360,000 to just over 200,000. Wages are ridiculously low, in large part because the government could argue that workers were really well off because of the value to social goods provided, and astonishingly, wages today are less than they were 25 years ago. Public infrastructure is deteriorating, especially in transport and electric power because of lack of money; there has been no significant expansion, and in fact, there is now a serious neglect of current maintenance and repair work.

FROZEN JAPAN

Japan's government finds it increasingly hard to avoid an economic fact: the Japanese economy is in serious need of structural reform: radical monetary easing; realignment of public spending; active efforts to loosen up the economy and get it to produce greater accommodation to many things. The government must finally face up to the poorly performing state enterprises, running forever at a loss, and draining funds from other public programs. There must be a whole change of intent in the governments use of regulations which are now oppressive, often overly restrictive, often out of date, and often simply stupid. The whole banking system is far too controlled and needs to be made more independent. But a reform involving an increase in the national value added tax from 5% to 8% actually produced negative results in the form of lower consumer spending, despite falling oil prices. Japan carries a huge debt (240% of GDP). President Abe has been planning to raise the VAT up to 10%, but now this has had to be canceled for perverse political reasons.

The weak yen has pushed up the price of imported goods. Rural and village residents loudly complain of a fall in their standard of living. Unemployment has been high, although lately it has come down a bit. Other needs are the liberalization of the rigid labor market; reform and restructuring of the electric power industry which is characterized by a powerful monopoly and needs to have production separated from distribution. It is very important to get rid of the monopolistic network of agricultural cooperatives and free up agriculture marketing and pricing, where the cost of overly protective government policies pursued by a massive bureaucracy reduces profits for actual farmers. Japan can no longer cling to outmoded labor-management practices such as ironclad worker protection laws, amounting to a de facto ban on firing. Also, the outdated Unemployment Compensation system needs overhaul. And the whole position of women in the economy and in society is badly in need of "modernization". In summary, Japan is an example where vested interests have been so defensive and rigid that they have hurt the national economy, and the political leadership either shares their rigidity or is too timid or cowardly to face up to the political need to sponsor and back structural adjustment. (6/12/14)

FAILURE OF THE CONTROL MENTALITY

In India, there is the growing feeling that the economy seems to be on an increasingly stable footing. Inflation has fallen by half after floating above 10% for years. The current account deficit has shrunk; the rupee is firm; the stock market has boomed, and even the slump in commodity prices like oil is a boon to the consumer. Much of this improvement centers around the force abandonment of the state Socialist system and mentality. Indian reform has moved, often reluctantly, toward its own version of a market based economy and the loosening of a notoriously excessive level of governmental control – of practically everything.

There are prospects of more reforms. Prime Minister Modi is trying to produce more results from fewer bureaucratic bureaucrats. India has a world class IT-services industry, but it lacks the kind of job creation that will absorb more than 100 million indifferently educated young people over the next decade. Land acquisition for public works is bottled up in old laws that favor rich land owners (who have long been supporters of the Congress Political Party). Also, the power system continues in bad shape: inadequate and inefficient and corrupt. Half of all manufacturers suffer power shortages of more than 5 hours each week. The whole system is too much embedded in SOEs and needs to be opened up to competition.

Perhaps worst and most intractable problem of all is the Indian government's long term propensity for huge, irrational, smothering regulation, including a massive tangle of labor laws linked to religious, ethnic, geographic and caste set-asides and preferments. The Indian "License Raj" still exists and a new "Regulation Raj" has been added.

INDIA'S MASSIVE BLACKOUT
(Newsweek Magazine, early October.)

"So you think <u>we</u> have problems?

The recent Indian power blackout was surely the biggest electricity failure in history, affecting a staggering 640 million people. Thus, the power outage has exposed the greatest vulnerability of the Asian economic miracle; it is fundamentally underpowered. In the past 10 years, according to BP, India's coal consumption has more than doubled, its oil consumption has increased by 52%, and its oil consumption has jumped by 131%. For China the figures are, respectively, 155 percent, 101 percent, and 376 percent. The McKinsey Global Institute expects India's economy to grow at an average rate of between 7 and 8% up to 2030. The bad news is that Asia's creaking institutions are not able to cope with the staggering social consequences. Urban populations will increase from 340 million in 2008 to around 590 million by 2030. India will then have 68 cities over a milllion, and three with more than 10 million. India therefore needs to invest at least $1.2 trillion over the next 20 years to upgrade urban infrastructure.

"India's electricity system is so dilapidated that 27 percent of power it carries is lost as a result of leakage and theft. And 300 million people – 25% of the total population – does not even have access to the system."

VENEZUELA: BLIND ARROGANT LEADERSHIP

Venezuela is the world's 9th largest oil producer, and the third largest exporter. In the country, gas for cars sells for about 7 cents per gallon. This subsidy costs the government about $ 9 billion/year; it is for the middle class, since the real poor tend to use public transportation (which is also subsidized).

But Venezuela suffers from a sagging and stagnant economy, heavy inflation (190% in 2015), a plunging currency (- 50% in 2012), an increasing number of scarcities, including even such necessities as milk and eggs, and including heating oil. Government subsidies were about 6.3 billion Bolivars in 1998, and in 2012, they were 48.5 billion Bolivars. The government created its own chain of food markets and deliberately filled them with subsidized products – chicken, lentils, milk, peas, beef, sugar, flour, rice, margerine. But inflation in the prices in these markets is actually higher than in private markets, and there are growing accusations of corruption – especially where food is stolen and sold at higher prices to private stores. Also subsidized is all aspects of agriculture, most fisheries, and many larger SOEs. In total, Venezuela is a heavily controlled economy, ranked 174th in global competition reports, and ranked 28th out of 29 economies in South and Central America. While the formal economy shrank, the informal economy has been growing rapidly, and is said now to employ 2.3 million workers or about 40% of the workforce.

Here is the general perception of the characteristics of the Chavez/Maduro regime: (See 2012 Index of Economic Freedom published by Heritage Foundation in cooperation with the Wall Street Journal).

* Heavy government interference in both economic and social matters, driven largely by heavy Socialist theory, mostly perverse. This has led to the fact that Venezuela now has the lowest rate of economic growth in the Americas.
* "Selective" price controls, many perceived to be for the purpose of subsidizing friends and punishing opponents.
* Rampant corruption; as government control and regulation expand, corruption expands, much of it by government officials.
* Stubborn retention of anti-free market policies.
* Serious and often vicious attacks on opposing politicians and other opponents of the regime.
* The outlawing of free speech, accompanied by the government that manufactures false information and invents enemies and threats to justify its oppression.
* Property rights have been shifted to government control, often without compensation. Many private companies have been nationalized against their will.

* The military has been greatly expanded, along with the intelligence service, whichi is increasingly used to spy on the people and their organizations.
* Foreign exchange is now government controlled, along with import/export controls. As a consequence, imports have declined more than 40% since 2012
* Control of electric production and distribution by the regime has resulted in chronic shortages and outages, and neglect of mainenance and repair.
* There are now almost constant and very serious shortages of even vital food items, and common consumer needs like soap, cosmetics, clothing, etc.
* There have been enormous increases in all forms of crime.

THE VULNERABILITIES OF GOVERNMENT CONTRACTING

Perhaps the most important home for government corruption lies in the fact that a government may have hundreds or even thousands of contracts in force, with additional contracts or contract renewals being let each year. Most governments suffer from inadequate resources to oversee these contracts, and in some cases, this shortage of oversight capability is deliberate, where corrupt politicians and officials want to keep oversight as ineffective as possible. The single most effective curb against contract corruption continues to be the mandated use of competitive bidding. A carefully drafted law mandating competition can be used as the basis for defending agency contracting practices, and giving leverage to reformers and those officials in agencies who genuinely want fair and legal contracting to prevail.

But a legislative mandate for competition even if it is achieved, is far from enough. Much depends on the willingness and ability of public officials to implement such laws fairly and free of corruption, and this is not easy. Each agency of government should be required to supplement the law with a carefully defined and published set of procedures for bid competition. All bidders should be made aware of these procedures, and bidders can and should police each other to make sure that the procedures are followed. The reputation of each bidding company can be tested by checking their performance on previous contracts and their financial and management ability to carry out the contract must be evaluated. The initial contractor selection process is critical because it is here that the likelihood of corruption will first manifest itself. If bad public officials and companies seize the contract at this point, it is likely that subsequent operations under the contract will be a constant problem. All contract bids should be subjected to an opaque evaluation process aimed at getting a realistic assessment of bidder capabilities. This evaluation should be open to review, at least for auditors and other bidders to examine. That way, if a selecting official makes a decision that runs counter to the technical evaluation, such an arbitrary selection can be more effectively challenged.

Another significant protection is created when the government has the authority to debar bidders from future contract opportunities if there is evidence of collusion, factual misrepresentation or intent to conceal relevant information. Debarment is an administrative action, and it puts the burden on the alleged offender to upset the decision either by law suit or by appealing for help from political allies who may regard it as dangerous to interfere. Even informally, any rumors or partial evidence of improper bidder practices can be made known to other contracting organizations in both government and the private sector.

Another important way for public officials to protect their position is for the government agency itself to prepare its own estimates of the expected costs for all significant elements of the intended contract. Such estimates should be available at the time of the contract competition so that the government officials have a basis for judging the costs proposed by bidders. This is especially valuable if there is the likelihood that few bids will be received, or that there may be bid rigging collusion among bidders. Substantial variances from the government cost estimate should be suspect. If the bids are too low, it may signal that the bidder is trying to "buy in" to the contract. If the bids are too high, it may signal that bidders think they can soak the government.

The need for government officials to have their own independent capability to evaluate costs is even more critical during the life of the contract because the potential to cheat is so high. Every single activity under the contract can be manipulated. Since corruption involves both sellers and buyers, every government agency must start with the premise that some improper approaches will take place. This means that the measures to protect against improper actions by the government's own staff are just as important as protections against outsiders. Special oversight of bidding processes can be provided by auditors, inspectors, or even outside investigators, and it should be made clear to the staff that such assessments are to be expected. Each agency should have formal procedures which clearly state that any form of bribery, collusion or improper information disclosure will be sought out and punished. The evaluation of bids should be conducted by multi-person teams, and their evaluation and recommendations should be in writing and signed.

The most difficult problem comes where the selection of a contractor rests with a political official who is not controlled by the mechanisms applied to the career staff. Many cabinet ministers or agency heads have broad and unchecked authority under agency enabling statutes. They may make arbitrary decisions based entirely on their own judgment, and on political factors not considered in the staff technical evaluation. Factors such as the geographical location of bidding companies, or contributions to political campaigns, or the desire to reward the allies of the regime are not uncommon. Few career officials will have either the authority or the courage to challenge such political distortions. In some countries, provision is made for a "Tender Board" or Contract Review Board that has independent authority to review the outcomes of bid processes and challenge any instance of serious impropriety. But again, these boards may be ineffective unless they have the courage to press their objections. At the very least, their challenge of a contract selection can serve to fix public attention on the suspect decision.

During the performance of each contract, there should be multiple responsibilities. First, the official in charge of the program under contract must be made clearly responsible for its effective management. This is the first and most important line of defense against impropriety, and no amount of post audit can substitute for it. This responsibility includes real time determination that the demands of the contract are being met, that only authorized work is performed and billed, that all costs are realistic and appropriate, and that costly overruns are avoided. To support these contract managers there should be allies in the agency who will audit, inspect or investigate contractor performance if necessary. Auditing and inspection should be performed constantly and not left to post audits months after the fact. These government oversight systems should extend down to subcontractors or suppliers of the prime contractor. Some form of appeals process is also valuable so that factual disputes can be reconciled, or contractors may appeal what they believe to be improper or incorrect actions by contracting officials.

X

THE CHALLENGES OF URBANIZATION
AND INADEQUATE SOCIAL SERVICES

In many countries, the national government formally delegates the provision of public services to states/provinces or cities, while at the same time keeping the flow of tax income at the top, and deliberately denying adequate funding to local governments to meet social services obligations. In the United States, this approach is termed "the unfunded mandates." But the reality is that cities have become the world of the future. Huge surges in world population, and an irresistible shift from the rural/village life to cities have created what is surely one of the most challenging problems in the modern world, and it is not clear that how these enormous problems can be dealt with. It will certainly not be dirty trickery with public funds.

What makes cities even more of a problem is their widespread reputation for being horribly managed. To begin with, even the best efforts of skilled and dedicated urban leadership might simply find that they are seriously overwhelmed by their problems. Add to this the fact that many urban officials are not skilled and dedicated at all, but are in office as the least worst from a selection of third rate politicians or first rate crooks. Modern cities are really two new kinds of cities wrapped in one. There is a new confused incoherent slum like areas laid in and around some older, sturdier, but declining traditional city centers. There then tends to be the emergence of a new and substantial middle class, growing out of the central core of the elitist leadership and their friends, the senior bureaucracy, the heads of SOEs, allies and hangers on. The new middle class tend to gravitate to the older more stable parts of the city where they will occupy new high rise apartments or gated communities, shop in the new malls, and send their children to the few new and tolerable schools.

But by far, the greater tide is the overwhelming mass of the new urban poor – undereducated, untrained, dead poor, usually unemployed and unemployable in the formal economy, living in miserable and often dangerous tents and shacks, taking work wherever they can get it, and running their own little illegal businesses. For most of them, everything is illegal, they are robbed or extorted, and the police and all officials are the enemy. These slums have, for millions, come to characterize many of the big cities of the world, and their informal economies are their work places. Their great hope is that their cities will somehow magically evolve so that real jobs will be created, water will be supplied, and electricity will flow for everybody all the time. Somehow, cardboard shacks will miraculously change into real houses, and sewers will appear so that people can stop wading through trash and garbage.

And yet, cities are better than the old countryside. Even when life might be better on a farm or in the villages, what they lack is vital – hope for the future.

It has become increasingly clear that the future, for good or ill, is now in the cities and what will happen to them. That is why it is absolutely vital for cities to learn how to deal with their slums. This cannot be left solely to governments. The vital "rescue" of the informal economies and the resurgence of national private sectors are forcing the retreat of the more stringent forms of state socialism which pervasively, have not worked well enough. National socialist governments have all (except Cuba, Venezuela and N. Korea) abandoned the old "cradle to grave" socialism of the Soviet Union and are attempting to move to retreat only to the "commanding heights" version of socialist economic control advocated initially by no less than Comrade Lenin himself. Urban areas will become the new base of economics "from the bottom up", rather than huge top down government programs. Millions of small new companies, individual initiatives, or innovative upgrades will try to transform cities back into the ancient vision of them as bee hives of economic activity. Nobody will be able to contain city limits; they will simply "sprawl".

In most countries, the people seem more ready, willing and able to change than their political leadership, which will stoutly resist, their instincts being to hang on to any form of their centrist power. They will see change as threat, and few centrist regimes can bring themselves to become the instruments for change. They will retreat slowly and reluctantly, and only if they think that they can hang on at least to their political control as the Communist Party has been able to do in China, and the Communist regimes seeks to do in Vietnam. The redesign and rebuilding of cities will inevitably produce winners and losers which produces political conflict which in turn produces political cowardice. And of course, the effort to expand, re-equip, and upgrade urban areas will be unbelievably, overpoweringly underline expensive -- billions and trillions of dollars much of which does not yet exist and cannot easily be created. So here again, governments will be forced to abandon their sacred top down centrist and elitist philosophies, and start thinking about their world from the bottom up and in the broadest dimensions.

URBANIZATION IN CHINA: MASSIVE REFORMS

As in countries all over the world, there is an almost inevitable tide of people movement from rural and small town areas to cities. In 2009, for the first time in world history more people in China are living in cities than on farms or in villages. The Chinese urban population is now about 480 million or 38% of the total population. The rural population is about 800 million. The urban workforce is about 248 million, only about 114 million of whom are in the "official" economy as authorized by the government, and are thus covered by the social security system. 72 million work in SOEs, 11 million are in collectives, 8 million are in foreign funded facilities and 23 million are in governments, the professions or self employed. At the same time, there are an estimated sixty to eighty million workers in cities who are "unofficial" residents, still legally residents of the place where they were born. In fact, there is a workforce "float" of around 180 million workers which includes these illegals, mostly in the informal economy, those who are in casual or part time work, those who are transients, and those who are simply unemployed.

There are now 661 cities in China, of which 89 are over 1 million in population. Of 177 world cities over 2 million in population, 21 are in China and 8 of those are over 5 million. Thus, the urbanization wave has now become the most extensive in world history, and it is expanding beyond the largest cities to many others, and creating new massive suburbs – and shanty towns.

Article 90 of the Constitution guaranteed citizens freedom of residence, but typically, the government ignored its own Constitution and a directive in the '50s from the Ministry of the Interior and the Ministry of Labor set out rules to "control the blind influx of peasants into cities." This in turn led to a huge and elaborate control system aimed at limiting the flow of migrants. The Household Registration System was first initiated in 1955, decayed, and was then reinstituted in 1978. Under this policy, every individual is tied to his/her place of official residence, and social services are available only at that place of official residence. First and foremost, this was a policy to monitor and control people. And most importantly, it was the principal means for controls against free movement, especially from farms to cities but also between work places. Linked to this work allocation was the allocation of other resources. Almost everything was rationed – food, shelter, health care, housing, education beyond primary, child care, fuel, and almost everything else. There were three main classifications: rural, "non-agricultural", and collectives. In many cases, workers and their families had no individual property but were only listed as a member of a collective or commune. Ration coupons were issued and often valid only at the official place of residence. Thus, migrant workers who could not yet get "formal" jobs were considered illegal and could not receive any social services, and were usually harassed and often ejected or arrested by the police. After years of failure, this whole elaborate system proved to be totally unworkable, and like so many communist/socialist blunders, has had to be abandoned. But the government retains the ability to arrest or harass its citizens whatever the laws may say.

Many environmental problems are ancient: floods, droughts, overgrazing, desertification, soil erosion, mining wastes. But there are also new problems that are a direct consequence of the economic development programs and most of them are urban, such as hundreds of thousands of new industrial sites dumping pollutants into the air or water; millions of new automobiles; exhausted water resources; huge wastage of energy and raw materials, and those rapidly expanding urban slums. Lack of raw materials and energy in turn tends to drive up prices. While China's <u>government</u> benefits greatly from foreign sales, it has not yet made satisfactory progress in meeting the consumer needs of its own people.

Urban air pollution is not being dealt with, and in fact, is getting worse every day, and in more cities and lung diseases now kill more people than any other cause. The depletion of urban underground water aquifers is permanent and irreversible, and the exhaustion of these resources is speeding up. Urban expansion requires more water resources, urban sanitation, waste water treatment and other public services which are not being developed. It also means the rise in the number of households, millions of urban transportation trips, huge truck traffic to bring in supplies, vastly increased oil and gas consumption, and heavy and unremitting construction activity.

Two thirds of the water in underground aquifers in 118 major cities is severely polluted, and these aquifers are also being exhausted. Almost every city in China faces an increasingly ominous future about the adequacy of its water supply. In some coastal cities, when underground aquifers are drawn down, they may be penetrated by seawater pollution which is permanent and irreversible.

The most "modern" of China's environmental disasters is in the air. The amounts of dangerous chemicals pumped into the air are now staggering and the air in China's major cities is almost toxic. China is now the world's largest producer of carbon dioxide. Air pollution also includes excessive and illegal levels of sulphur dioxide, chlorofleurocarbons, smoke, dust and soil. Even the government's own State Environmental Protection Administration (SEPA) admits that this is true, and that air pollution is getting worse, not better. It is typical that the Chinese government now has a full array of nicely drafted laws and regulations "controlling" air pollution, and there are standards setting limits for every form of emission. But two thirds of China's cities that have been tested cannot meet these standards, or similar standards set by the World Health Organization. Nor does anybody seem to have a clue how this pollution can be brought under control. On the contrary, the whole vast tide of industrialization and urbanization is guaranteed to make matters very much worse very fast. One needs only to think about the millions of new automobiles and trucks and airplanes, and the development of an additional 562 new coal fired power plants, and the addition of many thousands of new or expanded industrial facilities to realize what is making air pollution worse.

Finally, and most typically, these environmental disasters pose ever increasing threats to the health of China's citizens. An estimated 190 million Chinese have had illnesses connected with drinking contaminated water. Cities and villages alike have suffered from repeated epidemics of diarrhea, and heightened rates of cancer, tumors, poisoning from lead, mercury and other heavy metals. Air pollution alone is said to have been the cause of up to 300,000 deaths. Once again, China's record is worse than any other country on earth. Beijing has six times higher air pollution rates than New York. Past dust storms are so persistent and severe that many people in cities wear face masks against dust and chemicals. There are huge worker time losses from lung diseases, blood infections, heart diseases, strokes and diabetes. There are about 24 million cars today, but in 20 years there may be upwards of 100 million, most of them in already choked cities. 60-90% of rain in Guandong province is acid rain, and farmland losses would equal the farm land in Britain, Germany and France combined.

And these disasters are building. Shanghai is in many respects modern China in miniature. Consider this example: in the late 90s, the river basin northwest of Shanghai, which contains 110 million people, suffered from a further massive pollution of an already polluted river. "Hundreds of thousands of people were left without drinking water, several thousand were treated for dysentery, diarrhea, and vomiting, and 26 million pounds of fish were killed." Pollution came from several thousand factories: paper factories, leather, cloth dyeing, many more. Most factories are Township and Village Enterprises (TVEs) which are official elements of local governments, yet most workers are migrants and moonlighters at slave wages. While the government forces the closure of these small business plants (60,000 in 1999), the larger SOEs are left alone. And still Shanghai continues to grow.

Now, reluctantly, the official policy has evolved. Officials now concede the fact that an additional 300 million farmers are expected to move to cities in the next 20 years, and they cannot be prevented, and thus efforts had better be made to prepare for them. In recent years, urban housing has been largely privatized meaning that the government continues to own the land but the housing itself can be acquired either by purchase or long term lease. This creates two improvements: the government has shed itself of much of the huge costly obligation to maintain the housing stock, and cities have gained a whole variety of new forms of income – rental income and property taxes, various land use taxes, leasing fees, construction fees and other levies. On the negative side, much of this housing was neglected and now needs costly repairs and upgrading. Mortgages are not easy to obtain, and are still available only through state owned banks. Nevertheless, governments at all levels and both public and private developers have been pushing forward with very large programs to construct housing, all the way from basic apartment blocks to opulent gated communities in the American style.

Urban expenditures were held to a minimum for many years, largely because Mao did not trust cities or urban dwellers or bureaucrats. Thus, Mao precipitated the CCP's own period of stagnation for cities that lasted about 30 years. The only real urban activity lay in the construction, at enormous cost, of new industrial cities in the interior mostly based on the perceived need to protect military industry from unspecified foreign attack. When the collectives system was discontinued after Mao's death in 1976, the CCP finally had the courage to start rebuilding urban governments. The Household Responsibility System was reinstituted in 1978 under which the government set quotas for every kind of enterprise from farming to medical practice. Products/services up to the limit of the quota had to be furnished to the government at government dictated prices, but still, the change stimulated productivity to a remarkable degree because any such surplus above the government quotas could be privately sold at a better profit.

The official urban workforce were "entitled" populations who are given priority for subsidized housing, food, state-sector jobs, and many fringe benefits including health care, disability benefits, schools, pensions, and unemployment compensation. Throughout the 50s the newly formed state enterprises actively recruited rural labor in large numbers into these official jobs. This was a means of promoting the shift of populations from agriculture to manufacturing. At the same time, the government foolishly refused to allow workers to bring their families to the cities, because that would drive up costs to the state in the form of housing, health care, education, food subsidies and urban infrastructure. Only about 20% of the population ever achieved this full official urban status. Beginning in the mid 80s however the dam broke and an estimated 60 to 80 million workers came flooding into the cities despite official disapproval and active measures to prevent it. In addition to these floaters, there is also some percentage of official workers who are unemployed at any given time. Thus, half of the urban population was illegal and guilty of breaking the law.

The old nature of core cities, or even core suburbs, has been dramatically expanded to become endless huge sprawling complexes of industrial and commercial enterprises, public facilities like ports and power plants interwoven with residential enclaves ranging from glittering towers to intolerable cardboard hovels. Chongquing has a central city of about 3.3 million but a huge regional area population of almost 31 million. The Shanghai river basin region contains 17 to 20 million people. Beijing has about almost 15 million and Tianjin about 11 million.

Land grabbing by the government continues in almost every city in China. The bigger problem however is taxes because most cities are desperate for money so there are road taxes, a population tax, a grain tax, and every other kind of tax, applied rigidly and enforced ruthlessly. There are few central government subsidies for public programs and local officials are always desperate for funds to try and keep up with this enormous expansion, so they impose every tax they can think of and supplement their income through land grabs and the time honored manner of gouging the peasants for more taxes.

The initiation of the national reform program in the mid 80s, and the divestiture of SOEs led to the resurrection of something like full time professional city management. In many cases, cities were allowed to annex neighboring rural areas despite the Constitutional provision against such actions. In the process, they acquired access to land, which remains owned by the government but was generally controlled by collectives. Part of this resurrection was the institution of local People's Congresses that had authority to pass laws, make regulations, and approve certain administrative actions. Cities have been quietly jettisoning their communes and collectives, restructuring themselves, adding more professionalism to the staffs, and in general acting like real governments.

As the Chinese economy develops, barriers against urban migration are deteriorating. SOEs themselves are mutating and being liberated. The all-absorbing concentration on the growth of the manufacturing economy proved not to be enough to absorb even the entitled workers. The government officially discourages the workforce "float", but on the other hand, these workers contribute to the urban economy without the added costs of the service entitlements, so they are largely tolerated. There is no question that in whatever job they do, migrant workers can expect to be exploited. Working exceptionally long hours, they are usually paid below the mandated minimum wage. If they are young women, they can expect to be sexually harassed. Beyond that, health conditions at work are often in violation, with workers having virtually no protection against potential hazards such a chemical fumes. If overcome by tiredness or sickness, they can be dismissed at a moment's notice. In other cases, their identity documents can be withheld to insure that they work out the length of their work contract, which may be anywhere from one to three years. Many workers are housed in cramped dormitories, managed by the factory, where their grievances may be without recourse either to the government or to the unions, both of which will nearly always back the employer. So long as there is an unlimited supply of unskilled labor, these conditions of work are likely to continue. The government is now actually promoting a second great wave of urbanization, and that is the movement of rural workers to townships, villages (really small towns) and second level cities.

There has been a remarkable boom in urban construction. According to Campanella, there has been an explosion of building in most cities in addressing housing needs as well as industrial and commercial construction. But consider the formula for disaster this is building: first, the government continues to own and control almost all of the land. Then, public officials at local government level have world class reputations for corruption and pathological practices. Next, both public sector and private sector commercial developers have an even worse reputation for greediness. There is heavy competition for land lease deals with public officials, in which developers will "do anything" to win a lease. Next, there is little or no oversight over construction work, and even where there may be inspectors, it is likely that they will be bought off. Thus, a number of results are likely. There will be extensive bribery of public officials (in fact, due to recent reform activities, hundreds have already been caught, tried and convicted). There is the high likelihood that large numbers of buildings will be shoddy construction, and indeed examples of deterioration are already appearing. In addition, there is massive overbuilding, and as in Japan in the 90s, property values are being artificially inflated, and at some point, one can foresee heavy value losses as the market recedes to more realistic levels. If these problems are as serious as they appear to be, at some point they will start to scare off development money. And shoddy construction portends heavy unanticipated expenses for the unlucky owners in the form of either renovation or abandonment.

Older housing remains a big problem. Much of it was shoddy construction, and the State as landlord sadly neglected maintenance and repair, and many units provided by the State are being fixed up by their occupants or by managing cooperatives, at their own expense. But over half of all housing continues to be under the SOEs or government bodies. Rents are heavily subsidized, but the pattern is bad housing at low cost. Proposals to "marketize" rents are under way, but are stiffly resisted.

The number one complaint of urban dwellers is lack of commercial services. But more latitude for private and "informal" enterprise is reducing the past failures of the tight restrictions imposed by the government over the marketplace, and the older Communist communes, labor brigades and union cadres, while never officially repudiated, have been allowed to wither away. Most cities still suffer from lack of transport, and lack of child care. Also, millions of readers eagerly snap up the skyrocketing numbers of newspapers, journals and books. And wave after wave of new enthusiasms swept across China such as hobbies, tourism, fitness, computer games, or the Falung Gong. And gratefully, the older communist organizations such as communes or labor brigades or union cadres simply faded into the sunset.

The urban destitute are denied a political voice because the leadership doesn't want to hear the complaints, and can do little about them. The "cradle to grave" commitment never meant much except to those in the favored sectors of the economy; and as State resources have withered, things have only gotten worse. China's analog to the informal sector -- new neighborhood-run collective enterprises, urban private enterprises, and rural subcontracting -- are the most dynamic part of the economy. In truth, these sectors are faster on their feet than the SOE's as well.

YANGON, MYANMAR: A CITY HEADED FOR DISASTER

"Yangon has tripled in population to 7.4 million since 1984 – an absolutely astounding increase that has left the city and the national government far behind. Yangon has marvelous plans for economic development over the next 25 years, at the rate of about $ 5 billion per year. But actual investment is more like $ 900 million." (Economist, 01-31-15). These plans include a vast enlargement of the bumbling Public Sanitation Department, but many commenters are asking pointed questions. Instead of this grand scheme for enlargement, why not make the present department perform better? Why not actually fix hundreds of broken water pipes so that people don't have to buy expensive bottled water? Why not make the sewage system reach more than just 10% of the city population? Why is the power system so bad that big areas of the city suffer from congenital lapses in service? Instead of stumbling over trash in the streets, why not put out more trash recepticles and a few men in trucks to empty them?

The government's plans have led people to believe that big improvements are imminent, and it has made Yangon the focus of current and planned foreign investment in the country. But this has driven up the price of owning or renting decent buildings so much that people and small businesses have actually been driven out of the city. Then, new residents tend to be the poor from rural areas where things are even worse, seeking work, but not finding it. They then end up in the city's slums and the informal economy. In essence, the fancy picture of potential economic development masks the continued failure of both the national and the city governments to deal effectively with their human services problems.

MEXICO CITY: STUCK IN TRAFFIC

Every silver lining has a cloud. Mexico City is increasingly prosperous, but this has led to a huge surge in the number of automobiles on the city's streets. It now has more than 5.5 million cars, which has earned it two miserable distinctions: according to one estimate it is now the world's most congested city; and in 1992, the United Nations survey declared it's air as the most polluted of any city in the world (but there seems to be a lot of competition for this honor). Serious efforts have cleaned up the air so that it is "almost wholesome", but the auto problem is only growing worse. It is estimated that there will be more than 10 million cars on the streets by the end of the decade. The response of governments has been pitiful; it has merely banned cars on certain days of the week, meanwhile, expanding the street/road system. What Mexico City needs to do is to expand its rapid transit train and rapid bus systems, get rid of highly pollluting private microbuses, and stop demanding the provision of more and more parking spaces in the city. But all of this would be stubbornly resisted, not least because it will certainly be horribly expensive, and neither the Federal nor the city government has the money, or the courage to raise taxes to get it.

Part of the tax raising problem stems from another of government sins, found in all of Mexico including Mexico City. Governments and politicians throughout the country have a long and very sordid history of arrogant corruption, widely shared throughout Latin America. Scandals have occurred in Guatemala, Honduras, Chile, Argentina, Peru, Venezuela, and especially in Brazil, where literally millions of Brazilians have taken to the streets demanding the resignation or impeachment of its president, Dilma Rousseff. Protests and counter pressures on other governments have toppled presidents and invoked the creation of new ant-corruption laws, and anti-corruption commissions. It remains to be seen how effective these measures will be, in countries where there has been a lot of tolerance for leaders who "steal but get things done."

THAILAND: DRIVING CAN BE LETHAL

Thailand has now earned the dubious title of producing more traffic deaths per 100 thousand citizens than any other country in the world. The Far East has nine of the top ten worst countries in the world:Thailand, Vietnam, Malaysia, China, Cambodia, India, Indonesia, Philippines and Singapore. The capital, Bankok is an eternal traffic jam. Motorbikes and scooters flit in and out of traffic, and are involved in almost 75% of accidents, but few riders wear helmets. Police control efforts are overwhelmed; fines are small and seldom paid. Nobody gets punished. The air is polluted by smoke and carbons. Public transit is limited and the government seems reluctant to spend money on expansions. Things are getting worse, and the governments seem unable or unwilling to rise to the challenge.

AFRICA AND ASIA: GROWTH BY "SPRAWL"

Between 2005 and 2015, the cities of the world added more than 750 million people, and 80% of this surge took place in the cities of Africa and Asia. In addition, cities are hugely speading – they simply sprawl all over the land. Many cities are now really huge urban and suburban regional sprawls covering hundreds of thousands of acres and many millions of people beyond the city center. Unfortunately, these regions are chaotic messes; they lack any coherence in governance or the coordination of public infrastructure. Despite the fact that, in most cases, the governments own the land, they fail to lay out streets and roads, sewer systems, water distribution systems, power grids, or public transportation. In addition, because individuals and companies cannot own the land on which they want to build, this obsolete Socialist nonsense inhibits much economic investment. And the more sprawling and crowded these regions become, the harder it is to come in and retrofit these facilities. Far too many people live in miserable and dangerous slums and barrios. Others live in shoddy high rise apartments, poorly maintained. Next to opulent new homes and apartments, people are living is card board huts lacking even basic civic amenities.

NATIONAL EDUCATION SYSTEMS FAILURES

Despite almost universal acceptance of the importance of education, education systems have developed a very serious set of problems all their own. National political leaders all say the right comforting things about the values of education, but priorities for the allocation of scarce funds will usually leave education behind in favor economic development in any form, and very high expenditures on the military establishment. Elementary and secondary education is usually the responsibility of provincial and town levels of government with the full recognition that they seldom have the funds to support them properly. As a consequence, this long term neglect has resulted in entire national systems that are wretched: the physical plant tends to be poorly built, old, shabby, often filthy, ill maintained and repaired, and often lacking water, sanitation, and even heat or running water. Teachers lack adequate training, decent books, black boards or maps. And seldom can they hope for anything as astonishing as a classroom computer. The teachers themselves may be marginally educated, and most school systems seem never to have the money for the training, balanced distribution, economic wellbeing, in-service development and social wellbeing of this vital human resource. The reality often is "a flip chart under a tree."

And what is taught is all too often marginal. Textbooks, when available, tend to be obsolete and poorly written. The curricula are usually regarded as simplistic, out of date, and irrelevant. Far too much teaching is in the form of older patterns of recitation and memorization. There is constant frustration that modern concepts for the stimulation of independent student thinking are ideas that never actually penetrate the classroom. And yet, these systems seem to reward themselves. Administrative costs are usually very high, overhead costs are excessive, too many people are sitting in offices and too few are teaching in classrooms. Teacher salaries and benefits are seen as very generous (teachers vote!), and at the same time, classroom performance is heavily condemned as seriously inferior. There are usually very high drop out rates that school administrators and government officials do not want to acknowledge. About 15 percent of students do not complete even primary education, and 70 percent of those who fail to attend are girls. In some rural areas, more than 50 percent of girls never even <u>enter</u> school. While some countries such as Jordan and Syria (formerly) have achieved 95 percent student enrollments, half of the children in Sudan are not in school, and in parts of Egypt the enrollment is as low as 10 percent. Given this reality, it sad to see how educators surround themselves with a halo of virtue, setting noble objectives for school systems that are never realized. It is common for school administrators to publish good numbers of student enrollment, not admitting that "enrollment" is not the same as "attendance."

Too many schools teach useless subjects, but don't teach vital subjects. For example, most of the population still live on farms and in villages, but only about 2% of African college students study agriculture, technology development, or rural development, while 30% still study "literature". The performance of school administrators and of the teachers themselves are widely and bitterly criticized. Teacher unions in far too many countries have become a powerful political special interest, having little interest in dealing with the well being of either teachers or students. Teachers are notorious for failing to show up for work, and for stubbornly resisting any tampering with their generous salaries and benefits. Parents are forced to pay special fees just to get their children into school and to pay teachers to do their job. There is an urgent need for instruction that better prepares children for the workplace.

HIGHER EDUCATION

Education at the college/university level has also come under criticism. What happens when politics and reality are in conflict over a vital public program? The answer seems to be that politics wins. A case in point is the condition of British and other European universities. In Great Britain, the universities were taken over by the government as a part of the enthusiasm for socialist solutions that swept over the country following WW II. Universities are one place where the "cradle to grave" promises of social service are failing. Britain spends just one percent of its Gross Domestic Product on higher education compared to 2.7% in the United States. Since the government has assumed control of higher education (as well as elementary and secondary), and since most expenditure is in the form of government payments, then it is clear that the state of universities is now a government responsibility. And that state is one of deterioration. [iii] Increasingly, buildings are run down, classes are overcrowded, academic salaries are too low, research has declined, and the morale of the faculty, administration and students is universally low. In the name of equality of opportunity fees charges are uniform for all students and are deliberately set by the government at low levels to permit children from poor families to enroll. But the inevitable political syndrome has set in. As the number of students has risen there has been no matching increase in the level of government support leading inevitably to the deterioration that has grown so noticeable. In other words, the British government, deliberately and knowingly has enjoyed the political virtues of advocating general and equal university education and then avoided the politically unpopular responsibility to provide more money.

The politicians have squeezed university management deliberately. When university officials have pointed out the obvious adverse management consequences of this political hypocrisy, they have been largely ignored. Another element of this perverse politics is the doctrinal commitment to government enforced "equality" and the avoidance of any hint of variation either in financing or class content. Now, universities charge a uniform $1900 per semester per student. This fee seems to be covering something like half of the cost of an undergraduate education, and the only bright spot has been the continued high rate of enrollments of foreign students who pay much higher non-resident fees. Some universities have considerable income from research but the cost of teaching science and engineering is very high – perhaps $15,000 per semester – and such sums are frequently not available. As a consequence, research is declining. The downward pressure of low fee structures has "dumbed down" the range and variety of courses offered the quality of the faculty, and any form of innovation where funds might be crucial such as research or the introduction of new technology. Even a proposed increase in government-set fees up to a level of $3000 is still seen as too low to allow universities to recover their lost edge.

Everybody seems at least to agree that universities need to be upgraded, but as seems typical in such social services debates, the initial urge is to blame the sad state of universities on the lack of "social conscience" on the part of the British taxpayer, reasoning that, if they really cared, they would ungrudgingly pay higher taxes to cover needs. By now however it seems clearer that the British tax payer has stiffened resistance against such calls for tax increases. Both politicians and university administrators are therefore finally beginning to consider breaking away from the present box of government subsidy and price fixing and considering funding alternatives. Bills have finally been passed in Parliament permitting universities to charge varying fees depending on their degree of academic excellence as perceived by customers. The increases of about $1.8 billion would permit some salary increases and deal with some of the worst physical maintenance problems, but even if realized, are still likely to fall far short of permitting fundamental upgrades. The new legislation also makes provision for a student loan program for very poor students, including a loan repayment system similar to that in the United States.

The pathology of British university governance is that politicians have adhered stubbornly to an approach which the great majority of professional judgment recognizes as a failure. Knowing better, why did the politicians defy rationality for so long, and why are changes, when finally permitted, so weak and inconclusive? The answer is partly a stubborn adherence to an obsolete piece of doctrine, and partly the unwillingness of politicians to face up to reality.

Great Britain is not alone in facing this dilemma. In Germany, protests against new university budget cuts precipitated protests in Berlin, Frankfurt, Gottingen and Munich, and started a wave of challenges to current tight fisted policies. There is an obvious hypocritical split between language lauding the higher education system and the reality of budget cuts. According to the Economist (June 10, 2004), the regional government told Berlin's three universities to cut their budgets by $ 85 million a year by 2009. This would require releasing another 250 faculty after having cut the number by half to 1,000 in the last decade. There will be 125 students per professor, more than twice today's national average. Other state governments are imposing similar cuts."

A survey conducted for the European Commission estimates that more than 400,000 scientists of all kinds have left European countries to work in the United States where universities and university research are better funded. The study concludes that most of these scientists have left permanently and have no real intention to return. To again quote the Economist: "The financial problems of European universities stem from their near-total reliance on the public purse. Of the 1% of GDP that Germany spends on higher education (vs. 2.7% in the United States) only 0.1% comes from private sources. Students do not pay fees in France and Germany or in most other EU countries. State funding for universities is mean and under further pressure."

Here again, as in Great Britain, university managers and academics are highly vocal in pointing out the pathology of this form of cheapness. A country that is under-funding its educational institutions is losing the power to innovate and upgrade and thus is squandering its future. The old theology against tuition fees has been stubbornly retained despite ample statistical evidence and countless warnings. Centrist political theory and control is preventing competition for students among schools at all levels.

Societal differences are brought to bear on higher education. Because funds for higher education are very limited in poor countries, the government will play a dominant role in deciding who gets access to higher education funds. The children of poor families may not be excluded as a matter of policy, but the tendency would be for the richer stakeholders to find the best candidates for university education among their own children. This is true even where the elite could pay for education out of their own private resources.

Also, because funds are so scarce, the selection process includes decisions about what students should study. Usually there is a strongly developed strategy -- or at least some short term tactics -- guiding the allocation of public funds to train domestic talent either at home or abroad. This usually includes such fields as medicine, engineering, economics, and the military. There is also another strategy around the building of a faculty for national universities, and another to train a cadre for the civil service. Such government funded programs will also attempt to bind the recipients to a period of work in the home country because if their graduates flee to greener pastures elsewhere, the government's investment has been wasted.

Inherent in this binding process is an explicit or implicit promise that the young people sent for training will become leaders and rise rapidly in their chosen fields. They can also assume that the lack of funds will limit the number of competitors in their professions. Thus are elites maintained.

INDONESIA: BEHIND THE CURVE

The whole education system in Indonesia is "lousy". Why?

To begin with, the bureaucracy is horrible. Three separate ministries are involved. The Education Ministry oversees state primary, junior, secondary schools; the Ministry of Religious Affairs supervises the *Madrassas*, and the Ministry of Research and Technology is responsible for universities and polytechnic schools. Despite recent improvements in the last few years, there continue to be wide gaps in school completion rates between rich and poor students and between rural and urban students. Teachers avoid working in rural and remote areas. "Across the system, enrollment declines markedly with age. For every 100 students who enter the system, only 25 will come out meeting minimum (international) standards for literacy and understanding of number calculations. Scores in science have declined, and scores in mathematics and reading have been declining slowly for 15 years of testing. The system suffers from ill prepared teachers, shortages of teachers, and a pernicious corruption, including sales of test answers. As a consequence, Indonesia suffers from a shortage of people with modern skills and understanding. Teacher certification has produced little result. Only 10% of teacher training institutes are seen as much good. The President has instituted the "Indonesia Smart Card" program designed to provide school stipends to 24 million poor students, but the fear is that "it will stuff more students into bad schools." (Economist, 13 Dec. 14).

WEST AFRICA: STILL DOESN'T GET IT

Few west African governments have ever provided education to as much as half of the school age population, despite spending between a quarter and a third of their budgets on education. Much of the money is squandered or simply disappears, and many parents have to pay fees up front to get their children in school, and to get teachers to show up and teach. Civil services and teachers unions are considered as "voter pools" and not as the source of competent public management. According to a United Nations report, the 10 worst education systems in the world are: Niger, Burkina Faso, Mali, Central African Republic, Ethiopia, Eretria, Guinea, Pakistan, Gambia and Angola – nine of ten being countries in Africa.

INDIA: FILLING THE GAPS

In India, the political leadership never took the form of a unified elite. There has always been a serious divide and conflict between Hindu and Muslim, and this has always been reflected in politics. In addition, there have been huge gaps in wealth, especially between the rural/village population and the urban elites. There is a complex relationship between the distribution of wealth and the ancient Indian caste system, where there continues to be a "Brahma Elite" system with continued strength held by the "landed gentry". Part of this prejudice is that the elite do not think that the "lower classes, including women" deserve to be educated. And this kind of thinking ranges across many other elements of Indian life, including the Indian Civil Service. The struggle then has become "bottom up" opposition to these views, pursued, with some success, in the political arena. In India, "discrimination" often means positive discrimination, pursued as public policy. (Kumar, "Political Agenda of Education, p. 97).

The attitude about women and education has been forced to start deep, attacking the whole general gender, religious, legal and prejudicial attitudes within Indian society and culture. First some social justice is required; then social equity. For example, there has long been an attitude that there are "appropriate" education for girls and women: cooking, needle work, music, arts and crafts, nursing and education of other girls. And this has also been linked to a comparable need to reorient the socialization of men, especially of the "ruling" class.

EGYPT: TRYING TO PLAY CATCHUP

Recent efforts of the government to reform education at all levels have become far more serious, but remain underpowered because the country has an exploding population and the school system has had trouble trying to keep pace, much less upping their game. Growing demands have left the system underfunded, obsolete, and losing quality. Increasing numbers of graduates are unemployable for both economic and education reasons. The official curriculum is seen as largely irrelevant. Teachers are still underpaid, low in prestige, low in the quality of their teaching, and lacking contemporary professional and technical knowledge.

An over abundance of administrators created bad bureaucratic practices, and robbed classrooms of teachers. Facilities are old and in bad shape, classrooms are overcrowded, facilities and equipment are in constant shortage, and schools have often been forced to use two and even three shifts. There is a common pattern of having many students who are officially registered but never attend class. There are many complaints about rote learning, mechanistic learning, obsolete course content, obsolete knowledge bases by teachers, and lack of modern equipment, especially in information technologies. In addition, financing is always scarce, and parents have to pay high fees (10% of annual income) for their "free" schooling. This includes exam fees, uniform charges, enrollment fees, and even private tutoring, often by the same teachers who are underpaid in their official jobs. The rigid centralized bureaucracy is cumbersome and slow moving, and dedicated to keeping control at the center. And, in the grand traditional pattern, there is a vast surplus of grandiose plans and a vast shortage of actual accomplishment.

In fact, it must be said that Egypt has a two track educational system that runs in parallel. In Egypt as elsewhere in the Muslim world, religious teaching is seen by its practitioners not as a second system, but as the only system. Thus, Egypt has a system of Mosque Quranic schools (*kuttabs*); religious schools (*madrassas*); and separate Sufi schools. This system is seen as not simply supplying education, but as defining and inculcating a whole concept of a culture – and in fact, two – that of Islam and of Arabs. An interesting and successful idea has been creation of a number of rural welfare centers which offer limited health care and literacy education; there are almost 10 million illiterates between ages fifteen and thirty-five.

IRAN: EDUCATION = INDOCTRINATION

Iran has seen two waves of educational development. The first was under the regime of Shah Pahlavi from 1925 to 1979, in which the older traditional clerical based system was pursued in local primary schools and religious colleges, but the Pahlavi regime set as its main objectives the training of Iranians for modern occupations in administration, management, science, technology and economics, with a new and more highly educated teacher corps. The Shah envisioned a more European secular middle class.

The second wave occurred after the 1979 revolution when a total and swift "Islamization" of the system was undertaken. Universities were closed down between 1979 and 1982 while major changes were mandated. All students were segregated by gender. The Cultural Revolution Committee was formed to revamp the curriculum to reflect Islamic values. Professors who were not considered sufficiently "Islamic" were removed; the student body itself shrunk by as much as 75 percent between 1979 and 1983 in part because those who were not Muslim were often no longer admitted.

Again in May of 2011, Iran's Supreme Leader, Ayatollah Ali Khamenei said that, despite more than 30 years of enforced reform, the education system was once again damned as "imported" and argued once again that it needed to become more Iranian and Islamic. To this end, the authorities have launched about 10,000 new Quran Schools (toward an ultimate goal of 50,000 such schools) to act as cultural bases for student indoctrination. These schools will largely offer classes after regular school. But this is an extraordinary confession of some kind of failure. It says that, after more than 30 years, an education system designed heavily to produce the New Islamic Citizen, especially one who is also properly educated and useful, has failed to deliver. In fact, the serious debate within the country makes it clear that the regime has still not really figured out what such a citizen should be like, or how to teach both revolutionary ideology and modern knowledge to its children. Meanwhile, teachers struggle along, teaching to the text, because that is the only safe course of action.

Many parts of the education system are performing well. Despite general policies of gender separation, women have done particularly well in the last fifteen to twenty years. It is now estimated that they make up more than 50 percent of university students, with some fields of science and engineering, and Iran is said to have the highest female to male ratio in primary schools among world countries at 1.2: 1. Today, 77 percent of the population is literate. After 1989, private universities have been permitted. Secondary education at state institutions is free but there may be heavy fees borne by students. At the level of grades nine through eleven, two tracks are offered. One is the General/Academic track which offers areas of study in the literature and arts, natural sciences, physics and mathematics, and social sciences and economics. The other track is the Technical/Vocational track which aims to train for service occupations, technician skills, and agriculture. The reconstruction of the university system has permitted some emphasis on science, technology and management, and if there is a new trend, it is to provide more training at all levels in the skills that are needed by a modern economy.

Private schools have been permitted since 1989, but their record is mixed. They are expensive, they often use the same teachers that were trained for the public system, and they often use the same textbooks.

They are often suspected of padding their results to attract customers. But it seems that, whatever their reputation they are still seen as better than most public schools and their enrollments are still growing.

JORDAN: DOING IT RIGHT

Starting with almost nothing in the early 1920s, Jordan has built a comprehensive high quality education system with 2787 public schools, 1500 private schools 48 community colleges and 19 universities. Education is free, and there is about 95 percent enrollment. Women are educated, and they are now two thirds of community college enrollment and 45 percent of university enrollment. The system is trying to upgrade the curriculum to teach more "thinking". In total, Jordan has the third lowest illiteracy rate in the Muslim world. Jordan ranks 90th out of 177 nations in the Human Development Index – the best in the Arab world, and its graduates can usually be accepted in the best universities around the world. Its education policies are secular: to meet the needs of a knowledge-based economy; to upgrade the physical plant; and to promote early childhood education. In a next step, targets will shift to upgrading teacher qualifications and performance, curriculum modernization and better means for evaluating student performance.

Basic education is two years of pre-school, ten years of compulsory basic education, and a final two years of preparation for either academic or vocational education. The Jordanian population is very young, and almost one third of them are in some form of school. Schools have also enjoyed great success in dealing with gender equality, and in bringing rural education almost up to the level of urban education. At the secondary school level, Islamic studies are mandatory for all students except Christians. There has been some decline in vocational education, in part because the academic track is more popular, but vocational education is highly prized as an attractive pathway to good jobs, and the government wants to make this track stronger. The United Nations Relief and Works Agency (UNRWA) operates a region-wide school system for Palestinian refugees – one of the biggest such systems in the region.

Jordan shares a common pattern with other Muslim countries in that the education bureaucracy is seen as too narrow and self-aggrandizing, and does not recognize the fact that most education takes place outside of the formal state administered schools system. Over and above formal technical training organizations, most companies teach new employees how to do their jobs, including formal On the Job Training (OJT) programs, or just by coaching of new employees. In most Muslim countries, a large proportion of the economy is in the informal sector where jobs are largely self-taught. Much of what is taught in formal schools is intellectually correct, but of little relevance in the real world, but almost nobody in government thinks this way.

Meanwhile, the Jordanian government is supposedly pursuing an agenda of reform, including financial reforms, judiciary reforms, modernizing of administrative and service delivery systems, economic liberalization, attempts to shift the economy to higher value added products and services, and the development of more sophisticated legal bases. Part of this is the supposed modernization of the formal education system, whose advocates claim that education is the keystone to all else. But like most Muslim countries, Jordan's population is more than half under the age of 18, and each year, more young people enter the job market than the economy can accommodate.

MOROCCO: TRYING TO DO IT RIGHT

Morocco has the usual type of pattern: two years of pre-school (voluntary) plus five years of primary school and four years of secondary school. This is then followed by three years of general secondary school or technical education. In the primary schools, the language of instruction is Arabic, but French is used in the universities. This language requirement is seen as a real barrier to enrollment which Morocco can ill afford. At the time of Independence (1956) only 10 percent of children were enrolled in school, and only fifteen thousand boys were enrolled in secondary level – no girls allowed. In 1959, education was largely Koranic, but a pitiful 10 percent of children actually attended elementary schools, and fewer than 5 percent made it to any secondary school.

Morocco is a strange and frustrating story of continued, earnest efforts to improve the education system with disappointing results. In 2000, 50 percent of the population was still illiterate; only 30 percent of women could read or write. King Mohammad V and the government had to fight their way through a debilitating war with the religious and educational establishments to force the offering of such classes as mathematics, chemistry, physics, foreign languages, and especially, the education of women. Now, more than 50 years later, school systems remain marginal, despite all of the plans and committees and high sounding rhetoric. Literacy rates remain very low (52 percent), access to schools is still limited, especially in rural areas. Many students never make it to school, and for those who do, drop-out rates remain high (22 percent), and girls still are badly under served. In addition, schools have been generally underfunded, there is a congenital lack of decent facilities and equipment, teacher training is weak, and the children themselves seem to hate the whole thing. There seems, still, to be too much rote memorization, too much junk work, too much emphasis on cramming for the university exam, and little recognition in schools of the realities of life outside of schools. There are widespread feelings that students will never actually learn anything that will get them a job, or prepare them to deal with life's uncertainties. The Human Development Index ranks Morocco at one hundred thirtieth place.

Official policies aim at full integration of all school systems (public, Koranic, private). Private schools are usually independent, and are growing in numbers, mainly because many public schools are not very good and private schools are seen as preferred by those who can afford them. Almost 40% of vocational schools are privately run. At the university level, Morocco has 14 public universities and many private universities, but they are small and represent less than 3.5% of the university population.

PAKISTAN: ETERNAL PITIFUL TOTAL FAILURE

The government has been moving to devolve responsibility for schools down to provinces and municipalities, but proposals for education devolution have long been stalled by a legal case before the Supreme Court. Strong opposition to devolution has been led by academics, teachers, opposition political parties and even students. The general case is that provinces will not maintain curriculum uniformity, but perhaps the more compelling argument is that provinces do not have enough skills or the infrastructure to run schools, and that they don't have the money either. In addition, the government has sent thousands of students abroad to study, and students fear the death of that system. Further, if the provinces try to raise more money by higher school fees (rather than general taxation), it is suspected that parents can't afford such fees, and student attendance will suffer. In Islamabad, an increase in fees of 700 percent has just been enacted at a time when one fourth of the population is living under the $2 per day poverty line.

So what is the consequence of all of this? Pakistan's education system is one of the worst in the world. Even the government is forced to admit that the country is in the midst of an educational emergency because the current system has produced a disastrous human and economic result. A government study, reported on the BBC in March, 2011 (7) stated that funding for schools had been cut from about 2.5 percent of GDP to less than 1.5 percent in the last 7 years. Few of Pakistan's twenty-five million children will ever receive an adequate education. Three million will never ever attend classes in schools. Of those children who do attend school, a third will stay there for less than two years. Of those who attend, half of them are incapable of reading even the simplest of materials.

School system physical plant, never very good, has been allowed to deteriorate from prolonged neglect. Only about two thirds of schools have proper rest rooms or even drinking water. More than 20,000 schools do not even have a building. Overall, lack of funds, poor curricula, poor and limited teaching materials, inadequately trained teachers, high rates of absenteeism, and poor facilities all seem eternal and governments seem totally incapable of doing anything about them. Parents who can afford it will send their children to private schools, especially if they have any intention of sending them on to a university.

Private education is available at all levels, with little or no government assistance. Currently, the government spends just under 2 percent of GDP on education, and plans to increase this to 7 percent simply sound ludicrous. Expenditure has remained stagnant for most of the last thirty-seven years.

NIGERIA: TOO FAR BEHIND

The Nigerian government is so typical: it has a national "education development" plan which promises to cure all ills, but actual reform is far too little to deal with an education system that is far too weak, and the education system seems to be falling farther behind. In the national population there are now more than 45% of people under the age of 15. In addition, huge numbers of these young people are crowding into cities where the hope for work and service is far greater than in the countryside, so cities are especially overwhelmed. The country also suffers from two serious historical mistakes: it has forever failed to deal with the position of women in their society, and the education system has stubbornly ignored the female population. Second, there are heavy religious prejudices because the south of the country is largely Christian and the north is heavily Muslim, and both the government and society in general has had trouble dealing with this dilemma. Thus, there has been deliberate neglect of the children of the Muslim north, and any effort of the government to upgrade education there is now horribly complicated by the vicious incursions of the terrorist organization Boko Haram. This name is in fact approximately interpreted to mean "Western education is forbidden".

In general, the reforms are hypocritical: they brag about increases in "enrollment", and conceal the fact that enrollment is not the same as actual attendance. Thus, for children ages 6-11, 40% of them are not even in school, and less than 50% ever make it beyond the fifth grade. Parents are forced to pay a bunch of special fees just to get their children into school, and to get teachers to teach.

VIETNAM: SURPRISE!

Recent evaluations of student achievement in math, reading and science have produced the surprising perception that 15 year olds in rigid Communist Vietnam are achieving very good results, with scores higher than many Western countries. There appear to be several reasons for this result. While the highly centrist Communist government performs poorly, its record with respect to education seems surprisingly good. By 2010, it was spending more than 20% of GDP on education, and the central leadership seems genuinely committed to making education more universal, more proficient, and more relevant. The teacher corps is generally highly regarded and respected, committed to go beyond rote, or beyond government propaganda.

The centrist Communist government continues to be highly controlling, and tends to strongly defend the wrong things. The education system pushes to get out from under this negative centrist control and get far more "modern" than the central government likes. And one of the national problems is that almost 40% of 15 and older children are not in school -- excluded by high costs which parents have to pay, or the need to work to earn income for the family. In cities, the elite can afford to send their children to fairly expensive higher rated schools. But then, it is ironic that these schooling arrangements are embarrassingly locked in covert corruption. Vietnam can be proud of its primary educational systems, but it appears that its universities are still too much under control of a rigid reactionary government regime.

NATIONAL HEALTH CARE SYSTEMS

Many national health care systems were inferior even before the modern tide of wars, insurrections and terrorist attacks. In country after country, these armed conflicts have deeply harmed health care capability, even to the verge of destruction. This is true in Iraq, Afghanistan, Vietnam, Cambodia, Laos, Syria, Sudan and South Sudan, the Democratic Republic of Congo, the Central African Republic, Sudan, Rwanda and Yemen. In other countries such as Bangladesh, Eritrea, S. Africa, Egypt, and many others, a lack of resources, low government priority, bumbling incompetence and corruption have produced health care systems seriously inadequate for the needs of citizens. Some of the dysfunctional characteristics of such systems are as follows:

1. As part of the surge of State Socialism after WW II, and justified by the assertion of the need for "a caring government", much of the health care system in many countries, Socialist and otherwise, was taken over by the government. But what has emerged in country after country is the growing realization that most of these government based programs were serious failures. They have been characterized by a lack of even moderately good facilities, a shortage of medications and equipment, inexplicably low salaries for doctors, nurses and medical technicians, and a failure to adopt the advantages of new technology that has revolutionized medical practice. In many developing countries, there has been an understandable shortage of money, but his has produced a strange and damaging sense of priority, with money going for factories and highways, (or weapons) but not for health care or education.

2. As a consequence of these distortions, many national health care systems are totally inadequate, and this shortage has produced another level of problems. In country after country, the ruling elite have been able to take care of themselves and their friends and their employees, but the rest of the population goes begging. Cities are vastly favored over rural and village and small town areas. National health insurance almost never got seriously

developed in such countries, and even where it was offered, the benefits were wholly inadequate.

China for example, still insures less than 20% of its citizens in programs that pay far too little.

3. Many country systems are seen as losing ground, and falling behind many kinds of medical problems. For example, because of its wars and crises, Ethiopian health concerns include high infant mortality, malaria, tuberculosis, HIV/AIDS, extensive malnutrition, lack of clean water, lack of effective sanitation, and general shortages of health care facilities. In some countries, transportation is so bad that more than half of the population can't get to a hospital or clinic. Some of the old communicable diseases have staged some degree of comeback; a whole new range of non-communicable diseases have been expanding, including heart attacks, cancer, pulmonary problems, obesity, drug abuse and alcoholism. Finally many countries have been totally unable to deal with the surge of AIDS problems arising among their citizens. The elderly fare very poorly either in medical or economic terms, and there is little attention given to special problems posed by the handicapped, the mentally ill or the pathologically emotionally disturbed.

4. The failures of State Socialism begin in the economic world, and governments like Russia, China, India, Vietnam, S. Korea, Egypt and many others have been forced to retreat from strict adherence to Socialist policy, and move toward an economy relying more on market competition and the resurgence of the private sector in all of its economic and social dimensions. This tide has been extended to health care systems in the form of a retreat from strict state provision to one of a combination of public and private capabilities. As this has happened, more health care in general has been created, a competition has been created, and people have more choice. There has been a movement away from public facilities where they have been shown to be inferior. Private medical care is usually more expensive, but it is true that, in many cases, free public care was never "free", and patients were forced to pay a lot of money up front. Private medical care is

making serious inroads in urban areas where more people can afford the costs.

5. As the nature of national health care systems change, the service in rural and village areas has begun to improve, initially at the lowest but very useful level of walk-in health care clinics and service facilities. Women on rural areas are generally getting more care for pre and post natal care, family planning, child health care, and better nutrition. Gradually too, a greater number of hospitals are emerging at the provincial or regional levels where a full range of medical treatment is available.

HEALTH CARE IN BRAZIL (ECONOMIST, JULY, 30, 2011)

The 1988 Constitution declared health care to be the right of all citizens, and an obligation of the state. But (as usual) there is a gap between this lofty ambition and reality. Again as usual, funding is an inadequate hotch-potch of national and local government money, and service varies wildly from place to place. Brazil now has a Unified Health System (combined from formal and informal systems), but covered medical service reaches about 50% of the population; another 25% have private care, and the remainder are in remote rural areas or dangerous urban slums. Government payments are often inadeqate, and therefore about 60% of health care cost is private. (US = 53%)

Politicians have tended to be neglectful and the public passive, but the current political campaign is seeing health care as a dominating issue. Diagnoses suggest the system is not only underfunded and often lacking, but that it squanders money, especially on questionable deals with drug manufacturers. Some new competitors are challenging the government's near monopoly on health care for the low income patients including new lower cost health care plans, cheaper X-rays and more competition in the provision of other lab services.

SYRIA: WHAT'S LEFT OF IT

Before its current utterly tragic and distructive civil war, Syria had been making serious efforts to upgrade its health care system and its public provision of clean drinking water and adequate waste disposal systems, especially in urban slums. There was more money for hospitals and other health care facilities, and the salaries of doctors, nurses and technicians were gradually being improved. The usual gap existed between cities – especially Damascus, the capital – and the rest of the country, but to some extent, that gap had been narrowed. While health care was supposedly "free", patients had in fact to pay many fees in order to get care, and the state health insurance program was realistically available only to the ruling class, employees of the government and State Owned Enterprises, and the military. But still, statistics showed that many health care indicators showed measurable improvement in critical areas such as healthy child birth, child malnutrition, life expectancy, the incidence of many diseases, and the increase of child immunizations. The government's 10 Year Plan formuated in 2000 called for moving more public hospitals into independent status.

But then tragically, the country self distructed. More than 200,000 citizens have died, and another 11 million, or half of the pre-war population, has been displaced within the country or have fled to safety elsewhere. Hospitals have been destroyed. Doctors and nurses have fled the country. Medications are scarce or totally unavailable. Communicable diseases are resurging. Syria has ceased to exist as a viable country anymore.

EGYPT: REALLY UNREAL

Egyptian health care facilities have sunk to pitiful lows. "Today even Egypt's rulers avoid state hospitals. When the Prime Minister visited two hospitals, he saw uniformly grim conditions: obsolete and dirty equipment, overflowing sewage, patients surrounded by stray animals. Most Egyptians shun the state run system." (Economist, 20 June 15). A government insurance system covers about 54% of the population, mostly public workers (including the military) and their families and school children, but only 8% of those insured use public outpatient clinics. Nearly 75% of health costs are paid out-of-pocket. There is some provision of free services for the most needy and those suffering emergencies, but even those covered often face "informal charges" without which many facilities could not operate. Medical personnel are so badly paid that they often go on strikes and protest marches, and many shift to private providers or move abroad. "There are more Egyptian doctors in Saudi Arabia than in the Egyptian primary care system." Now, about 500 of Egypt's 4,000 state run clinics do not even have a doctor. Facilities are widely perceived as grossly mismanaged and they are so corrupt that 75% of all Egyptians think of them as crooked according to a Transparency International survey. This and similar views of other public services were heavy contributors to the Arab Spring insurgency that threw out President Hosni Mubarak.

The government spends about 1.75% of GDP on health care which is well below international standards. The Constitution was amended last year to require an expenditure of 3% of GDP, and some increase has occurred over the last two years. But huge amounts of money are still spent on political subsidies for bread, fuel and even sugar. And the government still plans to spend huge sums on a new national capital.

INDIA: A DECLARATION OF DEFEAT

Somewhere in time after independence, India measured the challenge posed by the health care needs of the nation – and seemingly declared defeat. Care in medical area after medical area is now among the worst in the world. Immunizations of children for various diseases are an arena of terrible neglect, and there is growing discontent. Increasingly, there have been strikes among doctors and other health care workers against low wages, lack of equipment and facilities, and a feeling of arrogant neglect. In addition, the people are also rising up to complain about overcrowding and poor service in public hospitals, to the extent that these facilities are being forced to hire more security forces. The media have almost totally neglected health care as a significant arena of interest. The political leadership has ignored the problems for decades. According to reports of the World Health Organization and UNICEF, measles alone is estimated to be killing 100,000 children each and every year. There is serious neglect of immunizations for diphtheria, polio, BCG and Hepatitis B. And this miserable record exists despite the facts that solutions are easily available, and that other often poor or developing countries are making the substantial improvements that the Indian health care bureaucracy somehow cannot manage.

Public expenditure on health care has been around 1% of GDP for more than the last 20 years – among the lowest rates in the world. Indian health care facilities are far too few, most are totally inadequate – poorly managed, lacking both facilities and equipment and adequately trained staff. According to Druze an Sen, "as reported in a recent study, absenteeism rates among health workers ranged between 35 and 58% in different Indian states – and in one district, more than half of the health care sub-centres were found to be closed during regular opening hours. Meanwhile, local residents suffered horrendous levels of morbidity: one third of all adults had a cold during the 30 days preceding a survey; 42% had body ache; 33% had fever; 23% suffered from fatigue; 11% had bad chest pains, and more than half suffered from anemia." This horrible pattern goes on and on.

The real issue is just exactly that: this terrible performance **has gone on and on** for decades of political and governmental neglect and indifference. This is the essence of India's declaration of defeat. Some of India's most significant human needs have gone unmet or seriously attacked or even seriously challenged. Part of this sense of defeat is the enormity of the need. India has more than 1.3 billion human beings, including more than 1 billion in rural and village locations that are hard to reach because of medieval transportation facilities. This enormous need seems to have intimidated generations of politicians, frightened the middle classes and wealthy property owners fearing the costs, and overwhelmed a totally inadequate health care structure and bureaucracy. It is part of the consequences of this colossal challenge that the Indian governments at all levels have punted and attempted to deny full health care responsibility, and have shifted much of the problem to the private sector, or forced it back on the patients themselves. Public facilities are widely inadequate, but private health care is not often much better – even for the rich.

Private providers are a chancy proposition: they are almost totally unregulated and seldom evaluated. Many are unscrupulous, and there is an unsavory record of fraud, over-treatment, improper pricing, unneeded and very expensive surgery, and shady deals with medical suppliers. This ineffective reliance on private provision has allowed the political leadership to avoid facing up to the inadequacies of public health care systems and performance, and thus improvement has been painfully slow and spastic. The realism of India's poor make it mandatory that a better public solution must be created. Rural poverty in India exceeds 34%. Urban poverty exceeds 28%. And even more seriously, poverty definitions are seen as too low and there are huge numbers of Indians who are desperately poor just above these lines. In total, it is estimated that 350 million people are living in poverty, with health care beyond their reach.

MYANMAR: URBAN CRISIS

Yangon, Myanmar has tripled to 7.4 million people since 1984 – an absolutely astounding increase that has left the city and the national government far behind. Yangon has marvelous plans for economic development over the next 25 years-- $5 billion this year. But actual investment is more like $900 million. But critics think this way: instead of fancy highway overpasses, why not just repair the broken stop signs? Instead of a plan for vastly increasing the Public Sanitation Department, why not put out lots more waste receptacles, and hire a few guys in a truck to empty them? Why do people have to buy bottled water; why not just fix the hundreds of broken pipes? Why has the sewage system not been upgraded since 1888, and why does it only serve about 10% of the population? Why is power so unreliable that there are large areas where users suffer extended cuts in service? The government's plans, however delayed, have made the city the focus of most foreign investment in the country. But as a consequence, rents in the limited supply of decent buildings have been driven up so much that people of lower income have literally been driven out of the city. And to an unfortunate degree, new residents are poor from rural areas in search of work, and not finding it. This is seen as a sure recipe for more and worse slums. In essence, a smoke screen of fancy "economic development" masks the continuing failure of both the national and city governments to deal effectively with their human services problems. (Economist, Jan. 31, 2015)

INDIA: CATCHING ON

Where China was heavily committed to Soviet-inspired heavy industrial production which is enormously polluting, India is developing more in the services sector which is far less polluting. Also, China stubbornly and deliberately ignored a whole range of serious environmental problems, but India seems to be learning from this experience and is moving more solidly on many fronts. Still, families still use smoky fuels for meal cooking and these fires "claim about 1 million lives a year". Stack gas scrubbing is well known, but very slow to be installed. As usual in India, what the law says and what the government or the people really do are two different things, and enforcement is both weak and corrupt. Also, the Indian power grid is so bad that many companies and homes have had to install local generators which are both inefficient and highly polluting. In China, the government tended to dump environmental problems on the provinces and cities, knowing full well they were totally unable to deal with them. In India, the local government structure has much more capability if they choose to use it.

HARM REDUCTION IN IRAN

Despite a heavy anti-drug campaign, Iran has become the principal transit country for drugs from Afghanistan, and in 2002, it accounted for ¼ of world opiate seizures. Iran itself suffers from high levels of addiction, added crime, and high costs for treatment and prevention. Opium production was prohibited by law in 1955; now the government has to run an opium maintenance program. After the Revolution, drug controls on the growth of opium poppies became ineffectual, in part because the regime was fixated by worries about alcohol, which is a Sharia prohibition. After the Revolution, health services facilities were closed in favor of compulsory "rehabilitation" camps, and the main policy was one of severe punishments. During the 80's, courts sent thousands of people to these centers or to prisons -- a total of 1.7 million. But in the last analysis, this heavy enforcement approach is considered a failure, and more and more, thinking has turned toward social rehabilitation and health prevention and treatment measures. Some of the outpatient clinics than had been closed down have been reopened, but not a lot of progress is evident. HID/AIDS treatment and prevention is still "a drop in the ocean". (Beckley Foundation, July, 2005)

But there seems to have been a fall in opium production in Iran itself, in favor of transshipping it from Afghanistan, which is now the largest producer of opium in the world. Iran serves markets in the Gulf, Russia, Turkey and Europe. 65% of all drug seizures are in Asia, and 25% of the world total is in Iran. 10% of the population in large cities are said to be addicted, despite mandatory drug screening before marriage, on application for government jobs, and even when applying for driving licenses. Official figures list about 1.2 million addicts, but other sources say the number is closer to 3.3 million.

The justice system processed about 270,000 offenders in 2000, with 80,000 prisoners already in jail. In the 90's, more than 140 officers and 900 offenders were killed. 94% of offenders are men; 94% are living with families, including many young men who can't find work. There now is a high rate of HIV/AIDS infection among injecting drug users, with widespread needle contamination.

In general, the UNODC now reports that more than half of the world's opiate users are in Asia (7.8 million), primarily in countries surrounding Afghanistan and Myanmar, especially in Iran, Kyrgyzstan and Laos, with new worries about Iraq. What has followed is economic decline, high unemployment, high medical and enforcement costs, and social dislocation. The sense is however, that this problem has little or nothing to do with religion, and while Imams are not really part of the problem, they are also not part of the solution, preferring to rely on traditional theological opposition to alcohol carrying over into drugs.

WORLD REFUGEE PROBLEMS

The world now is facing the worst refugee crisis since WW II, and it is not clear how this crisis can be successfully dealt with. The population of refugees/displaced persons in the world is now estimated to be 60 million – including both refugees and internally displaced persons. But there are millions more who are now living in half ruined cities, and further millions living in jails and prison camps. This does not include those who immigrate voluntarily, even if they do so if threatened. In fact, the dispossessed fall into several different categories:

1. Legal immigrants
2. Illegal immigrants
3. Asylum seekers fleeing government persecution
4. Refugees fleeing for self protection
5. Temporary job seekers
6. People internally displaced in their own country
7. People externally displaced, with the intent to return.

Countries with large refugee problems:

Bangladesh
DRC
Iraq
Kenya
Lebanon
Mali
Myanmar/Burma
Niger
Somalia
Sudan/S. Sudan
Syria
Guatemala
Eretria
Burundi
Afghanistan
Cameroon

CAR
Algeria
Chad
Ethiopia
Gaza/Palestine
Libya
Nigeria
Pakistan
Rwanda
Vietnam
Turkey
Yemen – 28 countries

Of the 60 million, 86% come from developing countries, but this includes Egypt, Turkey and Jordan. It is estimated that more than half of these refugees will never be able or willing to return to their country of origin. 50% of the true refugees are living in camps, while the other 50% are dispersed into the private world, and most of them are in cities where they stand a better chance of finding work and housing, and of being absorbed into the informal economy. In many countries (Iraq, the Central African Republic, S. Sudan, Syria, Yemen), there are new waves of an estimated 500,000 people who are in deep trouble, but are unable to flee. Iraq still has 2.4 million refugees, 4.5 million internally displaced, and another 8.2 million seriously at risk. In Syria, nearly one half of its 23 million people are in serious trouble. 7.6 million are displaced in the country; 3.3 million have fled to other countries and are mostly living in refugee camps -- 1.1 million in Lebanon; 1.2 million in Turkey; 620,000 in Jordan. In Sudan, there have been 2.9 million victims. 670,000 are refugees to other countries; 240,000 are internal refugees; and a further 2 million internally displaced. In Darfur, 450,000 people have been killed, 2.5 million are internally displaced, and more than 4 million are destitute. In total, it is estimated that the situation is so bad that about 7 million people out of a total population of about 30 million, are in desperate shape and need massive help. Massive conflicts disrupted agricultural planting, and the country is now facing serious shortages of food. Many public services scarcely function.

Refugees the world over are likely to be the poor imposing themselves on other poor; people who need homes and jobs and schools and medical care are descending on countries that already lack enough of these things. It is pitiful that refugees and displaced persons end up in ruined countries like Yemen, Iraq, Lebanon, Congo or Ethiopia. Half of these people end up in camps, where donor countries and volunteer organizations can work to provide for them. But astonishingly, the other half end up absorbed by the people of cities and villages.

The refugee camps face the usual daunting problems of finding enough food, shelter, water, clothing and sanitation for almost desperate human beings who are abjectly poor and often devoid of hope; and however sincere the assistance may be, it is seldom better than basic. A school may be a flip chart under a tree; medical care may be a band aid and an aspirin; shelter may be a piece of canvas or a card board lean-to. The great flood of refugees and displaced persons has washed up from the horrors of the Middle East and Africa into Turkey, Egypt and half of Europe, and it is marvelous to understand the very human response in these countries to provide care and assistance as best they can. In the refugee camps however, other kinds of human problems must be dealt with. People want to shift from place to place, hoping somehow to find better conditions, so transportation has become an urgent problem. Refugee camps will have people committing the usual human sins of fighting, cheating, and stealing, so there is a new and urgent need for some kind of policing and a legal frame of reference. Camps are also especially vulnerable to the intervention of communicable diseases, drug abuse and sanitary failures. And ominously, some camps are targets for predatory criminal groups, or recruitment sources for terrorist organizations. The universal fear has become that 60 million refugees and displaced persons are irretrievably destined for a life of pain and disaster, rather than some bright new future.

Many countries are now facing the dilemma of what to do with refugees and displaced persons, many of whom will be permanent and will never go back to their own country. It is a conflict of conscience vs. practicality. Even rich countries are reluctant to spend scarce money on a bunch of foreign people. In many countries, the unions see these foreigners as threats for a limited number of jobs. Many people who feel a heavy social conscience tend to think of the problem as needing a "cradle to grave" government provided solution. Others see the possibility for creating an attitude of providing opportunity; a program of fostering and assisting self reliance rather than a program of socialist handouts. Many of the refugees will find themselves entering the informal economy, which produces conflicts of its own.

The UN is trying to raise more than $16 billion of special funding to take care of the refugees most at risk. In fact, the UN is joining with its own United Nations High Commissioner for Refugees (UNHCR), and this strengthened combination is already thinking of the long term. It is now being assumed that many (most) of these refugees will never be able or willing to return to their old countries. So planning must start now with local governments for the bottom up provision of schooling, medical care, roads, and unemployment compensation. The social issues will multiply, since refugees are often competing for jobs and support with the residents of relatively poor countries. Thus, the deeper consequences of the horrible conflicts around the world are becoming more obvious and scarier. There is a whole new population of 50-60 million people who are not stable, and cannot rely either on a supportive government or the accumulation of their own personal resources. Part of the solution apparently will be a long term program of shifting refugees out of camps to countries willing to take them in a new citizens; that is, absorption from the bottom up.

LATIN AMERICAN CHALLENGES

Despite recent efforts througout the region to improve social services, most Latin American countries started from such a low base that there remains a serious core of people who have not benefitted much from this improvement. Poverty still remains a major problem in many countries. People still lack the skills, the understanding, and the motivation to prepare themselves for good jobs, or to find where they are. Many do not even know how to take advantage of available social programs and services. There tend to develop "communities" of very poor and underserved, many of them in urban slums. There is a growing feeling that even providing money in the form of cash transfer schemes is not successful. There is an increasing understanding that there is another form of social problem in the form of "the near poor", who may have inched up from abject poverty, but are still living pay check to pay check and are highly vulnerable to layoffs, emergencies, or family health problems. So, the double commitments to government aid and self-help arguments are coming into question. So too is the premise that, if the government would only provide education and health care, and fix the roads, and provide electricity, all will be corrected. Part of the problem is the increasing concern that, in relatively poor economies, either there is not enough money in total, or the ability to suck taxes out of the system has reached its limits.

In general, the United States and other countries and multi-government agencies in the area pursue the following policies:

1. Promote free trade
2. Promote local economic development
3. Strengthen legal systems
4. Equip and train police
5. Equip and train military units
6. Reduce the drug trafficking
7. Reduce the number of migrants to the U. S.

The translation of these policies: talk a good game, but don't get sucked into the gears.

VIETNAM AND ETHNIC CONFLICT

Vietnam has ethnic minorities totalling about 12 million of the country's total population of about 90 million. There is a long history of intractable conflict between them at various levels which has survived all kinds of governments from kingdoms to Communist centrism. The major group is the Kinh; a large minority is the Imong, but there are more than 50 other minority groups. The Kinh have dominated, and they see all other groups as underclasses of undeserving poor. There is the added growth of a new split between the old rural poor, and a growing urban middle class. As the Vietnamese retreated from rigorous State Socialism reluctantly toward a market based economy, ethnic minorities tend to be left behind; ignored, or tolerated, or perhaps cheated and robbed. Land grabs are prevalent, of two kinds; one, siezure of lands by the government for mines, plantations, dams, industrial sites, etc.; and second land grabs by crooks or corrupt government officials, without adequate compensation. The Montagnards are particularly hard hit, because the old guard that still infests the residual Communist leadership still resents the fact that they fought along with the S. Vietnamese and the Americans in the Vietnam War. The government resents and attacks any form of opposition, but it is must seriously concerned with these ethnic groups because of their extraordinary coherence and self-identity. Bad economics, Kinh preferment, corruption, prejudice and land grabbing means that grinding poverty in the hustings is still very obvious, and bitterly resented.

CHINA AND THE ENVIRONMENT

Consider the judgments of official sources and expert opinions both in China and from the outside, about China and the environment:

* Agricultural runoff is "the worst in the world"
* Soil erosion is "the worst in the world"
* Desertification is "the worst in the world"
* Air pollution: China is the world's largest producer of carbon dioxide
* China has 16 of the 20 world's most polluted cities
* China suffers from "the worst river water cessation in the world"
* The Yellow River is the most silt clogged in the world
* China is the world's largest user of coal, the world's largest producer of carbon dioxide, and acid rain falls in one third of the country
* Almost every river in the country is heavily polluted
* 25-40% of all mercury emissions in the world come from China

* Only 20% of waste water is treated
* In the last half century, 332 Chinese dams have failed, including "the worlds worst dam disaster" – the Banqiao and Shimanan dams in Henan Province which collapsed and killed an estimated 80,000 to 200,000 people. (Bingman, "Reforming China's Government")

Economic development in China has meant breakneck urbanization, heavy concentration on manufacturing, greatly expanded pollutants from coal fired electrical power generation, heavy metals dumped into the air, and nasty chemicals dumped into the water. Heavy metals in the water are highly concentrated – 2,000 times as high as the official government standard. Japan and Korea are suffering from acid rain produced by China's coal power electricity plants, and from dust storms carrying toxic dust. Scarce water resources are simply being recklessly dissipated. All of these problems are heavy contributors to environmental failures and crises, and all have been known by the government from the very beginning. The problem of environmental pollution was first addressed at a national conference on the subject in 1973, and six years later, the National People's Congress passed the Environmental Protection Law. Five years after that, in 1984, the National Environmental Protection Agency (NEPA) was formed. In 1998 it was promoted to ministerial level as the State Environmental Protection Administration (SEPA) under the State Council. The law was amended to require environmental impact studies for all major construction projects and for imposing stiff fines for violations. Many environmental groups were started, and public opinion polls were almost unanimous in calling for stricter enforcement.

But despite all of these official efforts, extraordinarily little has ever really been done. This is a classic example of the vital needs of China's citizens are being deliberately ignored by the government Environmental issues seem particularly difficult to resolve in the Chinese political system because of the continuing clash with economic development goals and understandable conflict with local governments over the money problem. So the government continues to issue pompous, sterile utterances about how they are solving these problems while all environmental problems continue to get worse.

The Chinese Communist Party (CCP) issued its 11th "Five Year Program" in 2005 which calls for a 20% improvement in energy efficiency by 2010 but 2010 has come and gone, and few goals have been met. Energy efficiency for example is a very expensive, highly technical and long term activity, and there seems to be no adequate current explanation of how the Chinese could achieve this goal. "Socialist industrialization" has been highly wasteful because land and water continue to be government owned, and these assets were given away (or peddled) usually in the name of economic development, and recklessly squandered. Water and energy have been supplied to favored cities either free or at highly subsidized rates. All governments and most State Owned Enterprises (SOEs) had positive motives to consume assets if it will produce more profit.

Nor is this really a matter of China being a poor country. The government now has large sums of money that it can deploy, but environmental problems continue to be low priority. The national government avoided responsibility by "delegating" responsibility for environmental problems to local governments – provinces, townships, counties and cities. But at the time, all of these jurisdictions were still very poor and seriously disorganized after the Maoist neglect. The commune system displaced much of the normal government apparatus with amateur incompetents, and forced pathological practices on the country. For example, hundreds of thousands of valuable trees were simply cut down to provide fuel for hundreds of thousands of back yard iron smelting furnaces, which were a total failure. It is true that deforestation had been going on for centuries, but the Maoist era simply made it very much worse very fast. Unrealistic production quotas forced overproduction, land wastage, more forest clearing, production of the wrong things, and the wasting of huge sums of scarce funds. Terracing and irrigation were rapidly expanded, often with disastrous consequences. Dams, terraces, reservoirs and cisterns were so poorly built that many quickly collapsed or have been abandoned, since they often served marginal land that had low production potential and high costs. Activities in the hands of collectives have been better, but still amateurish and exposing low managerial abilities.

Beijing has reacted typically: the government kept announcing bold new "30 Year Plans", but everybody knew that local governments have never had the money to implement them. In fact, there has never had a sufficiently sturdy source of funds for environmental problems, and the national government has never had any intention of filling the gap. The CCP likes to point out that it is "spending more than $10 billion on environmental concerns", which is truly a pitiful trivial sum. In addition, the CCP has also developed a tendency to shift part of the blame onto "multi-national corporations". But this is merely classic CCP thinking – find somebody else to blame, and conceal your own sins. "China's environmental problems stem as much from China's corrupt and indifferent political system as from Beijing's continued focus on economic growth. Local officials and enterprise leaders routinely – and with impunity – ignore environmental laws and regulations, illegally reallocate environmental protection funds or simply steal them. (Bingman, "Reforming China's Government).

The local governments feel that they have been unfairly stuck with these problems with absolutely no help from anybody else. The people at the bottom can't, and the people at the top won't. The SOEs for example have never been held responsible. The private sector doesn't want the added expense or the responsibility. Many environmental problems are ancient: floods, droughts, overgrazing, desertification, soil erosion, mining wastes. But there are also new problems that are a direct consequence of the economic development programs such as hundreds of thousands of new industrial sites dumping pollutants into the air or water; millions of new automobiles; accelerating exhaustion of water resources; and wastage of energy and raw materials. Over expansion of cities has created rapidly growing urban problems. Lack of raw materials and energy tends to drive up prices. While China's government benefits greatly from foreign sales, it has not yet made satisfactory progress in meeting the consumer needs of its own people.

The success of economic development is vital to the survival of the CCP itself, and this cannot and will not be changed any time soon. Economic development has been the compelling and overpowering driver in China for almost 35 years. Because of this, China will not stop burning coal and creating acid rain. It will not willingly close industrial plants that pollute the air unless there is the risk of fatal political disaster. The CCP will not reverse its policy of dumping environmental problems on local governments, nor will it fund these governments. Neither the CCP nor anybody else has any idea of what to do about desertification, soil erosion and river silting, and even if they did, these problems are so enormous and complex that they are simply "mission impossible". Urban air pollution is not being dealt with, and in fact, is getting worse every day, and in cities lung diseases now kill more people than any other cause. The depletion of urban underground water aquifers is permanent and irreversible, and the exhaustion of these resources is speeding up. Urban expansion requires more water resources, urban sanitation, waste water treatment and other public services. It also means the rise in the number of households, millions of urban transportation trips, huge truck traffic to bring in supplies, vastly increased oil and gas consumption, and heavy and unremitting construction activity. It was not until the late 90s that the CCP appeared finally to wake up, and that is only because it finally began to realize the heavy economic penalties it created by its pathological neglect of environmental degradations. But the basic dilemma remains for the CCP: how can it meet these increasingly urgent demands without retrenching its economic development commitments?

And how long can it address its monumental environmental problems with its pompous, sterile utterances?

XI

THE NATIONAL JUSTICE SYSTEM: THE POLICE, THE MILITARY AND INTELLIGENCE SERVICES

It is reasonable for governments to develop and maintain a strong justice system of courts and judges, prosecutors, police and a military establishment. This structure is created and buttressed by a body of laws defining the nature of governance, the rights of individuals and organizations, and the limitation that society wants to impose on them. This legal system can and should be one of the greatest "bottom up" protections for the people and institutions of the nation. At the same time, the justice system is also one of the most important instruments for top down control. Both the people and the officials of the justice system believe in its independence and the equitable rule of law, and this puts the system in constant conflict with the top down control of centrist regimes. Thus, the drafting of laws and their enforcement should be the urgent and constant concern of the bottom up influences in the country.

Americans and Europeans are used to the concept that the civilian government must exert control over this military establishment, but history is full of very important occasions where the military has assumed control, and where all security forces act all but independently of civilian control. In many countries, the intelligence services have used their secret status to gather intelligence on domestic people and organizations as leverage. Think of the USSR, Pakistan, Iraq, Iran, N. Korea, Peru, and yes, the United States.

In the period following World War II, there have been 40-50 significant military coups de etat, and in some countries there have been successions of military regimes replaced by civilian governments that were again overthrown.

It seems surprising then that the historical pattern shows very few successful long term military regimes. Of 40 military coups since WW II, many have survived for only brief periods of 3-5 years, and at least 23 military regimes have been ultimately replaced (with varying degrees of success) by some form of civilian government. This is even true where military regimes have had long runs: South Korea after 30 years; Nigeria after 36 years (with a brief 4 year civilian government); Peru for 20 years; Ghana for 26 years.

Several military coups have however resulted in permanent long term tenure where the government either remained a military regime, or it evolved into a civilianized structure still mainly controlled by the military. These regimes include Argentina, Egypt, Guinea, Libya, Myanmar (former Burma), Pakistan, Somalia, and Indonesia until 1998. But whether or not the military actually controls the government, in most countries it becomes and remains a powerful and often controlling influence. In several countries, the military establishment that emerged from a great revolution earned (or assumed) the mantle of "Guardian of the Revolution" – a role with substantial support from the public, who accepted the military as a sort of guarantor and last resort protection from oppressive, corrupt or incompetent civilian rule. In some cases, there may have been real or apparent threats to the post-revolution governments, but in most cases (e. g. the USSR, the Peoples Republic of China, Turkey, Vietnam, or Cuba) the reputation of defenders of the revolution has been used as justification for leveraging or even overthrowing the civilian government.

Intelligence services enjoy no such reputation, and are feared because of their secrecy and the sense that their power is perverted because it cannot be controlled or moderated. Many intelligence services like those in the U. S., Iran, Pakistan, N. Korea and Peru have operated in ways that are hidden even from their own governments, and have pursued policies or activities that are deliberately in conflict with overall national policy.

This complex set of organizations and interrelationships have been undergoing a new set of changes in recent years. The "enemy" now is not just a formal government but may be one of a series of armed insurgent groups of varying purpose which may be independent, but may be sponsored by some government, largely through its intelligence services. Conventional weapons may now be largely obsolete because they cannot be used effectively against small informal opponent groups imbedded in the general population. Aircraft carriers and huge tanks and large bodies of troops cannot be brought to bear against such imbedded opponents. Nuclear weapons are useless because they might kill hundreds of thousands of innocent people and destroy valuable property. Insurgent groups are highly mobile, do not recognize borders or civilized conventions, and are perfectly willing to destroy everything or kill anybody caught in their way.

In many countries, the military establishment is third rate and excessively expensive. It is to the advantage of the military to exaggerate the supposed threats their country faces in order to justify demands for more money. In Nigeria, the army was a source of endless corruption for its leaders, and then it proved to be very ineffective when attempting to quell the incursions of the Muslim militant group Boko Haram in the northeast of the country. There are many instances where the army sat out conflicts in their barracks while opposition to insurgent groups was given over to informal militia groups armed and funded by it. Many armies in modern conflict situations have been revealed to be seriously inferior: ill trained, badly armed, underpaid and badly treated by their generals who spend their time looting the budget. One need only remember the collapse of units of the Iraqi army in the face of ISIS assault. The "military-industrial complex" in such situations are a swamp of corruption.

It is almost always to the advantage of the military to links themselves to the party in power. When they are in power, they still need some form of credibility with the general public and critical special interests. One of the greatest reasons – and justifications – of military intervention is how seriously bad the civilian government is. Military regimes have a very mixed bag of results, and almost all have eventually returned to civilian rule. National "military/industrial complexes" have unsavory reputations for enthusiastic corruption.

CHARACTERISTICS OF MILITARY ESTABLISHMENTS (WHY GOVERNMENTS GO WRONG)

Perhaps the most valuable asset of any military establishment is the long tradition of insistence on rigid discipline, top down authority, and obedience to command. These make sense under battlefield conditions, but are often ill adapted to the far less rigid realities of civilian rule. Military commanders thrust into civilian roles seem to find it difficult to accept the need for negotiation with elements in society. They prefer simply to issue orders and are often surprised and outraged when orders are challenged or ignored. Military officer training may produce good management skills but bad political skills.

Military establishments, whether in control of the government or not, seem to share other common characteristics. They tend to be ultra conservative, preferring the status quo however bad, to any urges for reform and change. Most seem to respect technology, but are better at utilizing it for military rather than civilian purposes. Most seem to become "bottomless pits", where no military expenditure seems excessive and social services programs never seem to win out in competitions for funding. The political arts of negotiation and compromise are poorly accepted or understood, and independent organizations such as public interest groups in civil society seem to be confusing, disruptive and often threatening.

One of the most important characteristics of these military establishments is the degree to which they could become financially self sustaining. In the USSR, the unstinting support of the military in the face of the Cold War permitted it to gain control of many vital sectors of the Soviet economy such as the electronics industry in which the military had unquestioned top priority to the exclusion of almost every other need. In Indonesia, the military owned and operated hundreds of profit making companies ranging from production of military hardware down to luxury hotels and restaurants, none of which had anything whatever to do with military readiness. Similar ownership was also true in the Chinese Red Army and elsewhere. This relative financial independence extended as well to any portions of the military budget which came through the civilian government. In most cases, there was little or no review of military budget proposals. Nobody in the oversight processes of the executive or legislative had the temerity to challenge even the smallest of budget items, and almost always the military request was quickly rubber stamped.

In modern day Russia, the government has been able to confront the greatly weakened military establishment and force military controlled assets into privatization, or SOEs. In Indonesia, the surge of revulsion against the undemocratic and corrupt regime of President Suharto, and the overthrow of his regime was in large part attributed to the dominant and brutal military establishment. This led to the final death of the cover story of military "protection of the revolution". A revitalized and newly democratic Indonesian government is finally in a position to wrest away from the military hundreds of its economic assets. Even the Chinese are doing the same with the "glorious Red Army" based on its successes in moving toward a more productive market based economy and the extraordinary reduction of the numbers of people living in poverty.

Military regimes with these characteristics have produced some of the worlds most vicious and tragic failed governments. And in many cases, the military is able to avoid even its basic military role, through the sponsorship of paramilitary organizations which are funded by the government to fight its battles against various forms of insurgency. The military stays in its barracks and lets the paramilitaries do the fighting. Generals wear their brilliant, medal bedecked uniforms in their military headquarters, but seldom lead troops in the field.

DILEMMAS OF MILITARY ESTABLISHMENTS

Most contemporary wars are civil wars involving two or more power groups fighting for power with little or no real justification. Usually there is no real prospect that either side is competent to manage a country and run a government and thus neither side "deserves" to win. While in the past many insurrectionist groups were communist and therefore had a supposed concept and philosophy, the basis for wars are now primarily two: that the "ins" are incompetent crooks and the "outs" will be better; and that ethnic, religious, or regional groups are being oppressed and need to be protected. These civil wars are especially intractable because accusations against the incompetence of the incumbent government are all too often true, and because religious or ethnic conflicts usually have some legitimacy and reactions to oppression or neglect are emotional and irrational. They are more like big feuds, with past outrages justifying the next outrages. Such wars appear totally incomprehensible to outsiders seeking a basis for mediation. Many are never really won or lost but fumble on forever.

Given weak and corrupt governments, it takes very little real force to mount an insurrection, and there seems to be lots of people to volunteer. Rebel leaders lack the knowledge or skills to govern, or any real sense of purpose or public policy. Mostly, their only ability is that of a local bandit chief who can hold together a few hundred armed fighters. Even if the rebels triumph, the new government seldom proves better than the old. Peace may be imposed through dictatorial methods, but the basic conflicts are not resolved. In these conflicts, the real losers are the citizens and the economy. Prior to WW II, casualties in the civilian population were relatively low at around 10-15% of all casualties. WW II changed that, and the civilian and military casualties were about 50/50. Now, the civil war style means that up to 75% of all casualties are civilian; and even most of the young men coerced into fighting on both sides are civilians rather than professional soldiers.

What is now being more fully realized is that such wars usually result in the long term destruction of the economy, the public infrastructure, and the personal assets of citizens. The high cost of armaments and supplies for both sides drains resources from the economy and squanders them on inconclusive destruction. For the government, taxes are raised and funds are diverted from other more needed public services. As public infrastructure is destroyed or deteriorates rapidly there is little or no money or workers to maintain and repair much less to catch up with the real needs of citizens. The whole economy is disrupted. Small businesses are destroyed or vandalized. Sources of industrial supplies and equipment dry up, or can no longer be afforded. This pattern fatally deteriorates the base of confidence in the government, even when there may be public support for resistance to the insurgents. For the insurgents, resources are obtained by blackmail and seizure, or from outside sources; and this sours the public on the insurgents. People are forced to learn a harsh lesson: failure to demand and support an effective government may result in utter catastrophe.

INDIA: THE USE OF PARAMILITARY FORCES

The military capability of India is supported by an extraordinary complex of police and semi-military organizations grouped under the general heading of the Paramilitary Forces of India. The first and most important level of such forces are the Central Police Organizations which function as a national police force dealing with a whole range of law enforcement matters ranging from insurrections to parades. These organizations include the State Armed Police, which is a highly mobile and well armed force of more than 450,000 troops, and functions independent of the military, reporting to civilian bosses. It is supported and reinforced by the Central Reserve Police Force (CRPF) which is a volunteer force with more than 300,000 active members, plus a Home Guard and Civil Defense forces with almost one million more members. The Central Reserve Police Force also maintains a Rapid Action Force and the Anti-Riot Police to deal with particularly violent threats, and a new 10,000 man Rapid Action Battalion for Resolute Action (COBRA) has been formed under the CRPF specifically to deal with the Naxalite Maoist insurgents in northeast India.

Unfortunately, the police in India have a very bad reputation. According to an editorial in the Economic and Political Weekly of India "Indians view the police, the most visible arm of the State, with distrust and fear and consider it one of the most corrupt of the government agencies. It has the powers to detain and arrest citizens, and verify documents essential for citizen services. And as custodial deaths and rapes show, it is not uncommon for the police forces themselves to break the law and even violate basic human rights. In the last 30+ years, there have been at least eight major assessments by the National Police Commission promising major reforms, but little has really happened. Changing the police's image as the pliable instrument of the rich and powerful will require a complete overhaul of the colonial mindset that colours its attitude towards the ordinary citizen."

At a next level are the Central Paramilitary Forces which are linked more closely with the Indian Army, and during wartime, would serve directly under the armed forces chain of command. It includes such units as the Coast Guard, the Border Security Force, the Central Industrial Security Force, the Tibetan Border Police, and many other special purpose units. The total population of all of these units exceeds 8.7 million troops. All of these organizations are headed by a senior Indian Police Service Officer apparently to provide some coherent leadership to a very complex array of military and police establishments, which are hugely expensive.

SUDAN: POLICE AS THE DEFENDERS OF OPPRESSION

Sudan is a somber example of the failure of a military government to rise above its own narrow elitist motives. Sudan gained independence from Egypt and G. Britain in 1956. Within two years, the military has seized power, and is in power still. The military regime was very narrowly confined to Arab Islamists, with an extraordinary overlay of Marxist/Leninist doctrine, and it set out to impose, by force if necessary, both Arabization and Islam on a widely diverse country of 25 million people. They succeeded in alienating the devout elements of the Muslim community as well as the Christian/Animist South. The result was two civil wars: one from 1960 to 1972, and the second which began about 1982 and is still not fully resolved. Thus, over the 40 year period of national independence, 34 years have been spent in self destructive civil conflict and the current war is the longest running in modern African history. It is usual to characterize the main conflict as being religious – the Muslim North vs. the Christian/ Animist South. But the regime in Khartoum has also excluded non-Arab Muslims in parts of the country, and many of the motivations for conflict are not religious at all but deal with efforts to impose centrist authoritarian control over a population that is in fact a loose array of very localized tribal, village or town interests who want mainly to be left alone to work out their own futures. The military regime used savage repression, purges and executions, banning of communist organizations, removal of public officials, and banning political parties and the media.

The leaders of the independence movement, the Sudan People's Liberation Army (SPLA) however began to overcome many of the ancient tribal differences and initiated elements of civil government in areas they occupied, where the main policy was one of relying on and reinforcing local participation and chiefs as voices for the populace. This policy allowed them to build such a powerful alliance that the region was able to declare its independence from its northern Arab oppressors, and to create the world's newest country of South Sudan. Then, tragically, these suppressed conflicts have created S. Sudan's own horrible civil war.

SIERRA LEONE: ETERNAL CONFLICT

In Sierra Leone, independence from Great Britain in 1961 led to a much despised military regime that eliminated parliamentary governance and created a one party state in 1978 which precipitated a 25 year civil war. The Revolutionary United Front (RUF) was not a very attractive alternative, and was built around the worst elements of anti-social anti-establishment youths who were described as "a good-for-nothing bunch, best avoided." And yet both the government and the RUF cultivated these youths either as thugs to do the government's dirty work or as guerillas for the RUF army. These malcontents were, in later years joined by a more educated and activist set of youths who began to push for a more political agenda. In the 1980's, RUF had begun to receive substantial help from Liberia. Many of the fighters and some of the leaders were Liberian, and Liberia was used as a safe haven and training ground for RUF forces. By 1991, the RUF had gained enough strength to launch more serious attacks against the government, and were joined at times by elements of the army. They succeeded in overthrowing the president in 1997, only to have him restored by Nigerian led external forces. By 1999, RUF controlled half of the country, but a combination of the capture of their leader, Alfred Foday Sankoh, the collapse of critical assistance from Liberia, declining revenues from mining, rampant smuggling and corruption, and UN intervention with 17,000 troops, finally drove the parties to the negotiation table and produced a cease fire in 2002 which held to the point that the 11 year old war could be declared to be over. Here again, the military regime had little to offer the country except harsh centrist control. It had little or no skill in dealing with the civilian population, had no intention of negotiating or compromising, had no interest in civil administration, allowed the deterioration of civil government, social services and public infrastructure, and wallowed in incompetence and corruption. Eternal war, followed by eternal incompetence.

INDIA: CORRUPT POLICE

In India, the police are widely involved in corruption, usually of a minor nature. Edward Luce in his book "In Spite of the Gods" cites an example. In New Delhi, there are 500,000 people who operate bicycle rickshaws, yet there is an entirely arbitrary ceiling of 99,000 permits to operate. This means that the government forces more than 400,000 to operate illegally and the police force them to pay bribes to survive. Similarly, street hawkers are deliberately kept in a similar state of limbo. While the streets are theoretically free, in fact, the hawkers pay monthly fees to the police or to the excise department.

Or consider the provisional court judges and officials who have spent government funds illegally on cell phones, laptops, furniture, rail tickets, vacations, household goods, and so forth. Meanwhile, the police are seen as threatening and abusing innocent people to create a shield for influential offenders, including known criminals. "Police use "encounter officers". When a high level police official decides that an obvious criminal or corrupted official will not be arrested, or will not come to trial, or will never be convicted, the police official may assign an "encounter officer" to kill the crook." This does not, however, include the crooks who are the patrons of the police themselves.

India's government seems stubbornly unable to provide even the most basic of amenities to many of its poor, such as public toilets for the huge urban slums, or chalk for school teachers in the countryside, or clean syringes in the country's health clinics. Even in the massive food subsidy program, there are unbelievable diversions of both money and the food itself. In the state of Bihar, India's second poorest, with a population of 75 million, more than 80% of such food aid is stolen."

In The Central African Republic, the bitter failure of its leaders produced wars, insurrections, failed elections, massive corruption, State decay, an out of control military, bad laws, ignored laws, criminalization, false hopes, and 50 years of terror and oppression. Most of the responsibilities of government had passed out of the hands of the formal government – a masterpiece of abject failure.

In Afghanistan there was a civil war won by the Taliban in 1994, and while they have been dislodged, they continue to attack the government, and maintain alliance with the Taliban of Pakistan. Insurgencies of all kinds continue at high levels, involving the Afghan Taliban, the Haqqani Group, al-Qaeda, strange tie-ins with the Pakistani Taliban, and the Pakistani army Inter Service Intelligence (ISI) service. Thus, the huge unrest created by the Taliban has all but destroyed the country over a period of more than 20 years and counting. The Pakistani ISI has endlessly meddled for specious reasons, and often in direct conflict with the policies of the central government. It ranks as one of the most "out-of-control" intelligence services in the world.

In the Republic of Congo, private militias were created by conflicting political groups which rejected the formal military attacks. The winner then got "elected" and ruled as an ostensible Marxist-Leninist, but was really simply was an authoritarian military regime. This once again illustrates how difficult to tell one group of thugs from the other.

CHINA: FINALLY, THE BOOM IS LOWERED

In China which is notorious for its corrupt public officials, Zhou Yongkang has been in deep trouble, and most feel that it is about time. For the last five years, he has been largely responsible for the state security and intelligence apparatus. He has recently been arrested despite his exalted political status and is facing a variety of criminal charges. And once he had been arrested, investigators and the media were free to discuss him openly. What has been revealed is rotten for two reasons. First, Zhou has been a very nasty human being. "He is a thief, a bully, a philanderer, and a traitor who sold state secrets. He enriched himself, his family, his many mistresses and his cronies at vast loss to the government. Second, his arrest has now been added to a sobering array of other top Party and government officials who have been criminals. "Other party officials have faced criminal charges. Chen Xitong, Mayor of Beijing; Chen Leangyu, Mayor of Shanghai; Bo Xilai, former party secretary in Chongqing; and dozens of others at the second and third levels of party authority. The CCP believes it is now "saving face", but the real and more important question now being asked: why did the Party, for decades and in so many high places, put so many rotten people in positions of power?

These scandals come at a time when the CCP is attempting serious and genuinely needed reforms of the national military establishment. By 2015, it had been reduced another 300,000 to just about 2,000,000. There are some solid efforts to undertke a major reform of the overall military command and communications structure. It is agreed that there is a need to beef up the PLA Air Force and the PLA Navy, and it is expected that this will mean further cuts in the staffing and equipment of the ground army. The PLA tends to favor front line combat troops over staffs and services, but increasingly, this is seen as sort of outdated. "Many Chinese analysts argue that, as now constituted, the PLA would not be able to conduct modern information-intensive military operations, one purpose of which is to integrate all services properly. Another element, seldom even mentioned officially, is the long standing concern that many top generals have been highly corrupt. An anti-corruption purge is now apparently looking seriously at 50 of them.

INTERPOL: STEALING IS EASY

Ronald K. Noble, Secretary-General of Interpol reports how very easy it is to rob a bank electronically these days, no mask and gun needed. Organized criminal groups will go online and steal small amounts, maybe 1-2 thousand from medium sized accounts. They might do this in bank A for a month, then shift to bank B. This theft is seen as too small to be cost-effective to pursue. It is cross border, expensive to investigate, difficult to track, and crosses jurisdictions. Meanwhile, huge sums of money quietly disppear.

Interpol now has <u>20 million</u> stolen or lost passports and visas in their data base. In 2009, they did 300 million searches. "In 2009, there were over 500 million international arrivals where passports were **not** checked against the Interpol data base, which contains records on over 11 million stolen passports and 9 milliion other documents. We have technology to identify false passports being used by war criminals, terrorists, assassins, drug traffikers and fraudsters." Every time somebody is arrested for any form of terrorist or narcotics violation, his/her fingerprints, photos and DNA is taken. But six years later, there are only about 40 countries that do routinely screen passports. Where countries do real screening, crooks simply tend to shift their activity elsewhere.

Noble's wish list states that it is in every country's best interest to make sure their borders are monitored 24 hours a day, seven days a week. All countries should screen passports of all international air arrivals against Interpol data bases. All prison escapees, known terrorists or other dangerous people should be reported to Interpol. Like it or not, governments should track and corrupt officials, especially in law enforcement, and prevent their corrupt careers.

A BOTTOM UP APPROACH FOR FIGHTING TERRORISM

Terrorist groups are always oppressive and never rational. Their emotions may be in part religious: the desire to secure the triumph of the Righteous. They may be in part a reaction of the failures of national governments and societies: corruption, theft, lying, oppression, fear, and mind numbing unfairness or simply eternal bumbling incompetence. But in large part, they are wholly irrational; the willingness to blow oneself up to kill innocent civilians. The only substantial proposal these terrorist groups seem to offer is "Sharia Law", but dozens of countries, including most of the larger ones with substantial Muslim populations already offer some version of Sharia Law which exists compatibly with more secular laws from other sources.

There appears to be an increasing recognition that dealing with terrorist forces from the top down is not succeeding. Pompous speeches in the UN move nothing. The military has great difficulty dealing with opponents who conceal themselves within the civilian community, so aircraft carriers, heavy bombers, and 70 ton tanks are of little value. Civilian governments have such bad reputations that people are unwilling to rat out insurgents to governments they hate.

In a sense, it is the police and not the military that appear to be better designed to deal with terrorist groups and individuals. It is impossible for the police to decide in advance where terrorists may strike, and this is especially true with suicide bombers who look like all other citizens on the streets. And suicide bombers are the real "drones" in this conflict – not the pilotless aircraft that the military have come to love. Suicide bombers can hit almost any target, at almost any time, and they do not worry about killing or wounding innocent civilians;

in most cases, serious harm to civilians and public facilities is the very purpose of the attack.

Therefore, it appears that the best hope for the fight against terrorists is not from the top down but from the bottom up. The main weapons may be information and propaganda. These groups must be stigmatized. There must be more determined efforts to solicit the support and assistance of the general public on the basis of moral and humanitarian issues. In many countries, bad governance has been cited to justify the growth of terrorists as "liberators", and some serious reduction of oppressive government actions (police against civilians, corruption, false arrest, bribery, political arrests) may be a vital first step in gaining a greater degree of public support. Police and security organizations urgently need more public help in locating hidden terrorists, tracking their movements, anticipating their plans, seizing their weapons and explosives, cutting off their flow of funds, and putting them under arrest. Turncoats among terrorist groups can and should be cultivated. Religious groups must not be allowed to galvanize support for terrorists as a religious duty, and instead, they should be persuaded to support anti-terrorist activities as a manifestation of religious humanism and morality. Much of the countering of terrorism then is really a form of governing from the bottom up

So, what might constitute a more relevant strategy? It would certainly help if governments and non-government organizations would mount more effective information campaigns to point out the horrible damage done to innocent human beings for no sane reason. It can also more effectively be emphasized that these terrorists offer nothing of value – only pain and oppression. None is capable of running a government humanely or effectively. An ISIS government would be endless, mindless tyranny and fear.

Governments and external forces need also to generate stouter resistance against terrorists within each national community. This is not an argument for the extension of US or Western policy. It is an argument about how Muslim countries and others must become braver and stronger in the defense of their own society and their own lives.

It is also true that much of the future is bound up not in combat but on the ability of local people plus external support to deal with basic human needs like health, education, welfare, help for the very poor and the helpless elderly, and provision of basic safety and personal security. This is very bottom up. There are hundreds of non-government organizations at work in the world to do exactly this, often in circumstances where governments have massively failed to meet these needs.

Military organizations need to develop new forms of capability. They are increasingly being required to act like police: to work on the ground, door to door, to root out concealed enemies. So let them be trained like police, and let them begin to work more closely with local police.

As part of this line of reasoning, it is also true that governments defending themselves against concealed terrorism need better intelligence – but not the kind of intelligence now coming from intelligence services still fighting the Cold War. The best and most useful intelligence would probably come from the bottom up; from individuals who are willing to finger terrorists and reveal where they are living and acting. To gain this kind of cooperation however, governments have got to stop punishing their citizens for thinking or acting properly. Often, more cooperation will be achieved by local governments and organizations which provide real services and are not so compelled by top down power and control.

XII

PORTRAIT OF A BETTER WORLD

A NEW WORLD IS EMERGING, AND IT IS URBAN

The world is awakening to the fact that the future will be increasingly urban, and neither central governments nor cities themselves seem ready to cope. Many of the world's largest cities are already overwhelmed. The huge surge of people to cities has meant that especially the largest and most densely populated cities has dramatically increased the need for high quality public infrastructure has risen in importance, and as cities fall behind the power curve, it has become harder and harder to catch up again. When states fail and collapse, the process of disintegration mutilates institutions and destroys the underlying understandings between the government and the governed. This is precisely why state rebuilding must be sustained, and requires time, massive capacity building, large sums from the outside, debt relief, and appropriate forms of tutoring. But note: not even the U. N. or the U. S. are intended for, and willing to be responsible for, total state rebuilding. Many humanitarian voices advocate exactly that, but the only way to resurrect more than a hundred failed of floundering states is for each to remain responsible for their own fate.

The world is experiencing a huge surge in its population. There are about 7.4 billion of us now, and that number is expected to rise to 9 billion in 2050, and more than 11 billion by the year 2100. Almost every sector of every economy is becoming more sophisticated and more productive, and despite the most ominous of predictions, the world has almost never run out of critical resources. There have been major improvements, worldwide, in technology, education, the body of usable knowledge, in managerial skills, and in the value added nature of economic sectors. There is less reliance on primary economic sectors (farming, fishing, mining, forestry) and a movement upscale to more value added secondary and tertiary levels of economic activity. Here are some of the most important ways in which the world has become better:

1. Transportation: air travel has grown beyond belief; hundreds of millions of people now have their own automobiles; millions of miles of highways and urban streets have been provided; the cost per unit mile of travel is, remarkably, down.
2. Despite repeated ominous predictions of world wide starvation, food is far more widely available, in remarkable variation, at far more affordable cost.
3. The expected life span of humans in 1900 was 41. In 2000, it was 77, and it is close to 80 now.
4. Almost all forms of medicine are unbelievably advanced. Most of the horrible diseases of the past – plagues, small pox, measles, polio, influenza have largely been eliminated. New problems such as obesity, drug addition and AIDS are being dealt with as individual problems.
5. Humans are more willing and able to move to improve their lives. Immigration and emmigration are valuable. The tragedy is the fact that "mobiliity" is now so often the fate of refugees and displaced persons, but there is a substantial record of humane efforts to deal with these problems. Hundreds of millions of people have moved from farms and villages to urban areas to improve their opportunities.
6. Machines that replace human labor have multiplied, and greatly reduced the cost of producing most "things". Machines have enabled the greater expansion of economies, creating more wealth and new forms of work.
7. Communications have experienced a remarkable revolution, especially in the form of computers and cell phones, and the world of the average person will never be the same.
8. Home ownership is much more likely, and homes are totally better and more convenient: heating and air conditioning,

sanitation, labor saving appliances, furniture, clothing – at greatly reduced costs.

9. The base of formal education and further access to knowledge has been greatly expanded. An exceptional number of young people are now able to go to college.

10. The openness of society has been increasing. The roles of women and minorities have become more equal, more permissive and more relaxed.

11. As a result of these changes, real incomes have doubled between 1900 and today. In 1900, the "middle class" was just about 1% of the population. Now it is over 23%.

12. There is a very special reality that, through the 1980s and '90s, the U. S. accepted more than a million legal immigrants per year – more legal immigrants than all other nations of the world combined. In addition, there has been a huge flow of illegal immigrants. 11% of the U. S. population is foreign born – about 40 million people.

13. Factoring out immigration, the rise of American inequality disappears; for 89% of the American population, that is, native born, income inequality is declining since the 1960's. For African-Americans, family median incomes are currently rising twice as fast as the population as a whole.

14. 80% of the U. S. population has graduated from high school, and 25% have a college degree. The U. S. averages 12.3 years of education – the highest in the world. The current drop out rate is about 10%; but prior to 1940, most children dropped out – in order to work.

15. Health insurance did not exist until after WW I. In 1900, 42% of workers were in primary sectors of the economy; 38% were in industry; and 20 % were in "white collar" occupations. 47% of women's employment was as domestics. 58% of men and 52% of women are now in service sector. In 1850, the average work week was 66 hours; in 1900, it was 53 hours; in 2000, it was 42 hours. House keeping chores took 4 hours a day for 90% of housholds in 1900; in 2000, it is about 14%.

THE WORLD IS BETTER, BUT GOVERNMENTS ARE WORSE!

A disturbingly low number of countries have been able to take advantage of this new wealth and the opportunities and leverages which are becoming increasingly available. The tide that brought State Socialism to more than 70 countries after WW II is receding. The failure of hundreds of thousands of State Owned Enterprises (SOE), and such socialist policies as mandatory Central Plans, import substitution, price controls, state monopolies, controlled banking, closed borders, heavy import taxation, and controls of worker movement have made this retreat a vital necessity. State Socialism inhibited the development of national economies. SOEs proved to be inefficient, unproductive, debt ridden, loss making, unwilling to innovate and even unable to modernize or even to maintain its facilities. In case after case, the move away from State Socialism toward some form of market based economy has yielded remarkable economic improvements. **The most important truth to be grasped and understood is that the great traditional pattern of top down governance has, even in these modern times, produced a record of widespread dismal failure. The listing of more than 100 governments in serious trouble diagnosed earlier was necessary to help people to realize that this top down failure is worldwide, and of breathtaking dimensions.**

Can these miserable governments simply be thrown out? Unfortunately, no.

SHIFTING POWER FROM "TOP DOWN" TO "BOTTOM UP"

State reform and reconstruction may be very difficult and even dangerous, since it challenges the absolute control that is so demanded by ruling regimes. It is vital to strengthen the "bottom up" elements of national activity, and at the same time people must try to point these stronger elements toward resistance to top down authority. What are these "bottom up" elements? Local communities of people can and do form bonds of mutual support and self-interest. Strengths form around gender, race, religion, tribes and clans, neighborhoods, work places, and all of these bonds are very human and usually very sensible. Similarly, businesses have reasons to promote their own interests against negative government controls and pressures. Small businesses may not have the leverage to become influential "special interests", but they can form alliances among themselves, and often with their customers. A genuine environment of personal security and safety must be achieved to persuade people and businesses to take initiatives, to find work, to save and to invest.

We must learn how to deal with the differences between what governments say and what they really do. It is the same for individual people: what they say vs. how they really act. There is a growing interest in the huge problems inherent in the distribution of wealth, in part because people seem to believe that super wealth is perversely used to capture super power. There is a growing spirit of bottom up activism, putting greater levels of pressure on the ruling elites. The future will deal with attempted overrides of specific things such as getting rid of oppressive laws and regulations, refuting policies of excessive control, and shifting priorities from special interests to general interests. For example, it may be that the flow of aid money is shifting from top down funding of official governments to "bottom up" funding of locally based organizations, where the money never gets into the hands of the government officials. People are increasingly feeling that, even when our motives were decent, we ended up funding and supporting oppressive dictators and tyrants, and some of that money ended up buying weapons to kill people. It is extremely valuable to push where possible for the disaggregation of power: delegation and devolution to local governments, delegations to local elements of central governments, the separation of parties and the state, the provision of greater range and independence of the private elements of the economy. It can be argued that parliaments, even when they are captured or relatively inert are nevertheless the most useful forums for building resistance.

One of the greatest priorities of governments is surely public security and safety, which are widely seen as both a private and a public responsibility; the debate is how much of each. The public responsibility at least includes prevention of invasion or infiltration; loss of territory; elimination of domestic threats to national order and domestic security; and a means for citizens to resolve their differences in a peaceful and reasonable manner. The State should provide a means for the adjudication of disputes; regulation of misconduct; an enforceable body of laws; securing of property and contracts; and hopefully, a means for citizens to participate freely in the important aspects of society.

Most of the countries gaining independence after WW II created bad governments. Why? Many were military, and most military regimes were dictatorial and authoritarian. Half of the military governments were ousted, but the other half got replaced more or less peacefully. Most newly independent countries suffered from and initial 20-30 years or more of bad governments, and it has taken a long and messy period to get to decent governments. Some countries have never made it. It is amazing and unsettling how few countries ever seemed able to adopt representative government. As discussed earlier, more than half of the governments in the world are in <u>deep trouble,</u> defined by the presence of wars, insurrections, active internal conflict, mal-distribution of wealth, widespread poverty, rampant corruption, and serious lack of social services and public infrastructure, and by simple bumbling government incompetence. The world has suffered from literally hundreds of insurrection groups, rebel groups, terrorist groups, all of which differed in a whole complex number of ways. There does not seem to be a single pattern; all depend on "circumstances", most of which are inadvertent or irrelevant. Some differences are based on local conditions, but there have been some clear common elements: zeal, greed, lust for power. Disturbingly, most emerging governments really have had little or nothing useful or creative to offer. They can't really articulate why they should have the power. They utter platitudes, write noble constitutions and bodies of law, and then ignore them and govern like idiots.

Now and in the recent past, there have been 25-30 civil wars taking place: Abkhazia, Angola, Benin, Burundi, Cambodia, Central African Republic, Congo, Cote d'Ivoire, Croatia, Darfur, Eretria, Ethiopia, El Salvador, Liberia, Namibia, Nicaragua, Rwanda, Sierra Leone, Somalia, South Sudan, Sudan, Syria, Tajikistan, Vietnam, Yemen, Yugoslavia. Most of these wars have been totally out of control by the government or anybody else. This has forced the United Nations repeatedly into the role of peace keeper and often the military role of opposing and closing down active conflict and attempting to force some form of compromise between violent, irrational conflicting parties.

The potential here is that, even when actual combat has ceased, the internal conflicts still tear up the country and prevent its recovery, much less its advancement. It might be of great value if the UN and/ or some other agency could evoke stronger programs to help the emergence of decent, effective governments after the fighting is over. Recovering governments often spend decades struggling through the consequences of their own destruction because their governments are no better at directing effective recovery than they were in creating peace or steering clear of war making.

Is the surge of Islamist conflicts really any different? Is it really religious motivation or is it camouflage? The Muslim people are widely motivated by their religion, but their leadership is widely motivated by power and greed. Public opinion polls show very heavy disappointment with most governments by the people of the Muslim world. But where do the fighters come from and why? Where does the bribe money come from and who takes it and why? How many of the oppressive forces are government sponsored? In the Muslim wars and terrorist convulsions, is it not Muslims that are killing Muslims? Is it not mostly Muslims who are among the world's 50 million refugees and displaced persons?

Most liberated governments in Middle East and North Africa (MENA) lurched into dictatorships – either military or civilian. Many countries then went <u>decades</u> before they reached some degree of political stability. And these governments spent huge sums on weapons and soldiers. Social services tended to be very low on the scale of national priorities, behind the military, economic development, and corruption.

Every country produces a high level of corruption, and developing countries are the worst because the leadership has proved so venal, and the defenses against corruption are usually <u>deliberately</u> weak, and too many fail-safe protections fail. The most popular targets for the crooks: government contracts, tax systems, customs and import/export, land, authorizations, and any other activity involving real money. There is a apparent link between major corruption in an organization and minor corruption. "When the top people are stealing big, the little guys are stealing small." THE CROOKS ARE SMARTER THAN THE DEFENDERS, and what is urgently needed is far more effective protective systems. A lot of intellectual attention has been paid to these protective systems and procedures like auditors and inspectors and investigators, but this is useless when these systems can be ignored or even sabotaged. The rule of law is not enough when the laws themselves are perverted.

It is astonishing how few political organizations have any real philosophy or coherent agenda. Most are simply anti; "us vs. them"; or "ins vs. outs" (like the U. S. with "Democrats vs. Republicans"). Look at insurgency movements: how many are ever able to say what they stand for? For example, Muslim insurgents often say they want "Sharia Law" but this is essentially meaningless since there is no such thing as **"the"** Sharia Law. It varies from country to country. It already exists in some form or another is more than 30 countries. Fundamentalist Islamist zealotry shows that the urge to oppress transcends political philosophies and represents a universal and compelling human attribute, going back to the earliest understandings of human history – back to the kings and emperors, back to the Pharaohs, back to the tribes and clans emerging from the caves. Through most of history, there has been human acceptance of this centrist control, almost to the point of regarding it as the normal human condition. The rejection of such leadership was undertaken primarily when the centrist control was intolerably oppressive and painful and dangerous. And if a centrist regime was overthrown, it was usually replaced by another centrist regime, but hopefully somewhat more tolerable.

Almost none of these regimes were ever intended to be democratic, and seldom, as in the old Soviet Union or China or Iran North Korea or Venezuela was any latitude permitted for pleas for change from the bottom up. Where debate or argumentation was tolerated, it was forcefully closed down if it was perceived to be even moderately effective. If this universal pattern of centrist elite control is fully understood, then the surge of something like bottom up democracy must be seen as extremely painful and risky. Who has the courage to speak out? How can change be brought about against an all powerful centrist regime? In general, it must involve a significant degree of strengthening of people's "bottom up" capability. Peasants with pitch forks might be capable of unseating a regime, but they would not be capable of creating their own viable government to replace it. Several things must be undertaken for the long term.

One of the greatest of human attitudes is that **of self reliance and self protection.** For centuries, there was a willingness to share responsibility for both reliance and protection with narrow human groups. This has proved to be both good and bad; good because a lot of people benefitted; bad because help and protection – in thousands of cases – became oppressive and dysfunctional. The fault was not with the people, but with the governments. Yet even the worst of governments are capable of acting responsibly to provide positive impetus to good things for the country. Governments can be made to have positive impact on bottom up concerns.

But one immutable obligation must be met. Governments and societies must develop and implement programs to help the poor. Every country does have such programs, mostly constructed to provide at least a basic safety net for food, shelter, medical aid, safety and special provisions for people like mothers and babies. But it is very disturbing to realize how many governments are unable or unwilling to satisfy even these rudimentary levels of support. Even fewer governments are able to advance the level of their assistance to the point where all of the nation's poor are properly provided for. So the answer to the provision of programs to meet the needs of the poor is not to rely entirely on governments. In fact, the fate of the poor is dealt with at three levels:

1. <u>Self sufficiency:</u> the poor can and do help themselves – they have no choice. It is wise for governments and elements of society to urge people to become more self sufficient however possible, and to assist them however possible in doing so.

2. <u>Governments</u> must also construct and maintain at least a "no-frills" safety net, with emphasis on those most vulnerable in society – the mothers and children, the elderly, the disabled, and the disadvantaged. But it must be recognized that, with very rare exceptions, such government programs **will not be enough.**

3. <u>Society in General</u> has always played this vital third role. There are literally hundreds of thousands of private organizations in every country dedicated to providing help and care and assistance to the poor and disadvantaged. This is humanity at its best. These organizations range from small neighborhood groups to major international organizations. They are most often funded by private donations, and are heavy users of volunteer workers, but many are also agents of governments and receive sustained government financing. It is now increasingly true that many national or international donor organizations have been cheated and ill treated by governments, and have seen their donated funds being stolen or misappropriated. Many now prefer to funnel assistance funds for the poor through non-government organizations (NGOs) instead of to some corrupt and incompetent government agency. In other words, the policies and mechanisms for helping the poor are increasingly "bottom up" in attempting to provide the help that governments from the top down have proved unable or unwilling to provide.

But it still remains true that the greatest influence on the fate of the poor remains in the capacity of the national economy. The economy of each country simply must be large enough and effective enough to produce sufficient wealth and enough jobs to provide adequate, stable income for the poor and for the revenues of governments used to finance their social obligations. This is exactly what happened in the People's Republic of China, where the abandonment of the State Socialist economy and the emergence of a more competitive and productive market based economy produced a hugely galvanizing effect on the Chinese economy and a miraculous reduction of abject poverty, unmatched in modern world history.

The need to support and encourage the advancement of the poor will never end, but there are striking opportunities to expedite their advance. One of the most critical has been the rapid shift from life and work anchored in the very basic rural/village world, and the overwhelming shift to the urban world. This is not a change mandated by governments; in fact, most governments are totally bewildered and hopelessly behind the reality of the shift. The basic economic elements of the past – farming, animal husbandry, mining, forestry, and the basic manufacturing of simple things – all have faded in importance, in large part because they produced low value added economic results. The new expanding urban areas have, for many reasons, become the far superior generator of wealth and opportunity, so young people leave the farms and villages and flood to the cities, wanted or not, ready or not. And in case after case, cities, especially in developing countries are not ready. They are under skilled, underfinanced, bewildered and overpowered.

Perhaps the greatest bulwark against a centrist government **is a strong and self defending private sector,** ranging from huge powerful corporations down to street vendors. Governments exert much control over the private sector, often for legitimate reasons including prevention of illegal or dangerous practices, legal constraints on malpractice, and the generation of taxes for the public good. Private organizations, whether profit or non-profit form special interests, some so powerful that they dominate elements of the national economy. Special interest competition and the exercise of political power is one of the most significant mechanisms for bottom up leverage on centrist regimes. In fact, the private sector almost always provides public goods and services of great importance – transportation, energy, health care, education, housing, retailing and banking. It can compete with government, and it can perform contracts on behalf of government.

Another exceedingly important bottom up element in very many countries is the existence of what is known as **"the informal economy".** The informal economy is defined by De Soto as "the refuge of individuals who find that the costs of abiding by existing laws in the pursuit of legitimate economic objectives exceeds the benefits. It is essential that the state remember that before it can distribute the nation's wealth, the must *produce* wealth. And that in order to produce wealth it is necessary that the state's actions not obstruct the actions of its citizens, who, after all, know better than anyone what they want and what they have to do. The state must restore it its citizens the right to take on productive tasks, a right that it has been usurping and obstructing. The state must limit itself to functioning in those necessary areas in which private industry cannot function. This does not mean that the state will wither away and die."

A distinction is usually made between the informal economy and the so called "underground" economy which is broader and includes illegal activities such as drugs, prostitution, illegal betting and smuggling. The informal economy is not confined to poor countries, and in fact every country has a substantial informal sector in its economy. When the formal economy is too weak, people often have no option but to enter the informal economy as a means of survival. One of the pathologies of many governments is that they fail to recognize this reality, and view the informal economy as a form of crime, often called a "black market" existing only to avoid taxes and escape regulations. In truth, in many countries the informal economy is saving the country from economic collapse. The government can and does use laws and police enforcement to suppress the informal economy even when it knows that it provides employment and income that the state has failed to provide.

There are no barriers to entry into the informal economy. Anybody capable of performing a service or providing a good can become a provider. The most likely types of work in the informal economy are casual laborers, construction workers, personal services providers such as servants, janitors, trash collectors, porters, messengers, errand runners, delivery people, child care providers, street vendors, and even panhandlers. In addition, if some capital is available, other people may be able to become small retailers or customer service providers. One of the most frequent such service is transportation in urban areas where networks of jitney cars and minivans supplement scarce and inadequate public transportation. Small scale manufacturing is widespread, including the fine arts of making cheap copies of Gucci handbags and Omega watches. Many crafts are represented, including carpenters, plumbers, masons, electricians, tailors, and auto mechanics, and many of these entrepreneurs are capable of working in both the formal and informal economies at the same time, depending on what work is available.

The informal economy has many obvious downsides. First, while the activities are all legal in the formal sense, they are illegal when they escape the tax collection system and avoid most government regulation. Their small scale of operations often prevents them from economies of scale and mostly they must refrain from some management practices like advertising or internet linkages that can be traced. In many cases, there are added costs of business for bribing the police, or to buying off inspectors. Property ownership and the protection of physical facilities is difficult and often dangerous. Informal operators may be the victims of thieves and protection rackets since it is difficult to appeal for police protection. There is seldom any real job security, work may be uncertain, income and wages are often unstable and fluctuating since most informal activities are highly competitive, with too many workers seeking too few jobs. Few work benefits such as health care or unemployment compensation are possible. But surprisingly, wages in the informal sector often compare favorably with those in the formal economy, where an excess of workers may keep wages down.

On the other hand, the informal economy, especially in poor countries, is often the only starting point for young people who do not have the education or skills to enter more formal businesses. Many entrepreneurs are women who might be barred from prejudiced formal businesses, and who would have little chance of becoming owners or managers of their own formal enterprises. Nor is the informal economy the home of crooks and rip-off artists. In most instances, there is a surprising degree of organization and self discipline. Almost like the guilds of old, members of groups such as street vendors or transport providers create coordination groups to allocate locations, prevent rip-offs, set price ranges, and even organize the business of bribing police and other officials. Lenders have found that small "bottom up" borrowers have an excellent reputation for the proper repayment of their loans.

More recent examinations of informal economies reveal some startling facts. The World Bank has estimated that, in many less developed countries, the informal economy employs between one third and one half of the national labor force. Various studies estimate that the informal economies in developing countries in 2000 were about 40% of their official gross domestic product. In Zimbabwe, the figure is around 70%, and it clearly reflects the terrible damage inflicted on what was once a prosperous country by the pathological policies of the dictator, Robert Mugabe. Other countries such as Turkey, Brazil, Egypt, and the new Russia, the figure ranges from 40 to 60%. Even in developed countries, the number averages about 18%, and there seems to be a direct correlation between the size of the informal economy and a country's total tax burden and the intrusiveness of its economic regulation. Thus, among rich countries Spain, Belgium, Italy and Greece have large informal economies and the United States, Canada, Switzerland and Great Britain have far lower levels. In China, the informal economy has had a particularly vital significance. In an attempt to limit migration from rural to urban areas, the Chinese created a limited "official" workforce in cities, largely working in SOEs, and tried to prevent migrants in cities who were not eligible for this official status. But in addition to its migrants, Chinese cities attracted millions of people who settled into the informal economy whether the government liked it or not. As these realities are finally being recognized, it appears that the attitudes of governments are undergoing some change. Most people in the informal economy are really seeking to upgrade themselves and enter the formal economy if possible. It is irrational to live in the shadows, and on the edge of survival, and with some help, many informal businesses could make even greater contributions to the economy by being allowed to go formal. For example, women have demonstrated, in the face of much local prejudice, that they can run successful businesses, and it would be an easy jump for even the murkiest of governments to work out low cost loans for women to do just that in the formal framework. Much of the evolution of the economies of developing countries is not from massive state owned enterprises, but from the bottom up – from small entrepreneurs with the drive and ability to expand their informal businesses if allowed to do so.

Another of the most important elements of any country that is capable and willing to exert "bottom up" counter force against dominant centrism is that of **local governments.** Local governments include states/provinces, urban centers, intermediate bodies such as counties, districts or regional governments, on down to villages and tribal centers. There are two great pressures at work: centrism vs. disaggregation; and the level of government at which money can be generated. Centrist governments believe in absolute control of everything from the top. Local governments believe in "the three D's" – decentralization, delegation, and devolution.

Local governments, at the state, regional, county and urban levels are also almost always in contention with the central governments. Local governments contend for the independent right to collect revenue, rather than being forced to rely entirely on national government funding and the control that inevitably comes with it. Local citizens want to choose their own leaders instead of having them appointed by the central regime. Local governments should be favored because they are almost always more responsive to what their residents really want, and because, all over the world, local governments have proved that they can do a better job of delivering public goods and services better than central governments. It is at least possible that greater local governance will increase the ability for governments to control crime and corruption, and that people can more effectively see and expose the crime and corruption within the government itself.

Local governments would prefer having authority within the central government agencies delegated to the lower levels of the organization, because they function better at the lower levels. Local governments most prefer it when authority is positively decentralized, including authority to decide, and direct control of money at the lower levels. This view is strongly anchored by the strongly held view in the world of public administration that local government management of service delivery programs are far more responsive and far more effective at the local "bottom up" level. Finally, local governments believe in devolution, where the central government removes itself, and leaves a program entirely under local government responsibility.

What applies to programs also applies to **money**. Local governments hate it when central governments make them responsible for some program but retain the authority to tax to acquire the financing, and then, of course, fail to pass down the money, leaving the local government literally holding the (empty money) bag. Local governments want strong independent powers to tax so that they themselves can cover their financial needs.

Yet another form of bottom up strength is the dazzling array of **civic organizations**. By the hundreds of thousands all over the world, this great force for bottom up influence is astonishing in its endless variation. Every purpose under the sun can and does organize itself in some manner, and many are willing and able to exert serious influence on government and national affairs. Most are strictly local; some are huge and international, and of enormous influence such as those for environmentalism, or women's rights, or worker protection. Their size and breadth of pubic support make them one of the influences capable of leveraging even absolute dictatorships. And, they are inherently bottom up. When any of these civic organizations set out to exert influence, it is likely that their objective will be the passage of some law, and therein lies that greatest risk, since by demanding to have their interests locked in law, and then demanding the law's strict enforcement, they are acting very much like the dictatorial government itself. Civic groups can become special interests, and then engage in special interest politics, with all of the negative consequences that this entails. The saving grace is that the odds are that bottom up special interests are more likely to be constructive and democratic.

Is it not "bottom up" for **individuals to make up their own minds, and make their own choices,** even including the functioning of their

313

governments? But it is strongly argued that this is not correct: that controlled choice mandated by the government is wisdom because the choices of wise and caring government officials will be superior to the scattered and confused and ill advised choices of individuals. It is further argued that these top down choices must be enforced; that millions of individual choices would be too "messy" and "inefficient". It is probably true that many of the affairs of government must be framed in consistent systems and defined choices, and that such systems are reasonable and legitimate. The problems that arise are almost always tied to top down excess, ranging from an excess of zeal all the way up to fiercely enforced tyranny, and the reality is that these dangerous and harmful excesses are far too prevalent. It is therefore a serious need to find ways to restrain such top down oppression, and to promote the greatest possible independence of choice for people from the bottom up. The presumption is that bottom up independence works to the benefit of individuals, and not of the State, and that, in the long run, is a good thing.

In many countries in the Middle East and Africa and the Far East, there are strange and wonderful emerging revelations of some very old realities. In many countries it is being recognized that **ancient ties of tribes, clans, families, villages and religious bonds** still exercise powerful influence, even in this supposedly new and modern world. These forces are supremely "bottom up", not only in the preservation of their ancient alliances, but also in their frequent and forceful opposition to government domination and control. Tribal entities are vital in the affairs of Nigeria, Yemen, Sudan and South Sudan, and for the Kurds in Turkey, Syria, Iran and Iraq. There remains great coherence in Tibet and in Xinjiang Province, home of the Uyghur Muslims, the Basques in Spain, the Muslims in the Philippines, even the horrors of the Khmer Rouge in Cambodia, showing that many of these ties are destructive in their impact.

These traditional forces have slowly evolved into positions anchored in what is often called **common law** – things that people accept and believe in even though they may not be recorded in official law. Much of this common law rests on human beliefs about what is moral and ethical and "right", and these values have great weight against governments that are seen as immoral, unethical, corrupt and "wrong".

Many countries have formally defined Constitutions, and almost all of them deal in some way with the concept of **an independent judiciary** – a series of courts at several levels, culminating in some form of a "Supreme Court", and supposedly free to decide legal conflicts on their merits. Reality does not always achieve this mandate. In most governments, judges are appointed by the political leadership and it is simply understood that judges will do as they are told. In China for example, judges are invited to visit the office of the local director of the Communist Party (CCP) where they are told how to decide any individual case in which the Party has an interest.

Despite Constitutional legitimacy, the actual jurisdiction of courts may be severely limited. Courts may not be allowed to question any law, or may be precluded from questioning a decision or action taken by a public official. There may be no judicial review of government budgets or contractual relationships, or of government disposal of land and other public assets. And yet – people recognize that courts are vital, and that one of the greatest sins of governments is that they are terribly unfair. Fairness is one of those very human needs of the highest value, and therefore attempting to end the unfairness of the court system has become a rallying cry across the world – a rallying cry from the bottom up.

Beyond the courts themselves, there is a much broader justice system which includes **the police who investigate and public prosecutors who bring the wrongdoers to tria**l. Legal systems suffer from two serious disabilities. First, they may be fatally suborned by their own political leadership and made to function improperly. Second, they may be guilty of committing their own forms of corruption. Criminals and various kinds of scoundrels can be "overlooked"; honest citizens can be falsely accused and punished. Land and property can be illegally seized. Police across the globe are notorious for petty crookery all the way from free doughnuts to huge roadblock bribery operations. Police may be ordered to oppress citizens at the instruction of bad political leaders. Here again, these people rise up out of the general population, yearning for honesty, fairness, safety and security. Society in general must therefore bring greater moral and personal pressure to bear on their sons and daughters to resist serving any perverse direction from the very people that they ought to hate and need to resist.

The ultimate and perhaps the most significant forces in governments are often **the military establishment.** The military is by absolute definition a crucial element of a nation's top down authority, yet it is a force that is capable of acting from the bottom up. As with the police, every military organization consists of the sons and daughters of the national citizenry, and they are the bottom up in their views of life, their understanding of human morality, and their cultural imperatives. The difference lies in the nature of military leadership. There is a long and fascinating history where the military leadership rises above the role of oppressors for tyrannical regimes, and places itself somewhere between the role of referee of national affairs and that of honest brokers or national saviors. The role of the military may shift from time to time to adjust to circumstances in their country. Many military establishments properly accept the broad concept that they must respond to proper civilian control. Many, when faced with very bad leadership will resent and revolt, and will rise up to seize power. In short, military establishments have track records often better then the politicians who supposedly supervise them.

But the experience of the last 20 years has been negative. Many military establishments have proved to be seriously weak and flawed. Many have been defeated by inferior forces controlled by ISIS, al Qaeda and other terrorist groups, as witnessed by the collapse of Iraqi army units when attacked by ISIS, or the inability of the Nigerian Army to fend off the forces of Boko Haram. Horror stories persist about generals who can't lead; of funds for the military being stolen or misappropriated; of chronic shortages of weapons and equipment; of rapacious contractors and suppliers growing rich off of military contracts; of units untrained and badly led. In many cases, the United States or NATO or other regime allies have poured billions into national military establishments only to see them fail frequently and massively, or to be used as instruments of oppression.

Governance is the ultimate mechanism for directing the affairs of a nation, and it is, of necessity, the exercise of power because it is the primary official and approved instrument for the making national decisions. This remains true even where there is a strong and independent private sector which controls most of the economic life of the country, because even then, the government has enormous influence over the environment in which the private sector functions. If a government is dictatorial and authoritarian, chances are that decision-making is in the hands of a single individual or a small group of elite power holders. If a government is more democratic and representative, the power of the government must be focused by building a reasonable public consensus for major decisions. In either case, second and third level decisions are linked to the functioning of elaborate **structures of government agencies** with power designated by laws enacted by legislative bodies that own and operate mechanisms for negotiation, compromise, or decision by fiat.

The one absolute essential for curbing perverse political power is to generate and **focus public attention on the activities of the political leadership**. The public will always be concerned; the real question is whether such concern can develop real leverage on the political leaders. This is not mission impossible; there are in fact many ways in which this leverage can be built. Even in absolute tyrannies, there are tides running which offer opportunities for reformist action. Old tyrants die, and regimes change. Legislatures and judges find windows of opportunity to change pathological laws or call culprits to account, as witness the impeachment of Dilma Roussoff as president of Brazil. Internal conflicts between elements of the elite may split the regime and open up further opportunities. And even tyrannies can be overthrown, either by internal forces, or by external pressures. It helps to remember that, primarily by internal uprisings, gone are Duvalier and Marcos, apartheid in South Africa, Franco, Ceausescu, the Khmer Rouge, Charles Taylor and Edi Amin, Peron, Mao and many other seemingly invulnerable tyrants. And the world has acted to terminate the regimes of Hitler, Mussolini, Stalin, Tojo, Hussein, and Milosovic.

Despite their frustrations, **elections still are the one best hope, because they can be used to legitimize and focus opposition.**

A regime that is forced to steal an election is also revealing the bankruptcy of its national standing, and the narrowness of its elitist base. In the contemporary world, seriously corrupt elections may now precipitate world-wide attention and cause the monitoring of the next election by international evaluators, giving greater hope to the opposition.

In even the tamest of captive **legislatures,** there will be some members with the courage to oppose the creation of pathological laws. These people can be visibly supported by others in society, and they can identify bad law proposals so that opposition can be mobilized against them. Citizen groups can help protect honest politicians and public officials by giving them positive visibility and making it more risky to attack them. Hopefully, fewer bad laws can be sneaked through in secret. Existing bad laws stand a better chance of being mitigated or neutralized.

Just as police rely on informers for intelligence, so too can politicians or public officials obtain information from citizens and private organizations about what governments are doing wrong. The worse the regime the greater is the need to make such "**whistle blowers**" safe, secure and anonymous. But what is really needed are **people within the power structure** who will listen and perhaps act, and can be trusted not to shoot the messengers. It may be an honest politician, an anti-corruption agency, a newspaper reporter, or a trustworthy public official.

The generation of greater public interest in the machinations of their government is not easy and it may even be dangerous. Public interest relates to the wellbeing of the whole population, and should be clearly distinguished from the more self-serving special interest politics. But even a relatively small group of citizens or a small staffed organization can lock on to an issue such as elementary/secondary education, child care, or the failures of state owned enterprises, or the evidences of corruption. **A variety of people have useful skills to contribute: research, writing, evidence gathering, intelligence generation, internet communications and so on.** Often, the best sources of such intelligence are from employees of government agencies or state owned enterprises that cannot live with their own corrupt environment.

One of the targets for civic action must be the laws themselves, especially laws that protect the right to oppose the regime. First and foremost, this means the existence of a law that provides for honest elections. In addition, laws are needed that secure the right for people to meet and to protest, and to broaden as much as possible the range of subjects that can be debated without being considered as an attack on the State. Among these subjects should be the right to press for anti-corruption measures, the effective audit or evaluation of agency activities, and the rules under which corruption can be investigated, removed, or prosecuted.

Also if possible, **Constitutions or basic laws should provide mechanisms to prevent the abuse of presidential appointment powers**. Patronage is one of the most powerful tools of authoritarian regimes, and it conveys five great advantages. First, it is used to make sure that key jobs – particularly those which involve control of money or the allocation of valuable resources – are filled by regime loyalists who will do as they are told. Second, political allies and supporters can be rewarded for past services. In many cases, these payoff jobs are in lesser positions such as "commissions" or "boards" with little or nothing to do. Third, some appointments will be protective. For example, if a law requires the appointment of an Inspector General in an agency, the threat of that office to the corrupt can be mitigated by the appointment of a loyalist or an incompetent to the post. Fourth, appointments can reach down blow the crucial top positions. Unless the number and location of authorized positions is strictly controlled, the agency can be filled with numerous, largely meaningless jobs such as "special assistants", or "assistant deputies" or "deputy assistants", all of which provide comfortable salaries without the discomfort of doing any work.

Even in the U. S., where representative democracy is at its strongest, there are serious concerns about tthe concentration of too much power in the government in Washington, the huge disparities in wealth and income, the power possessed by huge corporations, and a growing concern that the whole "system" is failing. In other countries where governance is more or less adequate, top down control is much stronger. Think of China, Russia, Vietnam, Argentina, Iran and many others. But in more than 100 countries that are in deep trouble, top down tyranny has all but destroyed the country. Think Syria, Iraq, Afghanistan, Yemen, Somalia, Eritrea, Libya, Mali, the Central African Republic, South Sudan, and many others.

Will the governments of the world ever really turn to representative democracy? If so what forces would bring that about? One of the best ways to move toward representative democracy is to make sure that the country has **a functioning two party system**, even if the "out" party may be harassed or feeble – because a second party will help define the needs for reform and how they can be realized. People should urgently press for an independent justice system, including police forces that are watched and evaluated to keep them modulated and fair. Many governments, as a means to guard their power, will deliberately cultivate and exacerbate conflicts between element of society – white vs. black; religion vs. religion; gender conflicts; or rural vs. urban. But individual people can recognize that they are perfectly capable of accepting this diversity without serious conflict, and they should band together to resist such government misconduct. The citizenry should be asked to tag the bad guys, stigmatize their conduct, expose their corruption and demand appropriate justice.

Many Muslim countries in the world already function under some form of Sharia Law, and many terrorist organizations in the Muslim world unfortunately and menacingly favor harsh and oppressive versions of Sharia Law to be forced on all Muslims. But in fact, in a dozen of Islam's most important countries, **Sharia Law and secular law exist comfortably in combination**, along with much local native common law. Sharia Law in its moderate forms tends to be widely respected, especially in family matters, but it is commonly accepted that Sharia Law needs to be supplemented by newer forms of laws dealing with crime, contracting, property rights and agreements, patents and trademarks, communications, liability and even constitutional law.

Is it necessary to start a revolution in order to counter government oppression? No. There are some valuable alternatives. Even in the worst of tyrannical and corrupt regimes, there will be some who will try to do right. Even in the worst dictatorships there will be forces that are pushing against the regime. Old dictators die, some are pushed out and overthrown, **change is inevitable, and new forces emerge.** In many countries, those who oppose the regime have no intention to undertake an insurrection. Their strategy tends to be to work their way into the ruling structure with the hope of slowly changing it from the inside. Thus, there are counter pressures from legislatures against the executive and from judges with the courage to be independent, or from local government officials who are protecting their own responsibilities, or from civil servants who try to do the right thing. And there are courageous leaders who create significant resistance with the pubic – think of Lech Walesa or Nelson Mandela.

Of the twenty worst dictators of the 20th and 21st centuries, only five died a natural death. Pol Pot in Cambodia was overthrown; Idi Amin in Uganda fled. Auguste Pinochet in Chile was voted out. Ceausescu in Romania was executed in a coup; Saddam Hussein in Iraq was ousted from power by the U. S. invasion. Moamar Ghaddafi in Libya was ousted. Brazil's military government was, after 20 years, finally removed by election. Samosa in Nicaragua was shot. South Africa peacefully converted to black rule. South Sudan declared its independence from a dictatorial regime. The collapse of the Soviet Union created many new independent countries. Robert Mugabe in Zimbabwe is still in power in his 90s, and can't live forever (or can he?)

One of the lessons learned from the South African experience and that of many other countries is the absolute necessity for developing some positive means to damp down insurrections before they erupt, or to **find ways to produce reconciliation after the conflict** and to provide for the return of rebels to mainstream society. What are the critical forms of post conflict reconstruction? First, find ways to stop the shooting, and this may be enormously difficult. It may be possible through negotiation, or bribery. Or it may mean having to wipe out the hard core rebels. A lasting cease fire must be maintained even by force if necessary, but hopefully be amnesty, repatriation, and arms buy-back. Reinsertion into society means full access to mainstream services, perhaps supplemented by special provisions for free land, jobs, training, help for the ill or disabled or other forms of human accommodation. In fact, it is likely that, in countries devastated by heavy conflict, the whole country will need to make new special efforts to stabilize the economy, facilitate job creation, restore reduced crucial social services, and restore shattered public infrastructure. It is probably true that there will be an urgent need to upgrade management at all levels, and restore the concepts of excellence, productivity, quality control; efficiency; responsibility and accountability, and most of all FAIRNESS, FAIRNESS, FAIRNESS. The whole government must be redesigned to maximize service delivery from the bottom up, and not merely a return to the sterility and failure of the search for top down power.

We talk about the numbers of people killed and displaced in the world today, but the greatest impact is really downstream. Think Syria: hundreds of critical elements of the country have been destroyed or seriously reduced: schools, hospitals, small local businesses, housing, transport facilities, power facilities, sanitary systems, etc. Often, those who have fled have been those with the most valuable skills. The destruction of economic elements is very "bottom up" and especially damaging because small entrepreneurs lack the funding to repair or start over. Public services such as police, fire departments, sanitation departments, water and sewer providers, electronics and communications technologists and public transportation systems are all being decimated, and will take years and huge sums of money to recover.

But who is usually responsible for bringing about this kind of recovery? The same inepts that ruined things in the first place. Even if the old elite can be dislodged, chances are that they will be replaced by some new group of similar incompetents. As the mechanisms for running the government and serving the people's needs have foundered, often the winners have been the criminals and the corrupters. Despite brave words, there is a serious doubt that massive deteriorations can really be successfully dealt with. The failure goes beyond mere incompetence, and enters the realm of "mission impossible", and the inheritance of the long historical pattern of top down government. Rebuilding will have to be from the bottom up; and governments, including international ones, need to redesign themselves to support and encourage this fact.

The present international governing apparatus (UN, World Bank, IMF, NATO, etc.), seems unable to deal with the new terrorist world. **Global leadership** must go beyond the idea of global political cooperation and reach the level of **more powerful global action**. Too much of the current effort involves pompous speeches and broad statements of policy or objectives which are voluntary and not mandated and widely ignored. Some of the worst governments in the world gladly sign on the international agreements which they will vigorously undermine.

COMMON CHARACTERISTICS OF DEMOCRATIC GOVERNMENTS

One lesson that is being learned in international relations is that the concept of "representative democracy" is seen as a Western development and is not necessarily seen as the blueprint for other nations, especially in the Muslim world. But the good news is that Muslims and most other people love their own sense of "democracy", yearn for independence, and admire America for its world of freedom and openness. If there is an accepted pattern of what constitutes democratic governance in the world, it probably contains the following elements.

1. Deliberate diffusion of centrist power through the creation of strong elected governments at one or more sub-national levels, empowered by independent authority to raise their own revenues, and executing important people based programs delegated or devolved by the central government.
2. Since revenue is the universal solvent, they must design fairly complex independent tax systems and powers to give local governments a strong localized fiscal base and greater independence from central government control through the budget.
3. In recognition that centrist laws and regulations are almost always forms of centrist control, local governments must be able to creat whole new sets of laws and regulations for local jurisdictions. As the economy shifts, governments must keep up by redesigning the entire revenue stream for government to enhance public revenues by any reasonable means.
4. Creation of independent civil services that report to local officials. This requires new forms of motivation of the civil

service, and in most developing countries, serious and extensive training and education to produce motivation and competence.

5. Encourage and even create forms of public participation: public interest groups, professional and trade associations, a new "arms length" relationship with workers and unions.

6. It would probably be valuable to press for a rethinking and revamping of the whole range of public regulation: away from solely economic regulation and much more toward an enhancement of public health and safety regulation. But the main truth remains: laws and regulations are forms of control, and much of it oppressive and dysfunctional. So forms of enforcement must be created that are not elitist and tyrannical.

7. Similarly there usually needs to be a change the nature of law enforcement, away from public control to public protection in ways that are not merely rhetorical.

8. A special concern is corruption in public programs, which is extraordinarily hard to detect, much less prove. The world urgently needs to develop smarter and more powerful ways to deal with corruption in government.

9. In many retreating State Socialist governments, there is a heavy remainder of state ownership, from housing and businesses to water, power, and communictions facilities. Major programs will be necessary to revamp these patterns from government to private ownership.

10. The nature of the social contract must be redefined and most important public programs woven into either public responsibility, or shared responsibility with the emerging private sector.

In the last analysis, the message of this book is that the world of heavy governance from the top down has been such a failure on such a grand scale that the people of the world now need to rethink the nature of their own governance. The change needed now is that far more of the forces of governance must be from the bottom up. This in turn is also to argue that very large numbers of people have neglected their own governance, and that this neglect has burdened them with enormous negative consequences. Governance will continue to be top down; but there are real opportunities and methods for moderating its impact, mitigating its negative aspects, and making it more fair and humane.

APPENDIX A

ISLAM: THE "TERROR OF THE WORLD": ARAB CONQUESTS: 627-750

Syria – 629-640
Egypt – 639-640
Palestine – 638
Lebanon – 644
Iraq – 630 – 638, including Armenia
Caucasus – 641-642
Iran – 650
Turkmenistan – 650
Tunisia – 670
Morocco – 680
Libya – 680-710
Algeria – 701
Transoxonia – 701
Pakistan – 713
Sind – 713
Spain/Portugal - 716
Uzbekistan, Turkmenistan, Kyrgystan – 680-704

THE OTTOMAN EMPIRE CONQUESTS: 1071-1520

The Ottoman Empire peaked about 1520-30, and lasted until the end of WWI, and as some time included control of the following countries:

Romania
Parts of Russia
Austria
Hungary
Serbia, all of Yugoslavia
Greece
Ukraine
Moldova
Georgia
Armenia
Iraq
Arabia
Syria
Lebanon
Jordan
Egypt
Tunisia
Algeria
Libya
Sudan
Turkey
Macedonia
Rhodes
Cyprus
Crete

The Ottoman Empire peaked about 1520-1530, and lasted until the end of WW I.

SOURCES

I. INTRODUCTION

Country Reports on Terrorism, U. S. Department of State November 2009.

Corruption Perceptions Index 2012, Transparency International

Most Dangerously Polluted Cities, All Countries.org. 2011.

Inequality-adjusted Human Development Index, Human Development Report, 2010.

"A Haven for Malcontents", Economist, July 13, 2013, p. 42

"Africans Let Down by Governments", BBC News, 2004.

"Study Warns of Stagnation in Arab Societies", The New York Times, July 7, 2002.

Lynch, Marc, "The 2009 Arab Human Development Report", 2009.

"The World's Ten Most Authoritarian Leaders", World Policy Journal, Fall, 2012.

"How Anti-Rohingya Bengali Islamist Extremist Terrorists Campaigns Started", Burma News, June 13, 2012.

"Human Development Report: Five Arab Countries Among Top Leaders in Long Term Development Gains", United Nations Development Programme, November, 2010.

"Miserable and Weak Again", Economist, Nov. 16, 2013.

United States Department of State: National Consortium for the Study of Terrorism and Responses to Terrorism: Annex of Statistical Information, Country Reports on Terrorism, 2012.

"Life in Gaza", Washington Post, August 3, 2014, p. A15.

"The State of Africa", Washington Post, August 3, 2014, p. A13.

"Nasty Neighbourhood", Economist, Aug. 2, 2014, p. 41.

World Development Indicators, "Poverty", 2004.

"List of Ottoman Empire Territories", Wikipedia, July, 2011.

Feldman, Noah, "The Fall and Rise of the Islamic State", Council on Foreign Relations, Princeton U. Press, 2008.

Chandler, Michael, and Gunaratria, Rohan, "Countering Terrorism: Reaktion Books, 2007.

Diner, Dan, "Lost in the Sacred", Princeton U. Press, 2009.

Boston, Andrew G., Ed., "The Legacy of Jihad", New York, Prometheus Books, 2005.

Williams, Paul D. "War and Conflict in Africa", Cambridge, UK, Polity Press, 2011.

Ayittey, George B. N., "Africa Unchained: The Blueprint for Africa's Future", Palgrave Macmillan, 2005.

Ayittey, George B. N., "Africa in Chaos", St. Martins Press, 1998.

Ayittey, George B. N., "Africa Betrayed". St. Martins Press, 1992.

Zogby, James J., "What Arabs Think", Zogby International/The Arab Thought Foundation, 2002.

Rotberg, Robert, Ed., "When States Fail: Causes and Consequences", Princeton U. Press, 2004.

Villalon, Leonardo A., and VanDoepp, Peter, Eds., "The Fate of Africa's Democratic Experiments", Indiana U. Press, 2005.

Chellancy, Brahma, "Asian Juggernaut", Harper Business, 2006.

Smith, Lee, "The Strong Horse", Anchor Books, 2010.

Kuran, Timur, "The Long Divergence", Princeton U. Press, 2011.

Viorst, Milton, "Sandcastles" The Arabs in Search of the Modern World", Alfredd A. Knopf, 1994.

Rashid, Ahmed, "Taliban", Yale U. Press, 2000.

Wright, Robin, "Dreams and Shadows: The Future of the Middle East", Penguin Books, 2008.

Bueno De Mesquita, Bruce, and Smith, Alistair, "The Dictator's Handbook", Public Affairs, 2011.

Bhagwati, Jagdish, "Free Trade Today", Princeton U. Press, 2002.

Hayek, F. A. "The Fatal Conceit: The Errors of Socialism", U. of Chicago Press, 1988.

The Quran: The Dilemma, Volume I, TheQuran.com, 2011.

"UN and Government Specialists Discuss Global Anticorruption Efforts in Brazil", United Nations Development Programme, November, 2012.

Yergin, Daniel, and Stanislaw, Joseph, "The Commanding Heights", Simon and Schuster, 1998.

Herbst, Jeffery, "State and Power in Africa", Princeton U. Press, 2000.

Henderson, Harry, "Global Terrorism", Checkmark Books, 2001.

Roy, Olivier, "Secularism Confronts Islam", Columbia U. Press, 2007.

Bingman, Charles F., "Governments in the Muslim World", iUniverse Press, 2013.

Bingman, Charles F., "Changing Governments in India and China", Schiel and Denver Paperbacks, 2011.

Bingman, Charles F., "Reforming China's Government", Xlibris Press, 2010.

Bingman, Charles, F. "Why Governments Go Wrong", iUniverse Press,2006.

Cruvellier, Thierry, "The Master of Confessions: The Making of a Khmer Rouge Torturer", Paris, Editions Gallimard/Versilio, 2011.

Freedom House: "Freedom Country Rankings 2011 – Country Rankings

The World Fact Book: "The World's Most Populous Cities, Metropolitan Areas and Urban Agglomerations, 2008.

List of United Nations Peacekeeping Missions, 2015.

Numbeo: "Quality of Life Index for 2012.

II. THE CORROSIVE NATURE OF GOVERNMENTS

African Union: "All in a Nutshell", the Quest for Unity, 2015.

UNHCR: "Facts and Figures on Refugees", 2015.

"Great Lakes Refugee Crisis", Wikipedia, 2014.

Economist: "Despite Being a Woman: S. Asia is one of the worst places

in the world to be female", June, 13, 2015.

Washington Post, July 26, 2015, "Troubles at electric utility signal depth of Puerto Rico's crisis".

Refugees International, "Syria, Refugee Overview", 2006.

UNDP 2005: "Close to 43 million people worldwide are displaced because of conflict and persecution."

Foreign Affairs: "China's War on Terror: September 11 and Uighur Separatism", December, 2013.

Economist: "Vietnam and China: Through a Border Darkly", August 16, 2014.

The Weekly Standard, "North Korea Sponsors Terrorism", August, 2013.

Bechtol, Bruce E. Jr., "North Korea and Support to Terrorism: An Evolving Histrory", Berkeley Electronic Press, 2010.

McElroy, Damien, "US Threatens Eritrea Over Support for al-Qaeda-linked Terrorists", Telegraph Co., April, 2009.

Lewis, David, "High Times on the Silk Road: The Central Asian Paradox", World Policy Institute, 2010.

IRIN: "Congolese Refugee Camps in Rwanda are "Full", 2015.

UNHCR 2015 Country Operations Profile – Rwanda, 2015.

Economist: "Myanmar's Ethnic Conflicts: More Process Than Peace", Feb. 21, 2015

Economist: "Chad and Its Neighbors: Africa's Jihadists, On Their Way", July 26, 2014.

Entelis, John P., "Morocco's New Political Face", Project On Middle East Democracy, December, 2011.

Economist: "A Big Moment for Erdogan – and Turkey", May 30, 2015.

Tekeyh, Ray, "Iran's Weak Hand", Washington Post.

Economist: "La, tout n'est qu'ordre et beaute", "A Generational Shift Looms for South East Asia's Last Communist States"., May, 16, 2015.

Yarnell, Mark, "Struggling to Respond in South Sudan, CAR", Refugees International, March, 2014.

Economist: "Iraq: The Blighted City", The shocking decline of Iraq's oil capital, Nov. 21, 2015.

Washington Post, "Burundi's Perilous Times", 2016.

Economist: Nigeria: Opportunity Knocks", June 20, 2015.

AllCountries.org: "Most Dangerously Polluted Cities", 2004.

Economist: "Pollution in India and China: Indian Winter", Feb. 7, 2015.

World Policy Journal, Narizhnaya, Khristina, "Russians Go West", Spring, 2013.

Economist: "African Democracy: A Glass Half Full", Mar. 31, 2012.

Economist: "Secession in Mali: An Unholy Alliance", Jun. 2, 1012.

Wikipedia: "Khmer Rouge", December, 2015.

Economist: "Thailand's Violent South: Dreaming of a Sultanate", May 5, 2012.

Refugees International: "DR Congo: Overview", Aug. 2014.

Economist: "Brazil's President: Dilma's Disasters", Dec. 5, 2015.

Economist: "Kurdistan's Right to Secede: Set the Kurds Free", Feb. 21, 2015.

Economist: "Nigerian Politics: Please Don't Expect Miracles", Apr. 11, 2015.

Sanford, Victoria, "Victory in Guatamala? Not Yet", The New York Times, May 13, 2013.

III. GOVERNMENTS SUFFERING FROM MAJOR CONFLICTS

All sources

IV. RISE AND DECLINE OF STATE SOCIALISM AND STATE OWNED ENTERPRISES

Vatikiotis, Michael R. J., "Indonesian Politics Under Suharto", 1993; and Bresnan, John, "Managing Indonesia: the Modern Political Economy", 1993.

Yang, Dali L., "Remaking the Chinese Leviathan", Stanford U. Press, 2004. See also "Governance in China" by the OECD; and "Reforming China's Public Finances" from the International Monetary Fund.

Rotberg, Robert I., "Failed States in a World of Terror", Foreign Affairs Journal, July/August 2002.

Bhagwati, Jagdish, "India in Transition", Oxford, Clarendon Press, 1993.

Bhagwati, Jagdish, "Free Trade Today", Princeton U. Press, 2002.

Andrusz Gregory, Harloe, Michael, "Cities After Socialism", Oxford, Blackwell Publishers, 1996.

Bingman, Charles F. "China Struggles to Reform", Washington Institute of China Studies, Spring, 2006.

Das, Gurcheran, "India Unbound", New York, Anchor Books, 2002.

Friedman, John, "China's Urban Transition", U. of Minnesota Press, 2005.

Economist, "Reform in China: The good, the bad and the Ugly: the bloated state-owned sector", Sep. 12, 2015.

Fuller, Graham E., "The Future of Political Islam", New York, Palgrave Press, 2003.

Haggard, Stephen, Chung, H. Lee, Maxfield, Sylvia, "The Politics of Finance in Developing Countries", Cornell U. Press, 1993.

Hayek, F. A., "The Fatal Conceit: The Errors of Socialism", U. of Chicago Press, 1988.

Herbst, Jeffery, "States and Power in Africa", Princeton U. Press, 2000.

Isbister, John, "Promises Not Kept", Hartford, Conn., Kumarian Press, 1993.

Economist, "South Africa's State Owned Companies: Commanding Plights", Aug. 29, 2015.

"Making Sense of Subsidiarity", The Center for Economic Policy Research, London, 1993.

O'Donnell, Guillermo, and Shmitter, Phillipe, "Transitions from Authoritarian Rule", the Johns Hopkins U. Press, 1986.

Owen, Roger, "State, Power and Politics in the Making of the Middle East", New York, Routledge, 1992.

Pinder, John, "The European Community and Eastern Europe", New York, the Council of Foreign Relations, 1991.

Shleifer, Andrei, Vishny, Robert W., "The Grabbing Hand: Government Pathologies and Their Cures", Harvard U. Press, 1998.

Steinfeld, Edward S., "Forging Reform in China: The Fate of State-Owned Industry", Cambridge U. Press, 1998.

Waterbury, John, "Exposed to Innumerable Delusions", London, Cambridge U. Press, 1993.

McCargo, Duncan, "Rethinking Vietnam", New York, RoutledgeCurzon, 2004 Chol-Hwan, Kang, and Rigoulot, Pierre, "The Aquariums of Pyongyang", Basic Books, 2000.

Kohli, Atul, "State-Directed Development", Cambridge U. Press, 2004.

Dreze, Jean, and Sen, Amarta, "India: Economic Development and Social Opportunity", Oxford, Clarendon Press, 1995.

Villalon, Leonardo A., and VonDoepp, Peter, Eds. Indiana U. Press, 2005.

Waterbury, John, and Richards, Alan, "A Political Economy of the Middle East", Westview Press, 1990.

Michalski, Mark M., "Trade and Procurement Reform in Poland and China: Responding to the Next Globalization Wave of Interdependent Economies", Journal of the Washington Institute of China Studies, Fall, 2010.

"Reforming China's Enterprises", Organization for Economic Cooperation and Development, Washington, D. C., OECD Publishing, 2000.

Encylopedia of the Narions "Turkey: Infrastructure, Power, and Communications" Aug. 14, 2011.

V. GALVANIZING CHANGE IN THE MUSLIM WORLD

Wikipedia, "Islam by Country", 2007.

Arabicpaper.tripod.com, "Muslim Countries of the World", 2011.

Muslim Population: American Muslim Population, 2007.

Muslim Population: Asian Muslim Population, 2007.

Muslim Population: Middle East Muslim Population, 2007.

Pew Research Center: "The Future of the Global Muslim Population", 2011.

Zogby, James J., "What Arabs Think", Zogby International/The Arab Thought Foundation, 2002.

World Economic Forum, The Global Competitiveness Report 2010-2011, Middle East and North Africa.

World Policy Institute, "The More Things Change ... Political Reform in the Arab World", Summer, 2009.

Economist, "Sunni-Shia Strife" The Sword and the Word", May 12, 2012.

Economist, "The Shadow of the Caliphate: Concern Across Asia", Jun. 20, 2015.

WikiIslam, "Muslim Statistics (Terrorism), June, 2013.

Economist, "Salafism: Politics and the Puritanical" Jun. 27, 2015.

Organization of Islamic Cooperation, membership list. 2011.

Economist, "Malaysian Politics: Riding the Tiger", Apr. 4, 2015.

Otto, Jan Michiel, "Sharia Incorporated", Leiden U. Press, 2010.

YaleGlobal Online: "Where will the Muslim Brotherhood Take Egypt's Economy?", Feb. 18, 2012.

Economist, "The State and Islam: Converting the Preachers", Dec. 13, 2014.

Helm, Sarah, "ISIS in Gaza", The New York Review, January 2016.

Locke, Robert, "Islam: A Defective Civilization?", Frontpagemag.com, Jul. 30, 2011.

Economist, "Russia's Central Bank Governor: Putins Right-Hand Woman", Apr. 16, 2016.

Kepel, Gilles, "Jihad: The Trail of Political Islam", Harvard U. Press, 2002.

Economist, "Politics in the Middle East: The Arab Winter", Jan. 9, 2016.

Feldman, Noah, "The Fall and Rise of the Islamic State", Princeton U. Press, 2008.

Smith, Craig S., "Tunisia is Feared to be a New Base for Islamists – Africa and the Middle East, International Herald Tribune, Feb. 20, 2007.

About.com, "Bahrain", Mar. 20, 2011.

VI. GOVERNMENTS AGAINST THEMSELVES

Sulehria, Farooq, "Pervez Hoodbhoy: Miracles are Needed to Rescue Pakistan", Economic and Political Weekly, Jan. 29, 2011.

Economist: "Russia and the West: How Vladimir Putin Tries to Stay Strong", Apr.18, 2015.

Economist: "Vietnam: Lost Generations", May 2, 2015.

Ayittey, George B. N., "Africa Betrayed", St. Martins Press, 1992.

Ayittey, George B. N., "Africa in Chaos", St. Martins Press, 1998.

Ayittey, George B. N., "Africa Unchained: The Blueprint for Africa's Future", Palgrave Macmillan, 2005.

Economist: "The War in Yemen: from Aden to Camp David". May 16, 2015.

Hendawi, Hamza, "Revolutionary Guard Tightens Hold in Iran Crisis", The Seattle Times, Dec. 12, 2012.

Economist: "Repression in Egypt: Worse Than Mubarak", May 2, 2015.

Economist: "Ugandan Politics: Bored of the Big Man", Jun. 20, 2015.

Rotberg, Robert I., "Africa's Mess, Mugabe's Mayhem", Foreign Affairs Journal, Sep. Oct. 2002.

Crimi, Frank, "Eritrea: The Makings of a Terrorist State", Nov. 20, 2013.

Economist: "The Rohingyas: The Most Persecuted People on Earth?", Jun. 13, 2015.

Economist: "Crime and Politics in Bangladesh: Bang Bang Club", Feb. 8, 2014.

BBC News: South Asia: Sri Lanka Profile. Sep. 13, 2013.

Crescent International: "Muslims in Ethiopia Suffer Discrimination and Alienation", May, 2012.

BBC News: Africa: Liberia Profile. Oct. 2013.

Washington Post: "Thai army tightening its grip after coup", May 24, 2014.

Kaussler, Bernd, "Sunni Terrorists Strike Shi'a Mosque in Irans Sistan-Baluchistan Province", June, 2009.

Abramowitz, Morton and Barkley, Henri J., "Turkeky's Transformers: The AKP Sees Big", Foreign Affairs Journal, Nov./Dec. 2009.

Economist: "Turkish Politics: Everything is Possible", Mar. 1, 2014.

Ayboga, Ercan, "Turkey's Gap and its Impact in the Region", The Kurdish Herald, Sep. 2009.

Global Edge: "Turkey: Economy", Feb. 18, 2012.

U. S. State Department: Background Note: Turkey, 2015.

Economist: "Protests in Lebanon: Talking Trash", Aug. 29, 2015.

World Without Genocide: "Democratic Republic of Congo", May 20, 2015.

Economist: "Cambodia: Neither Truth nor Justice", Aug. 9, 2014.

Jubber, Nicholas, "Mali's Nomads: Bulwarks Against Jihad", World Policy Journal, Fall, 2014.

Economist: "The Palestinians: Glimpse of Unity", Apr. 26, 2014.

Waterbury, John, "Exposed to Innumerable Delusions", Cambridge U. Press, 1993.

African Economic Outlook: Sudan: Overview", Aug. 18, 2011. See also

Kandell, Jonathan, "Augusto Pinochet, Dictator Who Ruled by Terror in Chile, Dies at 91", New York Times, Dec. 11, 2006.

Economist: "Thailand: Peace, Order, Stagnation:, Aug. 9, 2014. See also: Economist: "Sudan: Downhill", Feb. 1, 2014.

"Thailand After the Coup: Uniform Reaction", Sep. 13, 2014.

Economist: "Politics in Pakistan: Army in the Middle", Sep. 6, 2014.

UNHCR Country Operations Profile, 2015: Central African Republic, May 5, 2015.

Economist: "Lighting Rural India: Out of the Gloom", Jul.20, 2013.

Economist: "Malawi's Mess: Banda and the Bandits", Dec. 7, 2013.

Hammer, Joshua, "When the Jihad Came to Mali", New York Review of Books, 2013.

Allison, Simon, "Mali: Five Key Facts About the Conflict", Guardian Africa Network, Jan. 22, 2013.

Economist: "Mass Arrests in Bangladesh: Round Up the Usual Suspects", Jun. 18, 2016.

Mt. Holyoke.edu: "History and Conflict in East Timor", Mar. 10, 2016.

UHNCR: "Some 16,000 refugees seek shelter in Cameroon following clashes in north-east Nigeria", May 5, 2015.

Washington Post: "Life in Gaza", Aug. 3, 2014. See also: Economist: "The Siege in Gaza: Cold Misery", Jan. 17, 2015.

VII. ECONOMIC DEVELOPMENT: TOP DOWN & BOTTOM UP

Richards, Alan, and Waterbury, John, "A Political Economy of the Middle East", Boulder, Colo., Westview Press, 1990.

Economist: "Infrastructure in Brazil: Not Many Aboard", Jul. 18, 2015.

Economist: "Japan and Abenomics: Moment of Reckoning", Dec. 6, 2014.

Gleick, Peter H., "Three Gorges Dam Project, Yangtze River, China", Water Briefs: The World's Water, 2008-2009.

Economist: "China: Mining Safety: Shaft of Light", Jul. 18, 2015.

Economist: "A Chance to fly: India Has a Rare Opportunity to Become the World's Most Dynamic Big Economy", Feb. 21, 2015.

London Conference on Afghanistan: "Summary: Afghanistan Economic Update, January, 2010.

Economist: "Corporate Debt in India: Power Cut", Dec. 6, 2014.

Economist: "India's Bad-Debt Problem: Rump Stake", Jun. 6, 2015.

Kuran, Timur, "The Long Divergence", Princeton U. Press, 2011.

Economst: "Oil in Nigeria: Problems at the Pump", May 30, 2015.

Morocco Economy Watch: "Morocco Central Bank Raises Interest Rates, Sep. 2008.

Saigon SGGP English Edition: "Market Economiy Does Good in Vietnam", Jul. 15, 2015.

Economist: "Reforming Cuba: Be More Libre", May 16, 2015.

Economist: "Women and the Property Market: Married to the Mortgage", Jul.11, 2013.

CIA World Fact Book: "Vietnam Economy Profile, 2013", Feb. 21, 2013.

TIME, WORLD: "Vietnamese Fight Bask Against Cop Corruption", Mar. 25, 2009.

Thamhmien News: "Vietnam's Economy Continues Perform Below Potential, World Bank Says". Jul. 15, 2014.

Wikipedia: "Economy of Syria", Feb. 12, 2012.

Wikipedia: "Economy of Saudi Arabia", Feb. 2012.

Wikipedia: "Economy of Afghanistan", Feb. 2012.

Economist: "Argentina's Debt Saga: Unsettling Times", Jul. 26, 2014.

Economic Growth in the Muslim World, UNDP: "The Arab Human Development Report,2015.

Economist: "China and Asia: Winners and Losers in the Great Chinese Rebalancing", Jul. 26, 2014.

Economist: "Manufacturing in Africa: An Awakening Giant", Feb. 8, 2014.

Weisbrot, Mark; Ray, Rebecca; Johnston, Jake, The Center for Economic and Policy Research, "Bolivia: The Economy During the Morales Administration", Dec. 2009.

Economist: "Latin American Economies: Passing the Baton", Aug. 2, 2014.

Economist: "Nigeria's Economy: To the Victor the Toils", Apr. 4, 2015.

Neuman, William, "Turnabout in Bolivia as Economy Rises From Instability", New York Times, Feb. 16, 2014.

Economist: "Nationalizing Utilities in Bolivia: From Tap to Socket", May 2, 2014.

Economist: "Electricity in Africa: Lighting a Dark Continent", Sep. 27, 2014.

Economist: "Russia and the Rouble: As Ye Sow, So Shall Ye Reap", Dec. 20, 2014.

Economist: "Pakistan: From the Graveyard", Dec. 20, 2014.

Plaut, Steven, "The Collapsing Syrian Economy", The Middle East Quarterly, Sep. 1999.

Economist: "Vietnam's Economy: Crying over Cheap Milk", Nov. 21, 2015.

Bingman, Charles F., "Reforming China's Government, iUniverse Publishers, 2010.

Economist: "Vision or Mirage? Saudi Arabia's Post-Oil Future", Apr. 30. 2016.

Economist: "Cuba's Economy: Picturesque, But Doing Poorly", May 16, 2015.

Economist: "Industrial Overcapacity: Gluts for Punishment", Apr. 9, 2016.

Economist: "Coming Up Roses: Kenya's Flower Export Business is a Rare Success, Apr. 16, 2016.

Economist: "Argentina's Debt Saga: No Movement", Aug. 2, 2014.

Kuran, Timur, "The Religious Undercurrents of Muslim Economic Grievances", Social Sciences Research Council, Sep. 2011.

Economist: "North Sea Oil: Offshore Fog", May 30, 2015.

Economist: "Trade With Africa: Tear Down These Walls", Feb. 2016.

Economist: "Industry in China: The March of the Zombies", Feb. 27, 2016.

World Economic Forum: The Global Competitiveness Report 2015-2016.

World Economic Indicators: Size of the Economy, 2016.

Economist: "Brazil's Sagging Economy: Recession's Sharp Bite", Sep. 19, 2015.

Economist: "Debt in China: Deleveraging Delayed", Oct. 24, 2015. See also, "China's Financial System: The Coming Debt Bust", May 7, 2016

Economist: "State Owned Enterprises: Fixing China Inc.", Aug. 30, 2014. See also, "If China Embarked on Mass Privatization – The Greatest Sale on Earth", Jul. 16, 2016.

Economist: "Pollution: Beijing v Belching Chimneys", Jul. 9, 2016.

Economist: "North Korea's Awful Economy: A Kim in His Counting House", Jan. 16, 2016.

Washington Post: "Living in the Dark: A World Shortage of Electricity", Nov. 8, 2015.

Kuhn, Anthony, "Indonesian Economy Booms, Its Infrastructure Groans" NPR, Feb. 17, 2012.

Economist: "Nigeria's Oil Company: Petrodollar Spill", Aug. 15, 2015.

VIII. DESTRUCTIVE UNIVERSAL CORRUPTION

The United Nations Convention Against Corruption, Dec.2003. The UN Declaration Against Corruption and Bribery, 1996.

Mbaku, John Mukum, "Bureaucratic Corruption in Africa: The Futility of Cleanups", The Cato Journal, Vol. 16 No. 1, Nov. 2012.

BBC News: "Africans Let Down by Governments", Nov. 14, 2012.

The Globalist: "A (Very) Brief History of Corruption", Jul. 1, 2012.

Wikipedia, "Corruption in India", Nov. 2012.

Anti-Corruption Resource Center, "Colombia: Overview of Corruption and Anti-corruption", Mar. 2013.

Onwuka Azuka, "It Pays to Be Corrupt in Nigeria", The Punch Newspaper, Feb. 26, 2013. See also: Smith, Daniel Jordan, "A Culture of Corruption: Everyday Deception and Popular Discontent in Nigeria", Princeton U. Press, Nov. 19, 2012.

UNDP: "UN and Government Specialists Discuss Globalization Anticorruption Efforts in Brazil", Nov. 11, 2012.

Economist: "Corruption in Brazil: Justice Delayed", Feb. 13, 2013.

Economist: "Corruption in South Africa: A Can of Worms", Jan. 28, 2013.

Hanson, Stephanie, "Corruption in Sub-Saharan Africa", Council on Foreign Relations, Aug. 6, 2009.

Quismundo, Tarra, "Corruption Abets Terror in the Philippines Says US", Asia News Network, Jul. 1, 2013.

Conde, Carlos H., "Philippines Most Corrupt Survey Says", New York Times, Jul. 1, 2013.

Economist: "Corruption in Romania: Immune System", Jun. 13, 2015.

Economist: "Bribery: Graft Work", Dec. 6, 2014.

Transparency International: Corruptions Perceptions Index, 2015.

Transparency International: Bribepayers Index, 2011.

Economist: "Kenya: Trotting Ahead", Mar. 15, 2014.

Latin American Herald Tribune: "Mexico: Cartels Pay Corrupt Cops $100 Million a Month", Jul. 20, 2014.

Economist: "Corruption in Ukraine: Dear Friends", Feb. 13, 2016.

Weiner, Lawrence, "From Sicily to Tiajuana, How Governments Perpetuate One Another", Jun. 25, 2013.

Althaus, Dudley, "Death and Corruption: Organized Crime and Local Government in Mexico", Oct. 18, 2013.

Economist: "Corruption and Natural Resources: A Fight for Light", Oct. 24, 2015.

Economist: "China: Business and Corruption: Robber Barons Beware", Oct. 24, 2015.

Business Anti-Corruption Portal: "Sudan Country Profile", Aug. 18, 2011.

IX. THE NEGLECT OF GOVERNMENT OPERATIONS, AND

X. THE CHALLENGES OF URBANIZATION AND INADEQUATE SOCIAL SERVICES

World Health Organization (WHO), "Health Performance Rank by Country", 2011.

Middle East Research and Information Project: "Iran: The Populist Treat to Democracy", 2006.

World Bank: "Tunisia: Poverty Alleviation: Preserving While Preparing for the Future", Aug. 9, 2012.

Asian Development Bank: "Pakistan: Causes of Poverty", 2010 Human Rights Report.

U. S. Dept. of State: "2010 Human Rights Report: Pakistan", Apr. 8, 2011.

The Guardian: "World Educational Rankings: Which Country Does Best at Reading, Maths, Science? Datablog, 2015.

Most Dangerously Polluted Cities, AllCountries.org, 2011.

BBC News: "Africans Let Down by Governments", 2004.

Factsanddetails.com: "Bureaucracy in China: Cadres, Hassles, the Hukou and Dead Souls", 2013.

Economist: "Still Standing Somehow: After a Disastrous Year, Greece's Prime Minister May Yet Win Re-election." Sep. 19, 2015.

Economist: "Libya's Civil War: Running Out of Time", Sep. 19, 2015.

Detter, Dag, and Folster, Stefan, "The Public Wealth of Nations: How Management of Public Assets Can Boost or Bust Economic Growth", New York, Palgrave McMillan, 2015.

Economist: "Arab Bureaucracies: The Region's Countries Desperately Need to Reform Their Public Sectors., Nov. 14, 2015.

Landzettel Marianne, "Pakistan Faces Educational Emergency Says Government", BBC News, South Asia, Mar. 2011.

Javedanfar, Meir, "The Worsening Housing Crisis in Iran", The Center for Iranian Studies, Jan. 2007.

Khalaj, Monavar, "Critics Give Iranian Education Low Marks", Financial Times, Jul. 11, 2011.

Turkey: Ministry of Education, "Basic Education in Turkey: Background Report", Jun. 2008.

African Economic Outlook: "Ethiopia: Economic and Political Governance", May 2, 2014.

Lomborg, Bjorn, "The Skeptical Environmentalist" Cambridge U. Press, 2001.

Pearce, Fred, "When the Rivers Run Dry", Boston, Beacon Press, 2006.

Economist: "Water Consumption: A Canal Too Far", Sep. 17, 2014.

Refugees International: South Sudan Field Report. See also Lebanon Field Report; Iraq Field Report; Mali Field Report; Somalia Field Report

Yang, Dali L., "Remaking the Chinese Leviathan", Stanford U. Press, 2004.

XI. THE NATIONAL JUSTICE SYSTEM: COURTS, POLICE, THE MILITARY AND INTELLIGENCE SERVICES

Wikepedia: "The Armed Forces of the Islamic Republic of Iran", Aug. 15, 2015.

Shah, Aquil, "Getting the Military Out of Pakistani Politics", World Policy Journal, Vol. 90, No. 3.

Economist: "The Death Penalty: Most of the World's Sharp Decline in Executions Can Be Credited to China", Aug. 3, 2013.

Economist: "Indian Military Power: All At Sea", Aug. 17, 3013.

Bingman, Charles F. "Changing Governments in India and China" Houston, Schiel and Denver, 2011.

Bingman, Charles F., "Reforming China's Government", Xlibris Publishers, 2010.

Wikepedia: "State Sponsors of Terrorism", Nov. 2, 2013.

World Development Indicators: "Assessing Vulnerability", 2004.

World Development Indicators: "Enhancing Security", 2004.

ENDNOTES

[i] See Waterbury p. 14.

[ii] See the Economist Magazine, Jan. 17, 2004, p. 13.

[iii] See the following Economist Newspaper articles: Sep. 27, 2003, p.16; Jan. 10, 2004, pp. 12-13; Jan. 24, 2004, pp. 23-25; Sep. 25, 2004, p. 68.

INDEX